AF290976

Mirror Images

"Few books capture as clearly the critical place and influence of popular culture on education. Silberman-Keller, Bekerman, Giroux, and Burbules have launched a collaboration that helps educators understand the learning process outside the confines of classroom pedagogy but provides the conditions of possibility for improving schools. Its expert contributors travel through social experiences that no educator can take for granted any longer as extra-curricular. If schooling is education of the whole person then this book takes us one step closer to that transformation."

Zeus Leonardo, University of California, Berkeley

Mirror Images

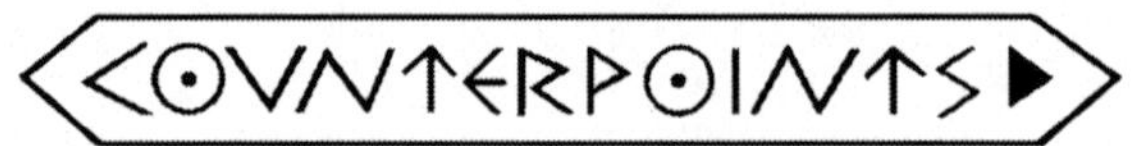

COUNTERPOINTS

Studies in the Postmodern Theory of Education

Joe L. Kincheloe and Shirley R. Steinberg
General Editors

Vol. 338

PETER LANG
New York • Washington, D.C./Baltimore • Bern
Frankfurt am Main • Berlin • Brussels • Vienna • Oxford

Mirror Images

Popular Culture and Education

EDITED BY
Diana Silberman Keller, Zvi Bekerman,
Henry A. Giroux, Nicholas C. Burbules

PETER LANG
New York • Washington, D.C./Baltimore • Bern
Frankfurt am Main • Berlin • Brussels • Vienna • Oxford

Library of Congress Cataloging-in-Publication Data

Mirror images: popular culture and education / Diana Silberman Keller ... [et al.].
p. cm. — (Counterpoints: studies in the postmodern theory of education; v. 338)
Includes bibliographical references and index.
1. Education—Sociological aspects. 2. Popular culture.
3. Postmodernism and education. I. Silberman-Keller, Diana.
LC191.M577   306.43'2—dc22   2007051151
ISBN 978-1-4331-0231-8 (hardcover)
ISBN 978-1-4331-0230-1 (paperback)
ISSN 1058-1634

Bibliographic information published by **Die Deutsche Bibliothek**.
Die Deutsche Bibliothek lists this publication in the "Deutsche
Nationalbibliografie"; detailed bibliographic data is available
on the Internet at http://dnb.ddb.de/.

Cover photo by Diana Silberman Keller
Cover design by Sophie Boorsch Appel

The paper in this book meets the guidelines for permanence and durability
of the Committee on Production Guidelines for Book Longevity
of the Council of Library Resources.

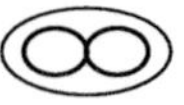

© 2008 Peter Lang Publishing, Inc., New York
29 Broadway, 18th floor, New York, NY 10006
www.peterlang.com

Printed in the United States of America

Table of Contents

Introduction

DIANA SILBERMAN-KELLER, ZVI BEKERMAN,
HENRY A. GIROUX, AND NICHOLAS C. BURBULES

The project to launch an edited volume on popular culture and education was intended to critically observe the topics' mutual reflections on each other. Mirrors, or reflections, were considered to be techniques that metonymically aroused a variety of possibilities through which seeing and seers' gazes could problematize the quasi-traditional questions in the study of the mutual relations between popular culture and education.

As brilliantly exposed by Apuleius, mirrors and reflections not only embody a variety of possibilities of visions and reflections but are also linked to a variety of questions that go *au-delà* of the "Baudrillardian" simulacra:

> … What do you think? Should not philosophers make all these problems subjects of research and inquiry and in solitary study look into mirrors of every kind, liquid and solid? There is also over and above these questions further matter for discussion. For instance, why is it that in flat mirrors all images and objects reflected are shown in almost precisely their original dimensions, whereas in convex and spherical mirrors everything is seen smaller, in concave mirrors on the other hand larger than nature? Why again and under what circumstances are left and right reversed? When does one and the same mirror seem now to withdraw the image into its depths, now to extrude it forth to view? Why do concave mirrors when held at right angles to the rays of the sun kindle tinder set opposite them? … (Apuleius's *Apology*, part 16)

Popular culture and education are two composed and complicated phenomena that studied reflected the one on the other seem to be leaving their narcissistic stage toward meeting Jacques Lacan's mirror stage. That is, overcoming the uncanniness of seeing themselves as the other, and adopting their whole body as composing their way to be in the world.

For this purpose the international group of scholars represented in the volume has adopted a variety of theoretical vantage points, media and political, social and cultural contexts, creating a catoptrical singular but plural possibility of breaking through by an effort to coalesce knowledge on education and popular culture studied as broad phenomena and not as a collection of case studies.

No less than education, popular culture is considered by most of this volume's authors as a transformative powerful medium; and by sometimes pointing at the first limitations and proposing the latter platforms and technologies in order to create user, seer, reader or listener and student options to better their life, they criticize racial, military, colonialist and limited definitions and modalities of knowledge transmittions.

Being so, and the *differences* among them remaining resolved, this volume doesn't deal with education and popular culture's mutual possibilities of applications in order to transform education in a more popular (as if a further popularization of massive education were possible at all) phenomena or to transform popular culture. It is clear to us that popular culture educates and that massive education, in its singular way, is a popular and centralized communication media. We offer instead considering the two as cultural phenomena that reflect the one on the other and in this way participate in cultural production and dissemination processes, sometimes by supporting each other and sometimes by creating dissenting images that open possibilities for real/quasi radical critique.

Popular culture and education mutual relations and reflections acquire in this volume figural poses and each chapter posits these mutual relations differently, reflecting an invaginated space where it is not possible to study the one without awakening the echo or traces of the other. This is perhaps the overriding message of this volume: If we are to theorize on education or popular culture, disciplinary and media boundaries are called into question in an effort to widen the possibility of enlarging the vocabulary and the verbs of all that stays unnamed by what is considered knowledge.

Moreover this volume proposes viewing popular culture as a pedagogical site that allows educators new opportunities to define the very nature of pedagogy, public commitment, the struggle over identities, subject positions, and values. Popular culture is not merely a subject that can be incorporated into the curriculum but is, in and of itself, a form of public pedagogy that demands a new theoretical and political understanding in terms of how it both shapes and can be shaped as a pedagogical and political form. It not only makes present the language of everyday life, but also offers educators an opportunity to connect their work with the experiences that bear down on students, while at the same time taking seriously that popular culture, in terms of both the technologies that drive it and the issues it addresses, demands a new form of literacy that must be taken seriously by educators. Schools and popular culture introduce learners to particular ways of life and their mutual study and critique problematize both the ways of life under discussion and what it would mean to address such issues through a pedagogy in which popular culture becomes central to the very task of learning itself. In this sense this volume includes itself in the vivid archive of popular culture and education history as depicted by Giroux (1994) recalling Richard Hoggart and Raymond Williams's work that addresses the issue of pedagogy in their early attempts to promote cultural studies in Britain:

> … As founding figures in the Birmingham Centre for Cultural Studies, Hoggart and Williams believed that pedagogy offered the opportunity to link cultural practice with the development of radical cultural theories. Not only did pedagogy connect questions of form and content, it also introduced a sense of how teaching, learning, textual studies, and knowledge could be addressed as political issues which foreground considerations of power and social agency. According to Williams, the advent of cultural studies in the 1930s and 1940s directly emerged out of the pedagogical work that was going on in Adult Education. The specificity of the content and context of adult education provided cultural studies with a number of issues that were to direct its subsequent developments in Birmingham. These included the refusal to accept the limitations of established academic boundaries and power structures, the demand for linking literature to the life situations of adult learners, and the call that schooling are empowering rather than merely humanizing … (Giroux, 1994)

Continuing this line, in Chapter 1 Mary Dalton introduces schools as constructed by Hollywood movies. Movies reveal schools to be places of fissure where people are placed into groups and separated by different needs in the scheme of things—needs that go largely unmet—with the largest rupture separating students from adults. This pattern holds true whether the school is an elite private school, a stereotypical inner city school, or a middle-class suburban school. Education in these movies causes some personal transformations along the way and a symbolic challenge to the uncaring system by a good teacher or a group of resistant students, but ultimately the status quo is protected, and the dominant ideology of maintaining the existing class structure (and as a byproduct maintaining segregation) stays intact. Despite some films such as *Elephant* and *American History X*, according to Dalton only a minority of films suggest possible alternatives to the dominant discourse and work on issues of social justice instead of perpetuating the status quo. Hollywood films then are seen as mirroring social and political situations; In this way they, no less than educational institutions in society, help to maintain the existing order.

In Chapter 2, whose suggesting title is "*Try to see this movie as an educational movie*," Gordon Alley-Young posits two themes of education films while recognizing that producers, critics, and viewers negotiate education films in a variety of ways. According to Young, it is important to study how popular films frame our perceptions on race and education. This chapter makes no definitive claims about education films as the genre continues to produce representations that require new criticism and study.

Henry Giroux's important contribution to this volume stresses a profound political critique calling for critical and protest activity toward the use of popular culture representations as educating toward militarization. Giroux explains and shows that unlike the old style of militarization in which all forms of civil authority are subordinate to military authority, the new ethos of militarization is organized to engulf the entire social order, legitimating its values as a central rather than peripheral aspect of American and worldwide public life. Giroux explains that the interface of military and popular culture has not only been valuable in providing video game technology for diverse military uses; it has also resulted in the armed forces developing partnerships with the video game industry to train and recruit soldiers. Army-Navy stores are doing brisk business selling not only American flags, gas masks, aviator sunglasses, night-vision goggles, and other military equipment, but also clothing with the camouflage look. Giroux warns that unless militarization is systemically exposed and resisted at every place where it appears in the culture, it will undermine the meaning of critical citizenship and do great harm to those institutions that are central to a democratic society.

Bekerman's chapter seeks to question the work done by those who seem to believe that popular culture and its use within educational settings have the potential of embellishing the educational scene and/or bettering the lot of those, mostly minorities, failed by the educational system. He posits that today's, popular culture and education research is one of those fussy fields that holds to a rhetoric of emancipation and questions what is it that present critical discourse on popular culture has to offer.

Critically discussing present conceptualizations of culture and education, Bekerman concludes by suggesting that we would serve the emancipatory cause better if we would realize that the school is not the domain within which to battle the hegemonic structures (in spite of it being the one that reproduces them) and suggests that we turn our efforts instead to the political/practical arena. As for schools, given present configurations, the best that we can hope for is that they will provide the indigent with equal access to the tools that will allow them to succeed within the present system, and it is toward this that we should turn our efforts.

Diana Silberman-Keller's chapter "Education and Popular Culture: Chiasmatic Reflections in Almodovar's *Bad Education* and Tarantino's *Kill Bill*" with its "*cri ecrit*" modality install itself in the discursive space of cultural production and reproduction and analyzes the way popular culture and education are constructed in these two films as a thematic cluster dealt inside the two movies themselves. Silberman-Keller posits that the two films representing an oblique gaze toward canonical cinematic and cultural bodies offer unusual opportunities for considering education and popular culture not as hierarchically qualified poles but as differences in cultural construction that work chiasmatically by the cathartic effects caused by transversion and exaggeration.

The next chapters of the volume propose different media as capable of bettering subjects and societal situation. Gonzalo Frasca finds that new developments in the video game industry, such as *advergaming* and *political games* are worth considering critically because they illustrate how ideas are conveyed in video games. According to Frasca this consideration is relevant because they can provide us with better tools for adapting video games for educational purposes particularly in subjects dealing in the humanities and the social science.

According to Frasca both *advergaming* and *political games* seek to persuade, even though the "products" showcased in political games are ideas.

Frasca concludes that good games reveal their secrets only after a lot of work. If we want to unlock the mysteries of game rhetoric we must indeed work hard. Clues are everywhere, not just in other games but also in other disciplines, thus suggesting an interdisciplinary approach to their analysis.

Kurt Squire enlarges Frasca's view about the possibility of educating through video games for although video games are nodes in a web of new media, technology, and social shifts, they are the quintessential site for examining how popular culture is having an impact on contemporary social institutions. Video games are the "medium of choice" for many millennials (or Nintendo) generations and a critical site recruiting, even requiring, new literacies. Fan message forums, DYI (or do-it-yourself) media production, and blogs have many of these same characteristics and are indeed frequently core components of gaming practices. However, video games can be considered the quintessential sites for studying such technologies because they are built on the logic of simulation and because they have been the predominant popular art form of the computer over the past twenty-five years. Squire contends that although schools remained shackled to literacies of print, media such as video games offer pedagogies of *interactivity* where players can inhabit possible worlds and participate in vibrant learning communities. Squire calls for a new critical studies, one that acknowledges how today popular culture is a powerful site for recruiting identities into sophisticated practices. These opportunities shift questions from mere *access* to technologies, or awareness of representations, to an understanding of how participants have differential access to social networks and social practices.

Not far from video games inquiry, Rebecca Ward Black's chapter defines the term *fanfiction* as encompassing an array of texts, ranging from uncommissioned sequels to Jane Austen's work all the way to love stories written by Star Trek fans about Captain Kirk and Mr. Spock.

Online fanfiction sites provide a unique context for study in that they incorporate an interplay of officially sanctioned forms of knowledge, such as traditional writing conventions and genres, and unofficial forms of knowledge, such as intimate knowledge of the characters and settings of television series, popular books, and video games.

Mary Stone Hanley examines some of the cultural complexities in Hip-hop culture and poetry and provides a historical context for the importance and possibilities of Hip-hop. From interviews with Black, White, and Latino youth about the arts and Hip-hop culture, poetry, and music to observations in classrooms, community sites, clubs, and coffee houses, Rap and Spoken Word are presented as culturally rooted verbal literacies that transform the consciousness of youth, their teachers, and society in general. Hip-hop culture creates social transformation through the form and content of their words. Embedded in culture and using Afrocentric art forms, they shape webs of meanings, hegemonic and counterhegemonic, in which young people are consciously and unconsciously caught.

In her chapter *Advertising and Consumerism: A Space for Pedagogical Practice*, Funes proposes the transformation of advertising into an educational opportunity, an opportunity to spark a flame of inquiry and to awaken a critical consciousness of advertising.

As well as being viewed as an enemy of the classroom, advertising inspires confusion and disjuncture in the teaching environment. This stems from an apparent contradiction between the ethics of teaching versus the ethics of advertising: the former centers on "duty" and "being," whereas the latter centers on "want" and "appearing."

This project considers the didactic application of advertising in formal education. Rather than just the transmission of content, the goal is that the students learn to learn. The methodology proposes a phased deconstruction of the traditional transmitter-message-receiver scheme in order to place the experience of the learner first. It is considered that practices focused on the analysis of media cultural texts will enable a distancing from which learners may go beyond being mere spectators and, through a progressive decentralization of their perceptive experiences, will be able to contextualize and, as a consequence, "defamiliarize" that which is generally accepted as obvious and normal. This process will enable the learning of a language used to express knowledge that escapes traditional textbooks and is deeply anchored in the cultural consumption of young people.

In an unusual gesture centered on style, Wong and Henriksen, in their chapter, claim that as educators they are envious of the intensity of observation and imagination associated with students' fascination with fashion. They wonder if only their own teaching could be as engaging. Thus, they propose that fascinating implications emerge from the question "What if ideas—substance of school—were fashion?" and discuss how the phenomenon of fashion can be a framework for thinking about teaching and learning.

Carlos Antonio Aguirre Rojas proposes a critical reflection on teaching history according to Carlo Ginzburg's theoretical insights on the history of subaltern cultures. According to Ginzburg, a subaltern culture *is not* something that is unitarian nor homogenous but rather a field of divided and contradictory forces that is always formed by two different universes—that of *hegemonic* culture (and not only of "dominant" culture) and that of multiple *subaltern* cultures (and not only of "popular" culture). Following Gramsci, Ginzburg conceives the culture of the dominant classes as being "hegemonic," that is, as a culture that exercises domination by means of not only imposition or total subjugation but also the creation of a certain cultural "consensus," at the same time forcing it to "take possession" of certain themes, motifs, and elements of the subaltern cultures, to deform them and use them as a weapon for their own legitimization, and urging it forward to permanently promote different efforts to diffuse her own culture within these subordinate classes, obviously directed toward firmly establishing and making the mentioned hegemonic culture acceptable on the part of those submitted classes themselves. Then Ginzburg considers the space of culture at the same time not only as a *permanent battlefield* where the hegemonic culture and the subaltern cultures incessantly face each other, but also and simultaneously as terrain identically marked by a movement of *constant circularity*, where both cultural versions constantly exchange cultural elements, cosmovisions, motifs, and configurations, as part of that same cultural battle that interconnects and overdetermines them in general.

Aguirre Rojas concludes that it is indeed an urgent and essential task for the critical, honest, and serious historians all over the world—that of again "saving our dead," as well as that of helping our living to fight, keeping lit up for some time that "spark of hope" that, from the grievances of the past and from the conflicts of the present, is always looking ahead and beyond in search of a better future.

In closing, but not concluding, it is worth paying attention to the fact that most of the popular culture contents dealt with in this volume are usually transmitted by media activated by electronic, cinematic, and digital technologies as Squires's chapter has suggested. Yet, almost forgetting McLuhan's *The Medium Is the Message*, most of the chapters do not deal directly with technology's traces on education or on popular culture.

Instead, mirrors and reflections as leading metaphors in the conversation on the reciprocal relation between education and popular culture were intended to stress that the "high tech concern with style and stylishness is not limited to questions of design; in high tech," as Rutsky writes (1999) "the very 'function' of technology becomes a matter of representation, style, aesthetics—a matter, that is, of technological reproducibility." Nevertheless, the inseparability between life and its representations as it has been focused in most of the chapters of this volume seems to reaffirm the Heideggerian notion of "the technological" evading the instrumentality of technology that usually "blinds us to" the broader sense of technology that links it to art and style, as it has been with *techne* in ancient Greece.

Technologically, education reproduces popular culture, which reproduces education and vice versa. This is why none of these phenomena together or separately can be considered as being superior or inferior to the other. Moreover, subjects experience these phenomena *al unison* and in their life they are (con)fused more than separated.

In the margins of practices it might be that it is important to deal with "remediations" strategies between education and popular culture. Still important is the fact that theoretical studies remain to be developed. Studying the cultural reproduction of qualities and modalities of a good education and a good popular culture is urgently needed.

CHAPTER ONE

The Hollywood View: Protecting THE Status Quo IN Schools Onscreen

MARY M. DALTON

INTRODUCTION

It has become clear from arguments made by cultural critics over the last twenty years or so that we are shaped by popular culture just as we shape popular texts. I have always found philosopher-historian John Fiske's description of this process particularly apt and elegant: "Because of their incompleteness, all popular texts have leaky boundaries; they flow into each other, they flow into everyday life" (p. 126). My own way of thinking about the connections among texts (including lived experience) is more narratively based. The scripts that we see on the screen give us "scripts" for our lives in the sense that popular texts inform our identities and our collective and personal sense of the possibilities and limitations our life stories hold.

In an earlier book, *The Hollywood Curriculum: Teachers in the Movies*, I categorized and analyzed over 100 Hollywood films spanning nearly seventy-five years of film history to examine the role of teachers. That work did not, however, look specifically at the institutional role played by schools in these films in replicating the dominant social, political, and economic systems of American culture. This chapter uses patterns displayed in many of the same films considered in the book but examines the films from an entirely different perspective: instead of foregrounding the role of teachers in these films, I look more closely at schools and how they are constructed cinematically. Another difference is the time frame considered. Although the primitive phase of the genre of good teacher movies appeared in the 1930s, Hollywood films that began to focus more overtly on schools and schooling were evident as the genre entered its classical phase with established codes and conventions, in the 1950s.[1]

Over the last fifty years, there have been scores of mainstream Hollywood films that exalt the good teacher. Typically, the good teacher in films inspires students to achieve despite the odds against academic achievement or to find personal enlightenment, depending on whether the students are lower class or upper class. This teacher is also presented as a stark contrast to repressive administrators and bad teachers who either are not interested in students or don't understand their needs. Some of these iconic good teachers are: Rick Dadier (Glenn Ford) in *Blackboard Jungle* (1955); Mark Thackery (Sidney Poitier) in *To Sir, with Love* (1967); Pat Conroy (Jon Voight) in *Conrack* (1974); John Keating (Robin Williams) in *Dead Poets Society* (1989); LouAnne Johnson (Michelle Pfeiffer) in *Dangerous Minds* (1995), and Katherine Ann Watson (Julia Roberts) in *Mona Lisa Smile* (2003). Two of these films, *Conrack* and *Dangerous Minds*, are biopics (biographical films) based on the autobiographies of inspiring teachers, which adds an air of authority to the film texts. This is just a sampling, but the type is well documented in stories that define the good teacher as one who exhibits most of the following traits: he or she is an outsider to the established system, the good teacher becomes personally involved with students, the good teacher has conflicts with administrators or other school officials, the good teacher frequently has a ready sense of humor, and the good teacher personalizes the curriculum to meet needs in students' everyday lives (Dalton, 2004, pp. 22–41).

Similarly, students have evolved over time into stock characters, such as those in *Stand and Deliver* (1987), who are difficult for the good teacher to form a connection with but worth the effort and others who have difficulties at home with parents who do not support their children's educational goals or interests. A common scenario features a good teacher's success being measured by his (or very occasionally her[2]) ability to reach the difficult student and help him (again, it is usually a male student in this important role) overcome adversity to graduate or even win a scholarship. For example, in *Stand and Deliver*, which has enjoyed a lasting popularity with audiences, the dedicated teacher Jaime Escalante (Edward James Olmos, who stars in yet another good teacher biopic) works hard to reach a gangbanger, Angel Guzman (Lou Diamond Phillips), with an affinity for higher-level mathematics. Such films present familiar patterns in which good teachers ostensibly side with the students to help them engage in self-actualization, but the teachers in mainstream Hollywood films really function as buffers to help ease students into the dominant culture they have resisted.

Despite the fact that films are complex narrative texts embedded with competing messages that invite a myriad of interpretations, they are also cultural artifacts. Movies, especially mainstream Hollywood fare, are powerful tools for identifying the dominant discourse in a given culture over time. Over the last fifty years, Hollywood films have repeatedly presented codes that constitute schools as sites of limited resistance staged by students and, sometimes, by a progressive teacher or two. Mostly, these good teachers are constructed as counterpoints to callous administrators and "bad" teachers who are either scared of students, bored by them, or eager to control them. Schools are constructed as spaces where the disconnect between what matters to students (and the good teachers who champion them) and what matters to faculty is a profound rupture and is not sutured in any convincing way by the final frames of most of the films. To the contrary, in the final scenes of most of these films, it becomes clear that, perhaps unwittingly, these good teachers are not supporting meaningful resistance. In fact, these teachers may even thwart the opportunity for systemic change by focusing on personal transformation for students instead of collective action against misguided policies of the institutions of education and the people representing those policies.

Certainly, while Jaime Escalante prepares his students to pass an Advanced Placement (AP) calculus exam, which they are later accused of cheating on because their high scores are suspicious to the racist company executives who market the test, he does not challenge the system that endorses tests that have been proven to be racially biased. Escalante does not question the dominant ethos of education that proclaims "accountability" as the buzzword of the era, effectively reducing the educational and intrinsic human value of individual students to test scores. Without this sympathetic teacher willing to question the status quo (that reduces these students to numbers), what chance do students have with administrators who are pushing policies fashioned from above and teachers who are not personally involved with the students? Very little to none. Escalante does provide an important role in building a bridge between the barrio that houses these students and his own middle-class lifestyle, but his choice to leave a lucrative job in industry and give something back to his community and the students' choice to work extra hours to prepare for the AP calculus exam does nothing to challenge the racial segregation of schools in the United States or to remedy the inequality of resources perpetuated by local funding that ensures that schools in rich neighborhoods enjoy a wealth of resources while schools in poor neighborhoods suffer from the lack of resources.[3]

Even if some good teachers are willing to challenge the status quo more directly and meaningfully in real life, Hollywood would be unlikely to canonize those stories onscreen. The commercial film industry in Hollywood is always geared toward the personal instead of the collective and many producers, directors, and writers strive to assume a cloak of political neutrality without realizing that ideology may be implicit or explicit, but never absent, in popular narratives. The industry executives in charge of deciding which films are "greenlighted" and which are "passed" would not choose to make movies with radical political objectives because those stories would not likely appeal to a mass audience and would be less profitable than more mainstream stories.[4]

Consider the aforementioned iconic teachers as representative of the main characters in the teacher movie genre across five decades. Four of the six teachers mentioned—in the films *To Sir, with Love, Conrack, Dead Poets Society*, and *Mona Lisa Smile*—are leaving their schools at the end of the movie and three of them have little choice in the matter. If good teachers challenge institutional rules, or even the mores of their institutions, there is no lasting place for them in schools, from the poor and isolated island off South Carolina where Pat Conroy taught black children abandoned by their school district to the elite hallways of Welton Academy where John Keating tried to inspire the rich, white male students to appreciate an aesthetic that transcends the pragmatism and prestige of the world in which they have been reared and groomed to inherit. *Conrack* and *Dead Poets Society* offer contrasting images of schools—one lacking in resources of every sort and another boasting every imaginable excess—but in the end both teachers are fired for challenging the dominant ideology of their institutions. In the Hollywood view, schools are sites where dramas are played out in hallways and classrooms. In these films, the personal dramas of students and teachers are primary to the superficial dramatic structure of these films but secondary to the deeper layers of narrative; they are ultimately secondary to the dominant discourse of the films as a whole, which is that schools provide a locus where the status quo must be restored or maintained and a space for inculcating students into the dominant culture.

This chapter looks closely at two films that depict schools in diverse ways. One of them, *High School High* (1996), parodies conventional Hollywood good teacher films, and it is a significant example because it reifies those genre films and, at the same time, calls attention to some of the disconnects between teachers and students and between the educational policies developed by government administrations and the practices in actual schools. In essence, although *High School High* comments on good teacher movies by making a joke of identifiable patterns that link those films, it also betrays the oversimplification and misrepresentation presented in those genre films. As a counterpoint to mainstream Hollywood cinema, Gus Van Sant's film *Elephant* (2003) is an elliptical and apocalyptic film that promises to be a slice of life drama inspired by the Columbine shootings. Perhaps Van Sant's film does not live up to its promise, but, despite its flaws, *Elephant* is a fascinating film that raises more questions than it answers. Raising relevant questions intentionally is something that is seldom seen in more conventional Hollywood fare. Though Van Sant's two earlier variations on good teacher movies, *Good Will Hunting* (1997) and *Finding Forrester* (2000), begin to broach the territory by tacking social class and race in the context of education, those films are each more conventional stories than *Elephant* and raise less troubling questions as they explore individual narratives of academic achievement "despite the odds." Both *High School High* and *Elephant* offer instructive counterpoints to the ways in which schools are usually depicted in Hollywood film.

High School High: The Power of Parody

High School High carries the tagline "There's a new teacha in the Hood!" and it is clearly an attempt to meld situations and images from films such as *Blackboard Jungle*, *Dangerous Minds*, *Music of the Heart*, *Stand and Deliver*, and *Lean on Me*. Although the good teachers sent into these "diverse" schools are often white such as Richard Clark (Jon Lovitz), there is an amazing lack of attention to racial politics in the conventional Hollywood films. *High School High* satirizes the racial/socioeconomic politics of other films in a two-step process. First, elite prep schools are lampooned in the opening sequence of the film. This model is familiar in mainstream films such as *Dead Poets Society* (1989), *The Emperor's Club* (2002), *Finding Forrester* (2000), *Goodbye, Mr. Chips* (1939), *The Prime of Miss Jean Brodie* (1969), and *School Ties* (1992). The particular target is Welton Academy, a prestigious northeastern prep school featured in *Dead Poets Society*.

 High School High opens with a shot of the manicured lawns and stately brick buildings of Wellington Academy (later referred to as The Wellington School for good measure). The interior of the school is equally well appointed and teeming with students in uniforms consisting of jackets and ties who look like future titans of industry and government leaders but murmur annoying and even cruel remarks to one another and to their history teacher, Mr. Clark. The competitiveness and smugness of the academy is palpable, and the classical music playing is pompous. The interior shot tracks over to the reception desk where a voice answers the phone, "Wellington Academy. Are you white? I'll put you right through." There is no pretense or omission here; Wellington Academy is clear on its racial politics because fostering elitism and an implicit but misguided sense of meritocracy is what sustains such an institution. The opening sequence is very brief: the establishing exterior shot of Wellington Academy and the shots of Clark hurrying through the foyer area past the reception desk and into a meeting room. There is a long table of old, white teachers who are mostly men. They all smoke identical pipes to denote their self-satisfaction and presumed intellectualism. Clark's father, a fitting choice given the traditions of legacy and nepotism that permeate such institutions, tells him that the meeting has been called in his honor to celebrate his promotion to "Assistant Vice Chairman of the History Department." Clark in turn announces that he has taken a job at Barry High School, and his obvious rejection of their standards and values stuns the other faculty members. It is a very brief but effective set up for the main narrative thread: the good (white) teacher comes to the blighted inner city ("diverse") school to save the students from themselves and from jaded or corrupt administrators.

The remainder of the film develops that central storyline. As Clark drives his rust-bucket heap of a Chrysler through leafy suburbs, the radio plays the Carpenters' 1974 hit song "Top of the World." The song stops abruptly when he passes a sign on the road that reads "Inner City," and as the setting changes from station to station, all Clark can tune in is an identical rap song. Above his California license plate there is a sign with a heart symbol followed by "2 Teach." As sight gags outside his car window indicate the deterioration of the neighborhood approaching the school, it becomes clear that Clark will need a passion for teaching to sustain him in this particular 'hood. The school itself looks like a burned-out war zone, and there is an explosion from a second-story window as he pulls into the parking lot. The lot features signs for "Student," "SWAT," "National Guard," and "Johnnie Cochran" parking, and Clark's clunker is stolen as soon as he turns his back upon exiting the vehicle. It is obvious that Clark is a long way from Wellington Academy now.

Other symbols of the degeneration of the school abound. This is Marion Barry High School, and students dismantle a statue of the former Washington DC mayor. They replace the flag Barry is holding with a bong pipe. There is darkness and chaos inside the school. Massive metal detectors are buzzing as students disarm (significantly, many will later exit the school with undetected weapons), a guy selling watches out of a case tries to interest Clark who declines only to discover that his own watch is missing, the halls are crowded and dark, and graffiti defaces every available surface. There is almost immediately a stand-off between a cool dude, Griff McReynolds (Mekhi Phifer), and a menacing guy, Paco Rodriguez (Guillermo Diaz), surrounded by his gang that Clark effectively and—intentionally—unconvincingly diffuses by getting them to shake hands and make nice.

Two events early in the school day reinforce the idea that schools are places where there is a profound disconnect between the interests of students and the interests of adults who control the agenda. Immediately following the confrontation between Griff and Paco in the front hallway of the school, a school nurse sits behind a desk handing out condoms beneath a banner proclaiming "Sexual Awareness Week." The nurse forcefully staples a brochure to a condom package (does she pierce the condom inside?) and bellows at the girl standing in front of her as she hands over the goods, "There you go, you little slut." Seldom have the mixed messages often given to students (in real schools and schools onscreen) been so clearly evoked in mainstream films. This is one of the reasons that film parodies are so useful in studying popular narratives: these films get at a layer of truth that is often disguised by the conventions of the genre being satirized, and, most often, parodies are single films that comment on an entire body of work, which presents an economy of meaning.

It is at this point in the film that a second event epitomizing the vast disconnect between student and institutional interests appears. A "Nurse Ratchett"-type character with a bullhorn and a bat emerges into the hallway evoking Joe Clark (the authoritarian principal in the biopic *Lean on Me*) as she clubs a student in the head with the bat. When Richard Clark protests to the imposing woman that he bets "the principal would frown on this sort of thing," she reveals that she is, in fact, Evelyn Doyle (Louise Fletcher), the principal of Barry High School.[5]

> Doyle: Look, pinhead, I don't know what nursery school you come from, but here you screw up, and you die. Every bad kid in the city is dumped into our laps.
>
> Clark: Excuse me, Miss Doyle, with all due respect, I don't think there is such a thing as a bad kid. At least, they don't start off that way.

At this point in the dialogue, a sexy staff member hears what he's saying and notices Clark.

> Clark: They just need someone they can relate to, and I can reach them. I know what's def, what's whack, what's jam, what's straight-up booty.
>
> Doyle: Mr. Clark, how long have you been teaching here? Clark stammers.
>
> Doyle: Twenty minutes! I've been here over 20 years. Don't you question my authority on this. Excuse me.

Clark has articulated the good teacher mantra about reaching students, he has challenged the uncaring administrator, and he has managed to get the attention of the supporting player who will become his love interest (because he is a male teacher, Clark is allowed this particular subplot) in short order, and her obvious interest in him validates Clark's challenge of the principal. Not insignificantly, his love interest is Victoria Chapell (Tia Carrere), who is a bombshell, Doyle's administrative assistant, and the head of the Drama Club.

Like so many of these films, there is a challenge presented early on—in the case of *High School High*, it is the Academic Proficiency Test that students must take and pass to go to college—that is both concrete and reductive in terms of what it can do to improve students' lives at a point so late in the academic game. There is a subplot involving Clark's romance with Chapell (in one scene that is a direct parody of a scene in *Blackboard Jungle*, Clark tries to thwart Chapell's attempted rape by Paco in the school library but injures her and endangers himself instead), another subplot involving Clark's attempt to "reach" Griff and turn his life around, and yet another subplot about gang activity in the school. As the students fall under Clark's influence, which is achieved by design in a manner that is both pat and unconvincing, they begin studying for the Academic Proficiency Test to learn in twelve weeks what has gone unlearned for twelve years. Simultaneously, they take over the school and paint, plant, and generally beautify so that Barry High School looks like a Hollywood near incarnation of Wellington Academy. If Barry is faux Wellington, it is clear that the veneer is just that because these students have been given no meaningful purpose beyond passing a particular test, and a coat of paint inside and some planted shrubs and blossoms outside are not enough to level this playing field.

In the end, *High School High* is a film that reveals the flaws beneath the veneer. At first it appears that none of the students passed the Academic Proficiency Test, which sends morale through the floor, and immediately the decay of school beautification project begins to mirror the loss of confidence. Doyle uses this opportunity to fire Clark without just cause for getting the students' hope up then letting them down. Clark will not give up, however, and he learns that the tests were stolen in a convoluted twist that links Miss Doyle to Paco in a scheme to keep the students demoralized and on drugs—drugs that she supplies. In fact, when order is restored, Doyle and Paco carted off to jail, and Griff averted from returning to the gang, it turns out that some of them did pass the test after all. The film ends as Principal Pro Tem Richard C. Clark presents diplomas to the six students who comprise the graduating class, including Griff McReynolds, the valedictorian with a 2.35 grade point average. Clark makes the grade, gets the girl, and—in the end—even gets the approval of his father, who arrives on the scene just in time to tell his son that he's proud of him.

In the final analysis, what are the most compelling readings of *High School High* that we can use to broaden our understanding of mainstream Hollywood good teacher movies? *High School High* directly addresses race and reveals in direct contrast the disparity between Wellington Academy and Barry High School. Even after the locally initiated school beautification project, there are no computers, or even extra books, in the classroom, and it is clear that the big cleanup has been mere window dressing. By presenting the Academic Proficiency Test as a bit of a sham, *High School High* reveals a common sentiment that such standardized tests are suspect and a poor measurement of meaningful learning and achievement. The test is dictated and constructed from some unseen administrative force and its implications in the real lives of these students seem nebulous, much murkier than the practical implications of the military recruiters who deploy to the Barry High School campus with regularity (and with the support of Principal

Doyle). The recruiter's sanctioned presence would be unimaginable at Wellington Academy. There is no common purpose that unites teachers or students at Barry High School in a way that rings true (even the way "Academic Proficiency Test" is articulated on screen seems tongue in cheek, an effect amplified by the inane facts that are reviewed in preparation for students to take the examination), just as there is nothing in particular that seems to link students to one another or to link school faculty. Other than Clark, there really aren't any teachers included who engage the students pedagogically other than Clark, and the only administrator who is woven into the storyline in a significant way is Doyle. Clark and Doyle are presented in dramatic conflict rather than in some coalition, but this is not so different from the conventional roles of good teachers and administrators in Hollywood films. In the final analysis, how do we read *High School High*? Race and social class matter in America, and schools provide a space that demonstrates the disparity between the country's "haves" and "have-nots," as well as a space that reveals the disconnect between students and the adults hired to teach and manage them.

Elephant: Raising Questions

If race and social class are glaring examples of cultural disconnects in inner city schools and elite prep schools, the divide between students and adults in predominately white, suburban public schools is equally glaring. Although the gap is mostly employed to celebrate youth culture in films such as *The Breakfast Club* (1985), *Clueless* (1995), *Dazed and Confused* (1993), *Election* (1999), *Fast Times at Ridgemont High* (1982), *Ferris Bueller's Day Off* (1986), *Heathers* (1988), *Mean Girls* (2004), *Orange County* (2002), *Pretty in Pink* (1986), *Pump Up the Volume* (1990), *Rock 'n' Roll High School* (1979), *Saved!* (2004), *Summer School* (1987), *Teaching Mrs. Tingle* (1999), and *Varsity Blues* (1999), some films made in the wake of the Columbine school shootings seek to explore how the anomie of students assigned to schools—where there is a divide between the stated goals of administrators and the centralized curriculum, on the one hand, and what is meaningful in students' daily lives, on the other hand—is a recipe for disaster. Although *Thirteen* (2003) is a riveting and rather harrowing look at how a thirteen-year-old girl with little guidance at school or at home falls under the unstable influence of a slightly older girl at her school, it is Gus Van Sant's film *Elephant* (2003) that takes us inside a Portland, Oregon, high school that could double as a movie set for most of the schools in the films listed above, but Van Sant's view of the school and the people in it is markedly different from the narratives of mainstream Hollywood cinema. His film may be fragmented and flawed, but this elliptical narrative follows several students around the school on what starts out as an average day and ends up as tragically as the April 20, 1999 attack on Columbine High School.

The value of such a work, when examined from the perspective of critics looking at popular culture and schools, is that *Elephant* includes many of the same dramatic elements found in the other films—students with crushes, with family problems or self-esteem issues or eating disorders, those who are bullied alongside those who are exalted among their peers, and those who seem well adjusted alongside those who are gay and struggling with their sexuality—and presents a series of vignettes about them in a nonjudgmental, documentary style that intentionally avoids contextualizing the relationships and events of the day to draw connections and reveal themes as a conventional narrative would.

Elephant is a students' eye view of an average school day; at least, the day is average until it turns tragic. What does the camera record? There's a turbulent gray sky punctuated by power cords and lots of lush, autumn foliage. The school itself is nondescript, modern and clean, large, and a bit institutional. It is an average suburban high school. The students appear mostly middle class to upper middle class and are predominately white. The students group together, talking about mundane events—especially those related to their social lives—or walk alone and do not interact with others, but there are noticeably few interactions with faculty, administrators, and staff. There is one notable scene in which an African American teacher is engaged in what seems more like a consciousness-raising session on gay teenagers than a class session, but our view of this episode is truncated, which suggests that honest exchanges between adults and students about issues that might be relevant to their lives are peripheral and fleeting. Notably, the students who seem to need this sort of intervention the most are not present to receive it. This scene is significant for its content and for the fact that it is eclipsed by much more mundane social encounters in school hallways, the cafeteria, the ball field, and even the library. This is where the real action seems to be rather than in classrooms, which are largely unexplored territory in the film.

In *Elephant*, the narrative unfolds from a camera that seems to follow students like a silent observer, but this camera knows neither temporal nor spatial bounds. The apparent randomness of its recording follows one student for awhile then another student before returning to a previous scene to record the perspective of yet another different student. The camera seems also to transcend time with the inclusion of flashbacks that are not clearly marked. The only students who are presented extensively at home rather than at school are Eric and Alex, boys who are bullied and largely ignored by adults who might have intervened. These two are linked together by common interests, they are linked to one another sexually, and they are linked indelibly by their plan to destroy their school and as many of the people in it as they can. How could they have been so alienated and yet so invisible to others? Van Sant's fragmented film depicts widespread anomie among students, but he offers no insight into why two of the disaffected youth plot and plan and return to their school clothed as mercenaries toting big bags of weapons and bombs bent on the destruction of as many of their peers, teachers, administrators, and staff as they can claim. Even to the end it seems a game to Eric and Alex, and it is more than we can ask of a film director to put that scenario into a context that renders it understandable.

CONCLUSION

Movies reveal schools to be places of fissure where people are placed into groups and separated by different needs in the scheme of things—needs that go largely unmet—with the largest rupture separating students from adults. This pattern holds true whether the school is an elite private school, a stereotypical inner city school, or a middle-class suburban school. These Hollywood schools may feature a good teacher who works hard to form connections with troubled students and smooth their transition into the implied "dominant culture" waiting outside the cinematic frame, but even these iconic teachers do not mount serious threats to the status quo, which is represented in these films by administrators and the institution of education. In other words, when the credits roll at the end of the picture, there may have been some personal transformations along the way and a symbolic challenge to the uncaring system by a good teacher or a group of resistant students, but ultimately the status quo has been protected and the dominant ideology of maintaining the existing class structure (and, as a by-product, of maintaining segregation) is intact.

The question arises that if media reflects culture and culture reflects media and all of us are learning "scripts" about the possibilities and limitations we face based on the narrative texts we encounter (both popular texts and lived experience), then how can we expand the possibilities presented to include a different type of narrative? How can we challenge the dominant discourse and work on issues of social justice instead of perpetuating the status quo? How can we suture the rupture between students' needs and adults' policies and curricular imperatives? One answer is suggested by the fleeting scene in *Elephant* of the African American teacher talking with students about their lives; the answer is open, honest discourse. Another film, *American History X* (1998) speaks to the power of discourse to join an African American teacher (turned administrator) in healing friendship with a former student who ultimately renounces his past as a white supremacist to turn informer on the group. The stakes are high and the sacrifices are great when serious issues are at stake. Open discourse among all invested parties should have the goal of identifying common values—like social justice and democratic engagement and rights of citizenship—and integrating those values into a curriculum that recognizes the worth of the political, of the aesthetic, and of the creative as well as instilling conventional skills designed to create a supply of competent workers. There can be no lasting suture in the hallways and classrooms of our schools—onscreen or off—without the voluntary investment of all parties in open discourse to try to make the tie that binds.

NOTES

1. *Blackboard Jungle* (1955) is an early example of a film that does not simply feature a good teacher as a character but begins to codify the conventions of the good teacher movie. A good teacher movie is a film in which an inspiring teacher, who contains the characteristics listed in this chapter, transforms the lives of individual students without challenging the established educational system. In the case of *Blackboard Jungle*, this good teacher is a member of the middle class who chooses to work in a poor, inner city school, and this popular film has paved the way for others such as, *Dangerous Minds* (1995), *High School High* (1996), *Music of the Heart* (1999), *Stand and Deliver* (1987), *Teachers* (1984), and *To Sir, with Love* (1967). Two variations on this theme bring in administrators who bring order to unruly schools, *Lean on Me* (1989, another biopic) and *The Principal* (1987). Of course, there are many variations on this theme in films featuring good teachers in elite prep schools, coaches who function as teachers in these films, teachers in suburban and rural schools, teachers who play important if not major roles in films about teenagers, and stories about professors or teachers in unconventional school environments.

2. Given the historical and continuing sexism of American culture, it is not surprising that there is a double standard employed for female teachers in the movies. What is surprising, perhaps, is that female teachers from the 1940s into the twenty-first century have *uniformly* been held to a different standard than male teachers and are not allowed to successfully sustain a personal life as long as they are teaching. Although male teachers are either married or usually have some sort of romantic interest in the films (whether they are straight or gay), female teachers who act on their sexuality in Hollywood films are punished for doing so (in films like *Looking for Mr. Goodbar* [1977], *Mona Lisa Smile* [2003], *The Prime of Miss Jean Brodie* [1969], *Rachel, Rachel* [1968], and *Songcatcher* [2000]) or, sometimes, even for acknowledging their sexuality (*The Children's Hour* [1962] and *These Three* [1936]). For most female teachers, however, punishment is not the issue—they are devoted so exclusively to their students (and in the case of Roberta Guaspari [Meryl Streep] in another biopic *Music of the Heart* [1999], to their own children as well as their students) that romantic involvements are a luxury they cannot seem to afford in Hollywood's incarnation of the good female teacher. See Dalton, pp. 82–122.

3. Nowhere has the injustice of this funding system for public education been more eloquently and compellingly argued than in Jonathan Kozol's influential and still topical book *Savage Inequalities*. In an interview in the *New York Times Magazine,* online September 4, 2005, Kozol commented with his usual candor on the state of segregation in U.S. public schools. "Our political establishment refuses to use the word 'segregated.' They call the schools diverse, which means half black, half Hispanic and maybe two white kids and three Asians. Diverse has become a synonym for segregated." This general pattern is readily apparent in the movies depicting urban schools.

4. There are very few exceptions to this common practice, but one is *Sarafina!* (1992), a joint production of France, South Africa, the United Kingdom, and the United States. This film tells the story

of Mary Masembuko (Whoopi Goldberg), a teacher in South Africa who defies the approved curriculum to tell her students what she sees as the truth about the repressive regime that governs them and she pays for her defiance with her life.

5. Louise Fletcher played Nurse Ratchett in *One Flew Over the Cuckoo's Nest* (1975). She was a cruel and authoritarian nurse who wanted people to obey at all costs the rules she set. Her casting as the cruel and authoritarian principal in *High School High* is ironic; in this case she appears to be another Nurse Ratchett but, in fact, subverts the rules to serve her own greed and criminal conduct.

BIBLIOGRAPHY

American History X. Dir. Tony Kaye. 1989.

Blackboard Jungle. Dir. Richard Brooks. 1955.

The Breakfast Club. Dir. John Hughes. 1985.

The Children's Hour. Dir. William Wyler. 1962.

Clueless. Dir. Amy Hecklerling. 1995.

Conrack. Dir. Martin Ritt. 1974.

Dalton, M.M. *The Hollywood curriculum: Teachers in the movies.* New York: Peter Lang, 2004.

Dangerous Minds. Dir. John N. Smith. 1995.

Dazed and Confused. Dir. Richard Linklater. 1993.

Dead Poets Society. Dir. Peter Weir. 1989.

Election. Dir. Alexander Payne. 1999.

Elephant. Dir. Gus Van Sant. 2003.

The Emperor's Club. Dir. Michael Hoffman. 2002.

Fast Times at Ridgemont High. Dir. Amy Heckerling. 1982.

Ferris Bueller's Day Off. Dir. John Hughes. 1986.

Finding Forrester. Dir. Gus Van Sant. 2000.

Fiske, John. *Understanding popular culture.* Boston: Unwin Hyman, 1989.

Goodbye, Mr. Chips. Dir. Sam Wood. 1939.

Good Will Hunting. Dir. Gus Van Sant. 1998.

Heathers. Dir. Michael Lehmann. 1988.

High School High. Dir. Hart Bochner. 1996.

Lean on Me. Dir. John G. Avildsen. 1989.

Looking for Mr. Goodbar. Dir. Richard Brooks. 1977.

Mean Girls. Dir. Mark Waters. 2004.

Mona Lisa Smile. Dir. Mike Newell. 2003.

Music of the Heart. Dir. Wes Craven. 1999.

New York Times Magazine, September 4, 2005.

One Flew Over the Cuckoo's Nest. Dir. Milos Forman. 1975.

Orange County. Dir. Jake Kasdan. 2002.

Pretty in Pink. Dir. Howard Deutch. 1986.

The Prime of Miss Jean Brodie. Dir. Ronald Neame. 1969.

The Principal. Dir. Christopher Cain. 1987.

Pump Up the Volume. Dir. Allan Moyle. 1990.

Rachel, Rachel. Dir. Paul Newman. 1968.

Rock 'n' Roll High School. Dir. Allan Arkush. 1979.

Sarafina! Dir. Darrell James Roodt. 1992.
Saved! Dir. Brian Dannelly. 2004.
School Ties. Dir. Robert Mandel. 1992.
Songcatcher. Dir. Maggie Greenwald. 2000.
Stand and Deliver. Dir. Ramon Menéndez. 1987.
Summer School. Dir. Carl Reiner. 1987.
Teaching Mrs. Tingle. Dir. Kevin Williamson. 1999.
These Three. Dir. William Wyler. 1936.
Thirteen. Dir. Catherine Hardwicke. 2003.
To Sir, with Love. Dir. James Clavell. 1967.
Varsity Blues. Dir. Brian Robbins. 1999.

CHAPTER TWO

"Try TO See THIS Movie AS AN Educational Movie About Life Will You": A Critical Cultural Study OF Race AND Education IN Popular Film

GORDON ALLEY-YOUNG

Quintilianus (Quintilianus and Butler, 1920) produced early representations of educational life, and countless novels have used academe as a backdrop for writing about alienation, elitism, and learning (Hinton, 1994). Popular film continues this tradition of educational representation but it is also criticized for its problematic depictions of race and pedagogy (Farhi, 1999; Giroux, 1997; Grant, 2002; Heilman, 1991). It became clear to me after several presentations on this topic that this film genre stirs up conflicting responses. Once a colleague approached me and sheepishly whispered, "I have to tell you that I loved that film." He disclosed how it was problematic that he was so entertained by a film that also clashed with his sensibilities as a critically minded educator and as a person of color. My colleague's dilemma characterizes some of the discourse surrounding popular representations of education, or education films, which evoke both criticism and praise from viewers and critics, sometimes simultaneously.

Some people criticize popular education films for problematically representing cultural difference, teaching, and learning. Other viewers look past these problematic aspects to instead find positive meanings and educational experiences from such films. What does this tell us about these viewers and the culture in which they operate? A variety of perspectives and understandings should be explored in order to better understand and further the study of popular films set in education. This chapter examines *Finding Forrester*, *Save the Last Dance*, and *The Emperor's Club* for selected themes that could prove fruitful in furthering the critical discussion of this genre.

Cultural studies methodology, specifically Fiske's (1987) trilevel method, provides a means to examine the various levels of meaning in a popular cultural text. This critical cultural study uses a version of Fiske's method that is applied with an awareness of critical perspectives on difference and education. Before elaborating on Fiske's method it is necessary to explore how race and education have been represented in selected popular films.

RACE AND EDUCATION IN POPULAR EDUCATION FILMS

Representations of education originated in teacher lore or stories by and about teachers and their work (Schubert and Ayers, 1992). Some people believe that stories can prompt positive reflection on and about education (Ackerman, Maslin-Ostrowski, and Christensen, 1996; Carter, 1993; Preskill, 1998). Lore can also be negative as Valenzuela (1999) notes that the teachers' lounge can be a place where some teachers narrate their disillusionment, frustration, and biases. Film broadens the scope of oral and written lore by bringing a variety of education stories to a wider audience. Film has been criticized for its representation of the educational process and especially for the representation of the convergence of race and education.

Critics charge that films on education present an irresponsible picture of education. Dalton (1999) critiques education films for emphasizing teaching of the creative arts. Ayers (1994) argues that teaching only the creative arts, like theatre on screen, creates a null curriculum making what happens outside of the classroom more important. When actual teaching work is represented in film it has caused scholars such as Delpit (1995) to note that we have no effective medium for communicating good teaching and Grant (2002) to argue that it creates lower expectations of teaching, especially in urban settings. This emphasis on pleasurable subjects could be a function of how many education films celebrate what Farhi (1999) calls the superteacher myth. The superteacher, usually white, is so celebrated because he/she is shown spending more time connecting personally with and saving disenfranchised students than doing classroom teaching.

Minority characters appear less frequently than white characters in education films. Giroux (1997) states that the film *Dangerous Minds* depicts black characters as the antithesis to intelligence, logic, and order. Films such as *Save the Last Dance* are similarly criticized for representing urban culture as merely "flava," meaning that black music, dance, and culture are juxtaposed against a proliferation of bad boy and gangster representations (Boyd, 2004). Hollywood is similarly charged with offering a simplistic view of urban environments by either characterizing them as treacherous urban jungles as in *Dangerous Minds* and *187* or providing nostalgic representations of cities such as the Bronx in *Finding Forrester* that gloss over the actual problems that exist in these contexts (Simpson, 2002).

Scholars are recognizing the potential of popular culture criticism for opening up conversations about the culture of education (Giroux and Shannon, 1997; Giroux and Simon, 1989; hooks, 1994; McLaren, 1993; Trier, 2003). Grant (2002) uses popular films in teacher education to allow student teachers to deconstruct myths about urban students and schools. Understanding how popular culture helps create meanings can help us to see how cultural difference and education are communicated and understood within society. Popular education films also celebrate fantasies of pleasurable and fulfilling education with messages about how education is a way to achieve the American Dream regardless of one's class, gender, or race. We can question whether such visions are realistic or rooted in Hollywood fantasy, but films contribute to how we think and talk about education and cultural difference. This chapter uses different levels of data to critically analyze how education films potentially inform this understanding.

This study asserts that popular education films warrant ongoing examination, in light of earlier studies of education films, with attention paid to their representation of race and difference. This is supported by Hall's (1996) idea that race is a floating signifier. It is the idea that the meaning of race is never fixed because it is premised on the context in which it is represented, and with each representation the context changes. Ongoing study is necessary so we can understand the new meanings that are being affixed to race across educational contexts and how this meaning making informs how the greater culture communicates about race within education. This chapter also discusses viewers' readings and critiques of popular education films to include audiences in the discussion. Finally, this study uses the Internet to explore meanings made by audiences. This is an emerging research technique in cultural and media studies that has both benefits and shortfalls. These counterpoints are explored in the following discussion of method.

METHOD

This study applies Fiske's (1987, 1989a, 1989 b) trilevel method for investigating popular culture phenomena to understand how popular films set in education work as popular cultural texts to understand the meanings that are derived from and attributed to them.

The first level in Fiske's (1987) method is the primary level of text. In this case the primary texts are the films *Finding Forrester*, *Save the Last Dance*, and *The Emperor's Club* that were selected from nearly forty popular education films televised over a twenty-four month period (January 2002–December 2003). These films were selected as representative primary texts because they engage and/or evade issues of cultural difference and they mirror other films in this genre. The films were analyzed for images, scenes, dialogue, and plot elements that seem to be communicating what it means to be culturally different within an educational setting. Films that were not chosen as primary texts are cited when they elaborate upon content seen in the primary film texts.

The secondary level of analysis requires locating and selecting from the criticism and publicity written about the primary level films. Criticism was found in newspapers (e.g., *USA Today*), magazines and e-zines (e.g., *Metro Active*, *Flakmagazine*), film criticism (e.g., *Cineaste*), and in critical studies of race and film. Film publicity included theater posters, promotional Web sites, and film trailers when relevant. Fiske (1987) notes that both criticism and publicity show producers and critics vying for control of the meaning of the primary text. Criticism suggests how a film is or will be read by viewers and upon what basis the film succeeds or fails. Publicity tells us what parts of the text that producers consider to be meanings central to understanding their film.

The third, or tertiary, level of analysis requires examination of viewer responses to the primary film texts. Tertiary level research examines viewers' bulletin board responses to the films on sites such as www.rottentomatoes.com, www.IMDb.com, www.yahoo.com, www.eopinions.com, and www.teachers.net. Internet bulletin boards can range in size from 50 to 1,000 messages on a single theme or contain several threads with individual messages varying from short sentences to several paragraphs.

The Internet facilitated data collection at this level by proving access to more subjects, who researchers note, act similarly to their offline counterparts (Joinson, 2001; Moon, 2000; Stewart, 2003). Fornäs, Klein, Ladendorf, Sundén, and Sveningsson (2002) also note that the bulletin or message board format can allow subjects more time to consider their contributions. Coomber (1997) criticizes online subject research, noting that white males dominate online discourse, whereas studies by Cornwell and Orbe (2002) and Lupton and Seymour (2003) affirm that marginalized groups such as African Americans and the disabled regularly use the Internet to engage in issues of identity and difference. The amount of data available at all three levels of textuality made it necessary to be selective in choosing the data to establish the themes that would be most relevant to the discussion from a critical interpretive perspective.

FINDINGS

The trilevel method assumes that similar and contradictory meanings can occur both between and within different textual levels. Bulletin board participants, publicity and criticism, and the actual films expressed a variety of content for critical analysis—from supporting the status quo to critically questioning, points between these perspectives. These films unite viewers and critics by evoking discussion and strong feelings, both of pleasure and discontent. Content that was extracted from primary-, secondary-, and third-level texts for closer examination was used to support critical themes. The themes are (1) white minds and black bodies, (2) images of education (with two subthemes). These themes represent a selection of the critical discourse surrounding education films and gives insight into how we negotiate race and education.

Theme One: White Minds and Black Bodies

This theme addresses how white and black students are characterized in unequal terms. Related to this theme is a discussion of students' adornment and dress. Representations of white students in education films emphasize order and logic. Early in *The Emperor's Club,* Professor Hundert corrects a lone student who runs across the lawn and suggests that he use the footpaths to "Walk with the great men who have walked before you." This emphasis on order extends to the classroom where students sit quietly, hands folded, and speak only when called upon to answer. One viewer is "bemused" by this representation noting, "The boys were all far too polite with hardly any rough edges at all … The teachers were far too nice—anyone from a Catholic school system will understand what I'm talking about here." This respondent contradicts the film representation of genteel students by stating his own experience of boarding school as one marked by disorderly conduct and overt discipline.

Black students are represented in ways that counter the orderly example of *The Emperor's Club.* In *Save the Last Dance* Sara, a white student from the suburbs, transfers to a predominantly black Chicago high school. The camera takes the perspective of Sara's eye in focusing on a security checkpoint where officers frisk a black male student. All students wear photo identification badges. In Sara's English class she answers a difficult literary question. Classmate Derek criticizes Sara's ignorance of African American authors and is encouraged by his classmates. Sara becomes silent, and the teacher interrupts the students' exchange.

These two representations evoke Descartes' mind-body dichotomy (Alenen, 2003). Mohanram (1999) notes how colonialism established a mind-body dichotomy to keep blacks in a subservient position by conceptualizing them as physical bodies requiring governance by whites who were depicted as having the qualities of the mind. In the education films discussed here whites are characterized as the mind and blacks are characterized as requiring surveillance and control. Giroux (1997) notes how in the film *Dangerous Minds* the black community is represented as illogically opposing and intimidating a forward-thinking white teacher. This white–black opposition is explored in various education films and film publicity. For example, in *Save the Last Dance* Derek challenges and opposes Sara's participation in class discussion. Derek is represented as visceral and reactive rather than intellectually proactive in the resulting exchange that reduces him to a physical presence or a foil to Sara's intellectual presence. One viewer wrote, "It bothered me that none of the black students were deemed intelligent to provide a reasonable answer except as a racial debate after Sara responds." The viewer's comments frame this classroom scene not as an educational exchange but as racial conflict. Similarly, in *Finding Forrester* when Forrester's deliveryman Massie activates his car alarm after seeing Jamal nearby Jamal reacts by aggressively shouting factual automotive knowledge at Massie. Like Derek, Jamal reacts to Massie's racist actions with knowledge, but his delivery shows a desire to react and oppose rather than to engage intellectually. So although characters such as Derek and Jamal draw upon their intellect, they do so reactively and defensively, whereas the white characters such as Sara act but resist reacting and produce emotionally detached, even passive, knowledge.

In film critic Dyer's (1997, p. 6) research the white body is characterized as "tightness, with self-control, self-consciousness, mind over body." Mohanram (1999) elaborates that from a white perspective the mind's control over the white body is preferable to a black body that is seen as acting on its own physicality. We see the white perspective when Sara's eye guides the camera to scenes in which black bodies are being frisked during her first introduction to the school. We see this white perspective later when Sara is distracted while walking with Derek's sister Chenille by a group of black students who show youthful abandon by listening to hip-hop and dancing. Chenille stops and takes Sara by the arm and says, "It's just a little hip-hop." Chenille words disrupt Sara's attempt to frame the women's physical involvement in contrast to her own stiffness. Chenille's words seem to be simultaneously directed at white viewers, who may view this scene the same way that Sara does.

The contrasting of white students in terms of the mind and black students in terms of the physical body is a key element in the plot of *Save the Last Dance*, as it is Derek who imparts his knowledge of hip-hop dance to Sara. Similarly, in *Finding Forrester* it is Derek who excels in basketball and tries to teach his white classmate Claire how to throw a basketball. Jamal and Derek excel in physical exploits such as dance and sports and are frequently shown teaching whites these skills. Dress and adornment, as an extension of the body, are also used to visually differentiate and identify characters based on race.

Derek's sister Chenille is praised on one hand for being a positive representation of an African American woman and also criticized by viewers for teaching stereotypical lessons. In one scene Sara plans to go to an urban nightspot with Chenille and her friends in an outfit purchased from The Gap. Chenille modifies Sara's outfit with her own jewelry and wraps Sara's hair with the Gap sweater. Chenille becomes an authority on bodily knowledge because she can take Sara from a mass-produced aesthetic and remake her body to reflect urban chic. One viewer posted, "Chenille and the sistaz will indoctrinate young Sara into the ghetoz way of life, dressing her up in ill-fitting and ludicrously unsuitable getup, doing her hair in a way that brings to mind Bob Marley." This viewer and others challenge why Chenille as a black woman has to be the expert on bodily adornment while also questioning how dress is used to align white and black characters with mass-produced culture versus alternative cultures respectfully.

How characters are dressed reminds us of their social position. Students in *The Emperor's Club* and *Finding Forrester* wear uniforms that reify their privileged status as prep school students. Postcolonial scholar Shome (1999) notes how Western school uniforms function to order the native body according to white Western standards of learning. Shome notes that for minority students such as Mehta, the only visible minority student in *The Emperor's Club*, uniformity is an illusion because the body of color marks one as different from white peers who also wear the uniform. Shome views the uniform as a white colonial move to elide nonwhite cultural difference.

In *Finding Forrester,* we see Jamal in a partial school uniform throughout the film (i.e., tie askew, jacket off). Jamal does not appear uniformed in exactly the same way as the other students until the end of the film once he decides to admit to a plagiarism that he did not commit for the sake of his school. In this scene, Forrester shows up and singles Jamal out from a class of similarly uniformed peers to praise him. The scene breaks the continuity of the uniform by setting Jamal apart via his race, scapegoat status, and Forrester's recognition, thus exposing the uniform's illusion of uniformity.

The theme of contrasting minority students with the homogenizing Western school uniforms occurs across education films. For example, in *Sarafina!* (Roodt, 1992) students celebrate Mandela's release and the end of apartheid by subverting their colonial school uniforms with Mandela T-shirts, berets, armbands, and grass skirts to show cultural freedom. In *School Ties* (Jaffe, Lansing, and Mandel, 1992), the school's characteristic necktie becomes a metaphor for assimilation as character David hides his Jewish identity behind this school necktie at an elite prep school. However wearing the uniform fails to override a Jewish ethnicity that ultimately prevents David from forging ties with his WASP classmates.

An urban uniform that comes from clothing that affiliates minority student characters with the inner-city streets counters the school uniform. Chenille attempts to provide Sara with a version of the urban uniform when they go out to the club. It is especially prominent in the film *Dangerous Minds* when white teacher Ms. Johnson is rebuffed by her black and Hispanic students, prompting her to abandon her teacher's uniform, consisting of a dowdy gray business suit with lace collars, in favor of the urban uniform of her students complete with her combat boots, leather jacket, baggy flannel shirt, and jeans. The urban uniform draws attention to the body by marking it as counter to authority, emphasizing and making body parts such as Sara's hair stand out.

In education films, the urban uniform disrupting the nondescript nature of the white body is represented in order to gain acceptance in an urban setting. The use of clothing is an extension of the differing representation of white and black characters. Intercultural representation is expressed in terms of the mind–body dichotomy to note how such characterizations not only establish difference but also unequal power relationships.

Theme Two: Images of Education

This theme addresses how popular films represent education and has two subthemes: (1) popular films as educational texts and (2) education versus educación.

Subtheme one: Popular films as educational texts. Viewers contrast education films from other media because of its perceived educational goals. One viewer writes, "The writers touched [interracial romance] without making it out to be an *ABC After School Special*. Both Sarah and Derek were made to realize that their relationship affected many different people in many different ways." Education films trump the *After School Special* because the latter preaches about social issues while film is less so with references to youth culture through music, dance, and language. Several education films have launched successful soundtracks. *Save the Last Dance* was so successful that Fox/Paramount Television coproduced an unaired TV pilot based on the film (Freydkin, 2002).

A viewer expressed having felt doubt about seeing *Save the Last Dance* because it was an MTV Films production, and she feared the subject would not be treated seriously. Perhaps she felt this way because some media critics associate MTV with a generation of media consumers who value style over substance. This viewer might remember MTV's first feature film—*Dead Man on Campus*, an education comedy in which two coeds plot to find a roommate who will commit suicide.

The coeds do this because they choose to believe the urban myth that you will be given an automatic 4.0 GPA in college if your roommate commits suicide.

Viewers expect education films to teach lessons as they are marketed this way. *The Emperor's Club* Web site, since the film debates character, invites visitors to play an interactive game to determine their moral character (Abraham and Hoffman, 2002). One viewer writes of *Finding Forrester*, "Try to see this movie as an educational movie about life will you." Another writes, "It was a great movie because of the lessons in the movie, not because it was action packed." Viewers discussing *The Emperor's Club* agree that the film teaches a lesson but disagree about whether the lesson is for students or teachers. In the case of *The Emperor's Club* and *Finding Forrester*, viewers extract lessons about having character, the nature of learning and knowledge, and living right.

Viewers agree that exploring racism is central to *Save the Last Dance* but disagree about who faces racism. A viewer writes, "This film takes a courageous stance, in showing the reverse racism that is as real as the 'classic' white against black." Another writes, "The movie showed that black people also have a lot of barriers to overcome in order not to discriminate against white people because of their color." Other viewers reject these claims as Sara is the focus of a movie with a mostly black cast. One viewer responds to claims of white racism writing, "Poor li'l Sara is subjected to so many cruel jibes focusing on her white skin. I can imagine that can be so very harsh! However." Two *Save the Last Dance* bulletin boards transition from discussing the film to personal reflection and arguments about race and interracial relationships apart from the film. This shows how education films participate in a larger discourse about race and difference.

Save the Last Dance is told from Sara's white perspective as she negotiates a black high school. In films that depict white students almost exclusively, the reverse is not true for minority characters. Mehta, in *The Emperor's Club*, interestingly faces no overt racism but remains more of a secondary character until the end of the film as much of the movie is told from the perspective of Professor Hundert. In *Legally Blonde*, Professor Stromwell taps the head of the one nameless black student in her law class and asks a white student, if he were a lawyer, would he risk the black student's life on his answer to an in-class question. The professor's lesson is on certainty, but she indirectly teaches about racism by framing this voiceless black student as the defendant and his white classmate as his attorney.

What makes an educational film pedagogical and not pedantic? This theme suggests that viewers expect education films to present a lesson that is accessible, relevant, and entertaining. A film's lesson is also in the eye of the viewer. Not all viewers will derive the same lessons from a film, yet the lessons deserve critical examination in promoting discussion of the intentional and unintentional curricula of education films.

Subtheme two: Education versus educación. hooks (1994, p. 164) states, "There's something else going on when we create spaces outside of the classroom for serious discussion." hooks is noting how critical pedagogy often finds spaces outside of the white classroom. Making separate spaces for white and nonwhite knowledge and learning is important to consider as this subtheme explores how learning is pursued both within and outside traditional contexts in education films.

The Mailer School in *Finding Forrester* emphasizes the white, Western literary canon as depicted in portraits on Professor Crawford's classroom walls. In the climactic scene Jamal confronts Professor Crawford by matching literary wits with him. This angers Crawford, who tells Jamal to leave class. As Jamal stands up to leave, his face is framed in a profile shot against a backdrop of similarly posed portraits of white literary figures. The shot seemingly comments both on Jamal's great potential and on Crawford's refusal to recognize great writing in anything other than a white writer represented in this canon. The film locates Jamal's learning outside the classroom in Forrester's apartment, where his mentor commands him to write from his own experience. In one scene Jamal is writing in bed despite the sounds of domestic violence and intercourse coming through his thin bedroom walls. The film posits that real learning is the love between student and mentor, challenging life experiences, and the actual doing of writing and not the formal relationships and disembodied rote learning that characterizes Crawford's classroom.

In *The Emperor's Club*, Professor Hundert's classroom similarly bears the portraits of Greek and Roman philosophers. Introducing the students to his Western Civilization course, Hundert states, "Aristotle, Caesar, Augustus, Plato, Cicero, Socrates: giants of history, men of profound character ... Their story is our story." Hundert here foreshadows how his largely white, male prep school students are poised to hold power and privilege. One viewer writes, "A modern Julius Caesar would most likely come to power in America with degrees from such an elite school—those matters lie unremarked [*sic*], glittering darkly in the heart of *The Emperor's Club*." In another scene, Mehta, the sole minority student, reads about Carthaginian general Hamilcar Barca in his dorm room. Hundert is amused to see Mehta reading outside of the classroom curriculum. The scene not only speaks to learning for its own sake but perhaps also reflects Mehta's desire for a more diverse learning experience than the classroom canon provides.

The juxtaposition of these learning experiences mirrors the difference that others have expressed as the difference between education and *educación.* Valenzuela (1999, p. 23) notes how *educación*, Spanish for education, also connotes building character and fostering students to be "caring, responsible, wellmannered, and respectful human beings." Valenzuela (1999) notes that *educación,* enacted through a mutually caring student–mentor relationship, must exist before education can happen. Some take *educación* as a rethinking of traditional educational relationships, what it means to learn, and what facilitates a learning experience. *Educación* is also cognizant that cultural differences of race, class, gender, ethnicity, and sexuality inform how we acquire knowledge and construct identity (Elenes, Gonzalez, Bernal, and Villenas, 2001).

Educación is implied in *Finding Forrester*. Jamal is stifled and stereotyped as a black athlete in the classroom, yet he flourishes as a writer and is validated in his identity in the gruff, but loving, atmosphere of Forrester's apartment. Although Professor Crawford teaches his students to surrender themselves to the great texts and his pedagogy, Forrester urges Jamal to discover himself through writing. Through their mutually caring relationship, Jamal and Forrester foster *educación*, which allows each man to better understand himself and thus to better engage with the world outside his own comfort level.

Educación is a frequent theme in education films with minority protagonists. *Real Women Have Curves* (La Voo, Brown, and Cardoso [2002]) begins with Ana, a Mexican American, graduating from high school, and the film ends with her going to college in the fall. She is shown learning not in the classroom but from the immigrant women, her mother, and her sister, who are her summer coworkers in a dress factory. At first Ana considers herself above these women, but she learns to appreciate her advantages, respect her culture, and embrace her plus-sized body. Similarly, in *A Lesson Before Dying* (Benedetti and Sargent, 1999), teacher Grant Wiggins bonds with death row inmate Jefferson, whom he has been enlisted to teach. Wiggins is teaching more than lessons as he prepares Jefferson to live and die as a man and not as the animal that Jefferson's attorney describes him as being. Learning happens not through the lessons that Wiggins teaches but through Wiggins and Jefferson's relationship that allows Jefferson and Wiggins to find community, dignity, and awareness as African American men in the segregated south.

Viewers appreciate new and nontraditional representations of education because it facilitates their fantasy of escaping or being rescued from what they perceive to be oppressive educational experiences. Viewers and critics consistently narrate their own negative educational experiences to validate these films' representation of learning. Film critic Sean Weitner (2001) claims that the shared desire to escape a repressive and "emotionally cloistered" school caused him to invest emotionally at screenings of *Finding Forrester* and *Dead Poets Society*. Poet and writer Terry Ehret, who relates to the scene from *Finding Forrester* of Jamal writing in bed while tuning out the sounds from other apartments. Ehret (cited in Templeton, 2001) notes, "I identified with his sense that there just has to be something more than what he had ... that writing was the way to bring something better into being, to invent a world where he'd be more at home ... That was me."

As a white woman, Ehret overlooks the cultural differences between herself and Jamal to focus how they share writing as both a tool of learning and as a means of escaping their circumstances. Teachers also escape into the fantasy world of education films. One viewer, a preservice teacher, reports how the school in which she works "squashed" a disadvantaged student's initiative and "predetermined" his future. She notes, "Watching *October Sky*, I made a new commitment to my future students and myself: I will do my very best to be a Ms. Riley to my students-I will believe in the unlucky ones." Education films allow viewers to escape as well as to connect to their own less than satisfying educational experiences. Seeing learning portrayed outside the classroom and in ways that focus on relationships and on self-discovery appeals to viewers who have experienced discontent as students and teachers.

The first theme in this chapter critiques education films' equation of non-white experience in terms of the physical body as juxtaposed to the white mind. This critique resonates here, as we are still not seeing culturally integrated classrooms onscreen. Certain classrooms, as depicted in the films discussed, are guided by white, Western canons of knowledge and leave minority students unrecognized and looking elsewhere for learning experience. Both Dalton (1999) and Ayers (1994) lament how education films represent the most significant learning as happening outside the classroom and the formal curricula. Why is this the case? This subtheme questions whether traditional classrooms and curricula can solely meet the learning needs of culturally and intellectually diverse students. Viewers question similarly and look for creative subjects and mentors, whether actual or fictional, that challenge and embrace them. As a genre, education films posit that learning requires life experiences that cannot be confined exclusively to the classroom, thus making the personal lives of students, and the superteachers who meddle in them, central for exploring alternate images of education.

DISCUSSION AND DIRECTIONS FOR FUTURE INQUIRY

This chapter posits two themes of education films while recognizing that producers, critics, and viewers negotiate education films in a variety of ways. This chapter focuses on the themes of (1) white minds and black bodies and (2) images of education with the subthemes of popular films as educational texts and as education versus *educación*. These themes are representative and not exhaustive of popular education films, as they were arrived at from a critical perspective on race and education. It is important to discuss these themes to understand how they frame our perceptions of race and education.

One representation of education on screen cannot capture all experience, and most viewers, as educational consumers, will inevitably evaluate these representations. Many education films attempt to replicate Farhi's (1999) superteacher or similar success narratives that position education, both good and bad, as a means to success and empowerment. The production and consumption of these narratives have also negatively impacted minority groups in need of empowering messages in a white-dominated society. Empowerment must not come at another's expense, and we must continue to revisit education films so as to reinforce this point with film producers and audiences.

Critically minded educators such as Grant (2002) remind us that negative representations can be used to foster necessary discussions. Message boards for the films *Save the Last Dance* and *Finding Forrester* transition from lighthearted discussions of the fictional characters to intense and personal discussions of race. The discussions were not always respectful of the differences, but they demonstrate how popular representations can be an impetus for communicating about race and difference. Arguably the representations are slowly changing as we see fewer bad students and more college-bound students, but old stereotypes linger and change needs to be hastened. Hopefully we will be able to mark positive change with each subsequent film that is released.

This chapter deals with mainstream films, but research for this chapter suggests that diverse educational stories are being told in partnership with cable television broadcasters. Tasker (1996) notes how important television is for film distribution. Hopefully the recent proliferation of diversity-oriented cable outlets will provide outlets for a greater diversity of education films. Television distribution of older films ensures that we keep these films in play for new audiences to critique and interrogate.

Limitations of this study include the inability to interrogate viewers in greater depth and to ask follow-up questions. Such an approach might resemble Fisherkeller's (2002) case study of one African American youth's interaction with American television culture from ages twelve to eighteen years. It is also important, in future extension of this study, to increase the focus on independent films.

This chapter makes no definitive claims about education films, as the genre continues to produce representations that require new criticism and study. Hall (1996) reminds us that race is a floating signifier and takes on new meanings with each representation. If education films really do have a lesson to teach, then maybe the producers working in this genre will learn from past mistakes to produce more inclusive images. The proliferation of education films and related narratives will fuel more studies as we strive to understand how these films contribute to creating a discursive space in which we formulate our perspectives on the related constructs of race and education.

REFERENCES

Abraham, M. (Producer) and Hoffman, M. (Director). (2002). *The emperor's club* [Universal Pictures movie].

Ackerman, R., Maslin-Ostrowski, P., and Christensen, C. (1996). Case stories: Telling tales about school. *Educational Leadership, 53,* 21–23.

Alenen, L (2003). *Descartes's concept of mind.* Cambridge: Harvard University Press.

Ayers, W.C. (1994). A teacher ain't nothing but a hero: Teachers and teaching in film. In P.B. Joseph and G.E. Burnaford (Eds.), *Images of schoolteachers in twentieth-century America: Paragons, Polarities, Complexities* (pp. 147–156). New York: St. Martin's Press.

Benedetti, R. (Producer), and Sargent, J. (Director). (1999). *A lesson before dying* [HBO movie].

Boyd, J. (2004). Dance, culture, and popular film: Considering representations in *Save the Last Dance. Feminist Media Studies, 4,* 67–83.

Carter, K. (1993). The place of the story in the study of teaching and teacher education. *Educational Researcher, 22,* 5–12.

Coomber, J. (1997). Using the internet for survey research. *Sociological Research Online, 2, 15.* Retrieved December 1, 2003 from http://www.socresonline.org.uk/2/2/2.html

Cornwell, N.C., and Orbe, M.P. (2002). "Keepin' it real" and/or "sellin' out to the man:" African-American responses to Aaron McGruder's *The Boondocks.* In R.R. Means Coleman (Ed.), *Say it loud: African-American audiences, media, and identity* (pp. 27–42). New York: Routledge.

Cort, R.W., and Madden, D. (Producers), and Carter, T. (Director). (2000). *Save the last dance* [Paramount Pictures movie].

Dalton, M.M. (1999). *The Hollywood curriculum: Teachers and teaching in the movies.* New York: Peter Lang.

Davey, B. (Producer), and Reynolds, K. (Director). (1997). *187* [Icon Productions movie].

Delpit, L. (1995). *Other people's children: Cultural conflict in the classroom.* New York: The New Press.

Dyer, R. (1997). *White.* London: Routledge.

Elenes, C.A., Gonzalez, F.E., Bernal, D.D., and Villenas, S. (2001). Introduction: Chicana/Mexicana feminist pedagogies: *Consejos, respeto, y educación* in everyday life. *Qualitative Studies in Education, 14,* 595–602.

Farhi, A. (1999). Recognizing the superteacher myth in film. *Clearing House, 72,* 157–159.

Fisherkeller, J. (2002). It's just like teaching people 'Do the right things'. In R.R. Means Coleman (Ed.), *Say it loud: African-American audiences, media, and identity* (pp. 147–185). New York: Routledge.

Fiske, J. (1987). *Television culture.* London: Routledge.

———. (1989a). *Reading the popular.* Boston: Unwin Hyman.

———. (1989b). *Understanding popular culture.* London: Routledge.

Fornäs, J., Klein, K., Ladendorf, M., Sundén, J., and Sveningsson, M. (Eds.). (2002). *Digital borderlands: Cultural studies of identity and interactivity on the internet.* New York: Peter Lang.

Freydkin, D. (2002, April 16). Dancing their way to TV. *USA Today,* pp. 3D.

Giroux, H.A. (1997). Race, pedagogy, and whiteness in *Dangerous Minds. Cineaste, 22,* 46–49.

Giroux, H.A., and Shannon, P. (1997). *Education and cultural studies: Towards a* performative practice. New York: Routledge.

Giroux, H.A., and Simon, R.I. (1989). *Popular culture, schooling, and everyday life.* Westport: Bergin and Garvey.

Grant, P. (2002). Using popular films to challenge preservice teachers' beliefs about teaching in urban schools. *Urban education, 37,* 77–95.

Hall, S. (1996). *Race: The floating signifier* [video]. Northhampton, MA: Media Education Foundation.

Heilman, R.B. (1991). The great-teacher myth. *American Scholar, 60,* 417–423.

Hinton, D.B. (1994). *Celluloid ivy: Higher education in the movies 1960–1990.* Metuchen, NJ: The Scarecrow Press.

hooks, b. (1994). *Teaching to transgress: Education as the practice of freedom.* New York: Routledge.

Jaffe, S.R., and Lansing, S. (Producers), and Mandel, R. (Director). (1992). *School ties* [Paramount Pictures movie].

Johnston, J. (Director). (1999). *October sky* [Universal Pictures movie].

Joinson, A.N. (2001). Knowing me, knowing you: Reciprocal self-disclosure in internet based surveys. *CyberPsychology & Behavior, 5,* 587–591.

La Voo, G., and Brown, E.T. (Producers), and Cardoso, P. (Director). (2002). *Real women have curves* [HBO Films movie].

Lupton, D., and Seymour, W. (2003). "I am normal on the 'net": Disability, computerized computer technologies and the embodied self. In J. Coupland and R. Gwyn (Eds.), *Discourse, the body, and identity* (pp. 246–265). Houndmills, Basingstoke, Hampshire, UK: Palgrave Macmillan Ltd.

McLaren, P. (1993). *Schooling as a ritual performance: Towards a political economy of education symbols and gestures.* New York: Routledge.

Mohanram, R. (1999). *Black body: Women, colonialism, and space.* Minneapolis: University of Minnesota Press.

Moon, Y. (2000). Intimate exchanges: Using computers to elicit self-disclosure from consumers. *Journal of Consumer Research, 26,* 323–339.

Preskill, S. (1998). Narratives of teaching and the quest for the second self. *Journal of Teacher Education, 49,* 344–357.

Quintilianus, M.F., and Butler H.E. (1920). *Institutio Oratoria: Loeb classical library.* Cambridge: Harvard University Press.

Roodt, D. (Director). (1992). *Sarafina!* [Buena Vista Pictures movie].

Schubert, W., and Ayers, W. (Eds.). (1992). *Teacher lore.* White Plains, NY: Longman.

Shome, R. (1999). Whiteness and the politics of location: Postcolonial reflections. In T.K. Nakayama and J.N. Martin (Eds.), *Whiteness: The communication of social identity* (pp. 107–128). Thousand Oaks, CA: Sage Publications.

Simpson, D., and Bruckheimer, J. (Producers), and Smith, J.N. (Director). (1995). *Dangerous minds* [Hollywood Pictures movie].

Simpson, K. (2002). Media images of the urban landscape: The South Bronx in film. *CENTRO Journal, 14,* 98–113.

Stewart, S. (2003). Casting the net: Using the internet for survey research. *British Journal of Midwifery, 11,* 543–546.

Tasker, Y. (1996). Approaches to the new Hollywood. In J. Curran, D. Morley, and V. Walkerdine (Eds.), *Cultural studies and communications* (pp. 213–228). New York: St. Martin's Press.

Templeton, D. (2001). Write turn: North Bay poet Terry Ehret critiques *Finding Forrester.* Retrieved from The Metro Active Web site: http://www.metroactive. com/papers/Sonoma/02.01.01/talk-pix-0105.html

Trier, J. (2003). Inquiring into "techniques of power" with preservice teachers through the "school film" *The Paper Chase. Teaching & Teacher Education, 19,* 543–557.

Valenzuela, A. (1999). *Subtractive schooling: US–Mexican youth and the politics of caring.* Albany: State University of New York Press.

Van Sant, G. (Director). (2000). *Finding Forrester* [Columbia Pictures movie].

Weitner, S. (2001). *Finding Forrester* [film review]. Retrieved December 11, 2003 from *The Flakmagazine* Web site: http://www.flakmag.com/film/finding.html

CHAPTER THREE

Militarization, Public Pedagogy, AND THE Biopolitics OF Popular Culture

HENRY A. GIROUX

Under the Bush administration, American power is being restructured domestically around a growing culture of fear and a rapidly increasing militarization of public space and popular culture. As United States military action is spreading abroad under the guise of an unlimited war against terrorism, popular spheres on the domestic front are increasingly being organized around values supporting a highly militarized, patriarchal, and jingoistic culture that is undermining "centuries of democratic gains."[1] Americans are not only obsessed with military power, but a kind of military metaphysics "has become central to" their "national identity."[2] Andrew J. Bacevich develops this position by arguing that Americans have fallen prey to a dangerous form of militarism. He writes:

> To state the matter bluntly, Americans in our own time have fallen prey to militarism, manifesting itself in a romanticized view of soldiers, a tendency to see military power as the truest measure of national greatness, and outsized expectations regarding the efficacy of force. To a degree without precedent in U.S. history, Americans have come to define the nation's strength and well-being in terms of military preparedness. Military action, and the fostering of (or nostalgia for) military ideals.[3]

How else is one to explain the fact that the United States has "725 official military bases outside the country and 969 at home"? Or that it "spends more on 'defense' than all the rest of the world put together ...." or the fact that "this country is obsessed with war: rumors of war, images of war, 'preemptive' war, 'preventive' war, 'surgical' war, 'prophylactic' war, 'permanent' war"? As President Bush explained at a news conference on April 13, 2004, "This country must go on the offense and stay on the offense."[4] The process of militarization—the increasing centrality of the military in shaping American culture, society, and foreign policy—has a long history in the United States and takes on different forms under different historical conditions.[5] Catherine Lutz provides a further helpful definition of militarization:

> [Militarization is] an intensification of the labor and resources allocated to military purposes, including the shaping of other institutions in synchrony with military goals. Militarization is simultaneously a discursive process, involving a shift in general societal beliefs and values in ways necessary to legitimate the use of force, the organization of large standing armies and their leaders, and the higher taxes or tribute used to pay for them. Militarization is intimately connected not only to the obvious increase in the size of armies and resurgence of militant nationalisms and militant fundamentalisms but also to the less visible deformation of human potentials into the hierarchies of race, class, gender, and sexuality, and to the shaping of national histories in ways that glorify and legitimate military action.[6]

Unlike the old style of militarization in which all forms of civil authority are subordinate to military authority, the new ethos of militarization is organized to engulf the entire social order, legitimating its values as a central rather than peripheral aspect of American public life. Moreover, the values of militarism are no longer limited to a particular group or sphere of society. On the contrary, Jorge Mariscal points out:

> In liberal democracies, in particular, the values of militarism do not reside in a single group but are diffused across a wide variety of cultural locations. In twenty-first century America, no one is exempt from militaristic values because the processes of militarization allow those values to permeate the fabric of everyday life.[7]

The growing influence of the military presence and ideology in American society is made visible, in part, by the fact that the United States has now more police personnel, prisons, spies, weapons, and soldiers than at any other time in its history. This radical shift in the size, scope, and influence of the military can be seen in the redistribution of domestic resources and government funding—less to social programs and more to military-oriented security measures—at home and war abroad. As Richard Falk pointed out, "The US Government is devoting huge resources to the monopolistic militarization of space, the development of more usable nuclear weapons, and the strengthening of its world-girdling ring of military bases and its global navy, as the most tangible way to discourage any strategic challenges to its preeminence."[8] According to journalist George Monbiot, the federal government "is now spending as much on war as it is on education, public health, housing, employment, pensions, food aid and welfare put together."[9] Moreover, the state is being radically transformed into a national security state, and increasingly put under the sway of the military–corporate–industrial–educational complex. The military logic of fear, surveillance, and control is gradually permeating our public schools, universities, streets, popular culture, and criminal justice system.

Since the events of 9/11 and the wars in Afghanistan and Iraq, the military has assumed a privileged place in American society. President Bush not only celebrates the military presence in American culture, but he also cultivates it by going out of his way to give speeches at military facilities, talk to military personnel, and address veterans' groups. He often wears a military uniform when speaking to "captive audiences at military bases, defense plants, and on aircraft carriers."[10] He also takes advantage of the campaign value of military culture by using military symbolism as a political prop to attract the widest possible media attention. One glaring example was evident on May 1, 2003, when Bush landed in full aviator flight uniform on the USS *Abraham Lincoln* in the Pacific Ocean, where he officially proclaimed the end of the Iraq war. There was also the secret trip to Baghdad to spend Thanksgiving Day (2003) with the troops, an event that attracted worldwide coverage in all the media. Since his reelection in 2004, Bush has showcased defense experts, such as Dick Cheney, Robert Gates, and Condoleezza Rice as the most visible and key representatives of a government whose power reflects what President Eisenhower had long ago labeled the "military–industrial complex" and had viewed as a dire threat to American democracy.[11] But Bush has done more than take advantage of the military as a campaign prop to sell his domestic and foreign policies. His administration, along with the Republican Party, developed a new, if not dangerous, "and unprecedented confluence of our democratic institutions and the military."[12]

Writing in *Harper's Magazine*, Kevin Baker claims that the military "has become the most revered institution in the country."[13] Soon after the Iraq War was declared, a Gallup Poll reported that more than 76 percent of Americans "expressed 'a great deal' or 'quite a lot' of confidence in their nation's military." In a poll of 1,200 students conducted by Harvard University, 75 percent believed that the military would most of the time "do the right thing." In addition, the students "characterized themselves as hawks over doves by a ratio of two to one."[14] Popular fears about domestic safety and internal threats, accentuated by endless terror alerts, have created a society that increasingly accepts the notion of a "war without limits" as a normal state of affairs. But fear and insecurity do more than produce a collective anxiety among Americans; they have been brainwashed into believing that they should vote Republican because it is the only political party that can protect them. In addition to producing manufactured political loyalty, such fears can also be manipulated into a kind of "war fever." In such cases, as Robert Lifton points out, "War then becomes heroic, even mythic, a task that must be carried out for the defense of one's nation, to sustain its special historical destiny and immortality of its people."[15] The war fever, intensified through a politics and culture of fear, carries with it a kind of paranoid edge, and is endlessly stoked by government alerts and repressive laws; it has been used "to create the most extensive national security apparatus in our nation's history."[16] Military support is also reproduced in the Foxified media, which, in addition to constantly marketing the flag and interminably implying that critics of American foreign policy are traitors, offer seemingly endless images of brave troops on the frontline, heroic stories of released American prisoners, and utterly privatized commentaries on those wounded or killed in battle.[17] *TIME* magazine embodied this representational indulgence in military culture by naming the American soldier the 2003 "Person of the Year." Not only have such ongoing and largely uncritical depictions of war injected a constant military presence in American life, but they have also helped to create a civil society that has become aggressive in its warlike enthusiasm. But more is at work here than just the exploitation of troops for higher ratings or the attempts by right-wing political strategists to keep the American public in a state of permanent fear and to remove pressing domestic issues from public debate. There is also the attempt by the Bush administration to convince as many Americans as possible that, under the current "state of emergency," the use of the military in domestic affairs is perfectly acceptable. This is evident in the increasing propensity to use the military establishment "to incarcerate and interrogate suspected terrorists and 'enemy combatants' and keep them beyond the reach of the civilian judicial system, even if they are American citizens."[18] It is also evident in the attempts of the federal government to try terrorists in military courts and to detain prisoners "outside the provisions of the Geneva Convention as prisoners of war. … at the US Marine Corps base at Guantanamo, Cuba because that facility is outside of the reach of the American courts."[19]

As the military becomes more popular in American life, its underlying values, social relations, ideology, and hypermasculine aesthetic begin to spill out into other aspects of American culture. Representations of fear are coupled with representations of hypermasculinity as a legitimating nod toward legitimating violence as central to the new biopolitics of militarized culture. Citizens are recruited as foot soldiers in the war on terrorism; they are urged to spy on their neighbors' behaviors, watch for suspicious-looking people, and supply data to government sources in the war on terrorism. As permanent war becomes a staple of everyday life, flags increasingly appear on storefront windows, lapels, cars, houses, SUVs, and everywhere else, as a show of support for both the expanding interests of empire abroad and the increasing militarization of the culture and social order at home. Major universities now compete for defense contracts and rush to create courses and programs that cater to the interests of the Department of Homeland Security. Congress recently passed legislation that would "stiffen penalties for colleges that bar military recruiters from their campuses."[20] JROTC (Junior Reserve Officers' Training Corps) programs are increasingly becoming a conventional part of the school day. As a result of President Bush's No Child Left Behind Act, "schools risk losing all federal aid if they fail to provide military recruiters full access to their students; the aid is contingent with complying with federal law."[21] Schools were once viewed as democratic public spheres that would teach students how to resist the militarization of democratic life, or at least to learn the skills to peacefully engage with domestic and international problems. Now they serve as recruiting stations that will send students to fight enemies at home and abroad.

Militarization abroad cannot be separated from the increasing militarization of society at home. War takes on a new meaning in American life as wars are waged on drugs; social policies are criminalized; youth are tried as adults; incarceration rates soar among the poor, especially people of color, and; schools are increasingly modeled after prisons. Schools represent one of the most serious public spheres to come under the influence of military culture and values. Tough love now translates into zero tolerance policies that turn public schools into disciplinary institutions that increasingly fail to recognize students' rights. In addition, as educators turn over their responsibility for school safety to the police, the new security culture in public schools has turned them into "learning prisons,"[22] most evident in the ways in which schools are being "reformed" with the addition of armed guards, barbed-wire security fences, and lockdown drills. In Goose Creek, South Carolina, police conducted an early-morning drug sweep at Stratford High School. When the police arrived they drew guns on students, handcuffed them, and made them kneel facing the wall.[23] No drugs were found in the raid. Although this incident was aired on the national news, there were barely any protests from the public.

Judging from Bush's 2007 State of the Union Address, the Bush administration will continue to allocate funds for "educational reform" intended both to strip young people of the capacity to think critically by teaching them that learning is largely about test-taking and to prepare them for a culture in which punishment has become the central principle of reform. Bush cannot fully fund his own educational reform act, but he pledged in his 2007 State of the Union Address additional funds to promote drug testing of students in public schools. Moreover, the political conceit and hypocrisy that informs Bush's public concern for young people was on display recently when he vetoed the SCHIP Bill, designed to provides millions of poor children with health insurance. Once again, fear, punishment, and containment override the need to provide healthcare for 9.3 million uninsured children, increase the ranks of new teachers by at least 100,000, fully support Head Start programs, repair deteriorating schools, and improve those youth services that will break the direct pipeline from school to the local police station, the courts, or prison for many poor students.

The rampant combination of fear and insecurity that is so much a part of a permanent war culture in the United States seems to bear down particularly hard on children. In many poor schools districts, specialists are being laid off and crucial mental health services are being cut back. As Sara Rimer recently pointed out in the *New York Times*, much needed student-based services and traditional, if not compassionate, ways of dealing with student problems are now being replaced by the juvenile justice system, which functions "as a dumping ground for poor minority kids with mental health and special-education problems. … The juvenile detention center has become an extension of the principal's office."[24] For example, in some cities, ordinances have been passed that "allow for the filing of misdemeanor charges against students for anything from disrupting a class to assaulting a teacher."[25] Children are no longer given a second chance for minor behavior infractions, nor are they simply sent to the guidance counselor, principal, or to detention. They now come under the jurisdiction of the courts and the juvenile justice system.

The militarization of public high schools has become so commonplace that, even in the face of the most flagrant disregard for children's rights, it is justified by both administrators and the public on the grounds that it keeps kids safe. At the same time, as children encounter a profound distrust on the part of adult society, they are being educated to passively accept military-sanctioned practices organized around maintaining control, surveillance, and unquestioned authority, all conditions central to a police state and to a unique form of authoritarianism. It gets worse. Some schools are actually using sting operations in which undercover agents who pretend to be students are used to catch young people suspected of selling drugs or committing any one of a number of school infractions. The consequences of such actions are far-reaching. As Randall Beger points out,

> Opponents of school-based sting operations say they not only create a climate of mistrust between students and police, but they also put innocent students at risk of wrongful arrest due to faulty tips and overzealous police work. When asked about his role in a recent undercover probe at a high school near Atlanta, a young-looking police officer who attended classes and went to parties with students replied: "I knew I had to fit in, make kids trust me and then turn around and take them to jail."[26]

Under the auspices of a national security state and the militarization of domestic life, containment policies become the principal means to discipline working-class youth and restrict their ability to think critically and engage in oppositional practices. Marginalized students learn quickly that they are surplus populations and that the journey from home to school no longer means they will move into a job after completing school; on the contrary, school now becomes a training ground for their "graduation" into containment centers such as prisons and jails that keep them out of sight, patrolled, and monitored to prevent them from becoming a social canker or political liability to the white and middle-class populations concerned about their own safety. Schools increasingly function as zoning mechanisms to separate students marginalized by class and color and, as such, have become prisonlike in their role as social institutions. This follows the argument of David Garland, who points out, "Large-scale incarceration functions as a mode of economic and social placement, a zoning mechanism that segregates those populations rejected by the depleted institutions of family, work, and welfare and places them behind the scenes of social life."[27]

Instances of domestic militarization, the rise of the punishing state, and the war at home can also be seen in the rise of the prison–industrial–educational complex and the militarization of the criminal justice system. The traditional "distinctions between military, police, and criminal justice are blurring."[28] The police now work in close collaboration with the military. This takes the form of receipt of surplus weapons, technology/information transfers, the introduction of SWAT teams modeled after the Navy Seals—all of which are experiencing a steep growth in police departments throughout the United States—and a growing reliance on military models of crime control.[29] This growth of the military model in American life has played a crucial role in the paramilitarizing of the culture, which provides both a narrative and legitimation "for recent trends in corrections, including the normalization of special response teams, the increasingly popular Supermax prisons, and drug war boot camps."[30] In the paramilitaristic perspective, crime is no longer seen as a social problem. Crime is now viewed both as an individual pathology and as a matter of punishing rather than rehabilitating the "enemy." Unsurprisingly, paramilitary culture increasingly embodies a racist and class-specific discourse, and "reflects the discrediting of the social and its related narratives."[31] This is particularly evident as America's inner cities are being singled out as dangerous enclaves of crime and violence. The consequences for these communities have been catastrophic, as can be seen in the cataclysmic rise of the prison-industrial complex. As Sanho Tree points out,

> With more than 2 million people behind bars (there are only 8 million prisoners in the entire world), the United States—with one-twenty-second of the world's population—has one-quarter of the planet's prisoners. We operate the largest penal system in the world, and approximately one-quarter of all our prisoners (nearly half a million people) are there for nonviolent drug offenses.[32]

Of the 2 million people behind bars, nearly 70 percent of the inmates are people of color: 50 percent are African American and 17 percent are Latino.[33] In addition, over 5 million people are either on probation, parole, or under supervision of the criminal justice system. When poor youth of color are not being warehoused in dilapidated schools or incarcerated, they are being aggressively recruited by the army to fight the war in Iraq. For example, Carl Chery recently reported:

> With help from *The Source* magazine, the U.S. military is targeting hip-hop fans with custom made Hummers, throwback jerseys and trucker hats. The yellow Hummer, spray-painted with two black men in military uniform, is the vehicle of choice for the U.S. Army's "Take It to the Streets campaign"—a sponsored mission aimed at recruiting young African Americans into the military ranks.[34]

It seems that the army has discovered hip-hop and urban culture and rather than listening to the searing indictment of poverty, joblessness, and despair that is one of their central messages, the army recruiters appeal to their most commodified elements by letting the "potential recruits hang out in the Hummer, where they can pep the sound system or watch recruitment videos."[35] Of course, they will not view any videos of Hummers being blown up in the war-torn streets of Baghdad.

Domestic militarization is also widespread in the realm of culture and it functions as a mode of public pedagogy, instilling the values and the aesthetic of militarization through a wide variety of pedagogical sites and cultural venues. From video games to Hollywood films to children's toys, popular culture is increasingly bombarded with militarized values, symbols, and images. For instance, Humvee ads offer the fantasy of military glamour and machismo masculinity, marketed to suggest that ownership of these military-designed vehicles, first used in Desert Storm, guarantees virility for its owners and promotes a mixture of fear and admiration from everyone else. One of the fastest-growing sports for middle-class suburban youth is the game of paintball "in which teenagers stalk and shoot each other on 'battlefields' (in San Diego, California, paintball participants pay an additional $50 to hone their skills at the Camp Pendleton Marine Base)."[36] Military recruitment ads flood all modes of entertainment; they use sophisticated marketing tools and offer messages that resonate powerfully with young people with appeals to particular forms of masculinity that directly serve as an enticement for recruitment. For example, the Web site for the US Marines, www.marines.com, opens with the sound of gunfire and then provides the following message:

> We are the warriors, one and all. Born to defend, built to conquer. The steel we wear is the steel within ourselves, forged by the hot fires of discipline and training. We are fierce in a way no other can be. We are the marines.

The military has found numerous ways to take advantage of the intersection between popular culture and the new electronic technologies. Even as such technologies are being used to recruit and train military personnel, they are also tapping into the realm of popular culture with its celebration of video games, computer technology, the Internet, and other elements of visual culture used by teenagers.[37] Video games such as *Doom* have a long history of using violent graphics and shooting techniques that appeal to the most hypermodes of masculinity. The Marine Corps was so taken in the mid-1990s with *Doom* that they produced their own version of the game, *Marine Doom*, and made it available for free download. One of the developers of the game, Lieutenant Scott Barnett, claimed at the time that it was a useful game to keep Marines entertained. The interface of military and popular culture has not only been valuable in providing video game technology for diverse military uses, but it has also resulted in the armed forces developing partnerships "with the video game industry to train and recruit soldiers."[38] The military uses the games to train recruits, and the game makers offer products that have the imprimatur of a first-class fighting machine. Moreover, the popularity of militarized war games is on the rise. Nick Turse argues that the line between entertainment and war is disappearing:

> [A] "military-entertainment complex" [has] sprung up to feed both the military's desire to bring out ever-more-realistic computer and video combat games. Through video games, the military and its partners in academia and the entertainment industry are creating an arm of media culture geared toward preparing young Americans for armed conflict.[39]

Combat teaching games offer a perfect fit between the Pentagon, with its accelerating military budget, and the entertainment industry, with annual revenues of $479 billion, which include $40 billion from the video game industry. The entertainment industry offers a stamp of approval for the Pentagon's war games, and the Defense Department provides an aura of authenticity for corporate America's war-based products. Although collaboration between the Defense Department and the entertainment industry has been going on since for years, the permanent war culture that now grips the United States has given this partnership a new life and has greatly expanded its presence in popular culture.

The US Army purchased and now maintains its own video game production studio, developing online software that appeals to computer-literate recruits. Capitalizing on its link with industry, a host of new war games are in production. The most attractive feature of the software is the shooting game "that actually simulates battle and strategic-warfare situations."[40] When asked about the violence the games portray, Brian Ball, the lead developer of the game was crystal clear about the purpose of the video: "We don't downplay the fact that the Army manages violence. We hope that this will help people understand the role of the military in American life."[41] One of the most popular and successful recruiting video games, *America's Army*, teaches young people how "to kill enemy soldiers while wearing your pajamas [and also provides] plenty of suggestions about visiting your local recruiter and joining the real US Army."[42] Clive Thompson argues that "more than 10 million people have downloaded … *America's Army* [which] the Army gives away as a recruiting tool."[43] The game, offered free on many gaming Web sites and also distributed as a free CD-ROM, has become so popular that the army staged a tournament in New York City and had recruiters waiting at the door.[44] In fact, *America's Army* is one of the most popular video games of all time.

Using the latest versions of satellite technology, military–industry collaboration has also produced *Kuma:War*. This game was developed by the Department of Defense and Kuma Reality Games, and was slated for release in 2004. It is a subscription-based product that "prepares gamers for actual missions based on real-world conflicts" and is updated weekly.[45] The game allows players to recreate actual news stories such as the raid American forces conducted in Mosul, Iraq, in which Saddam Hussein's two sons, Uday and Qusay, were killed. Gamers can take advantage of real "true to life satellite imagery and authentic military intelligence, to jump from the headlines right into the frontlines of international conflict."[46] Of course, the realities of carrying 80-pound knapsacks in 120-degree heat, the panic-inducing anxiety and fear of real people shooting real bullets or planting real bombs to kill or maim you and your fellow soldiers, and the months, if not years away from family, are not among those experiences reproduced for instruction or entertainment. Young people no longer learn military values in training camps or in military-oriented schools. These values are now disseminated through the pedagogical force of popular culture, which has become a major tool used by the armed forces to educate young people about the ideology and social relations that inform military life—minus a few of the unpleasantries. The collaboration between the military–entertainment complex offers a form of public pedagogy that "may help to produce great battlefield decision makers, but … strike from debate the most crucial decisions young people can make in regard to the morality of a war–choosing whether or not to fight and for what cause."[47]

In light of the militaristic transformation of the country, attitudes toward war play have changed dramatically and can be observed in the huge increase in the sales, marketing, and consumption of military toys, games, videos, and clothing. Corporations recognize that there are big profits to be made at a time when military symbolism is getting a boost from the war in Iraq and from the upsurge in patriotic jingoism. The popularity of militarized culture is apparent not only in the sales of video combat games but also in the sales of children's toys. Major retailers and major chain stores across the country are selling out their war-related toys. KB Toys retail stores in San Antonio, Texas, sold out in one day an entire shipment of fatigue-clad plush hamsters that dance to military music, and store managers were instructed "to feature military toys in the front of their stores."[48] Moreover, sales of action figures have soared. And when toy retailer Small Blue Planet launched a series of figures called Special Forces: Showdown with Iraq, two of the four models sold out immediately.[49] KB Toys took advantage of the infatuation with action toys related to the war in Iraq by marketing a doll that is a pint-sized model of George W. Bush dressed in the US pilot regalia he wore when he landed on the USS *Abraham Lincoln*. Japanese electronic giant SONY attempted to cash in on the war in Iraq by patenting the term "Shock and Awe" for use with video and computer games. The phrase, referring to the massive air bombardment planned for Baghdad in the initial stages of the war, was coined by Pentagon strategists as part of a scare tactic to be used against Iraq. Additionally, the *New York Times* reported that after September 11, 2001, "nearly two-dozen applications were filed for the phrase, 'Let's Roll.'" The term was made famous by one of the passengers on the ill-fated hijacked plane that crashed in a field in Pennsylvania.

Even in the world of fashion, the ever-spreading chic of militarization and patriotism is making its mark. Army–Navy stores are doing a brisk business not only selling American flags, gas masks, aviator sunglasses, night-vision goggles, and other military equipment but also clothing with the camouflage look.[50] Even chic designers are getting into the act. For instance, at a recent fashion show in Milan, Italy, many designers were "drawn to G.I. uniforms [and were] fascinated by the construction of military uniforms." One designer "had beefy models in commando gear scramble over tabletops and explode balloons."[51]

Authoritarianism in both its old and new forms views life as a form of permanent warfare and, in doing so, subordinates society to the military, rather than viewing the military as subordinate to the needs of a democratic social order. Militarism in this scenario diminishes both the legitimate reasons for a military presence in society and the necessary struggle for the promise of democracy itself. As Umberto Eco points out, under the rubric of its aggressive militarism, protofascist ideology argues that "there is no struggle for life but, rather, life is lived for struggle."[52] The ideology of militarization is central to any understanding of protofascism, as it appeals to a form of irrationality that is at odds with any viable notion of democracy. For instance, militarization uses fear to drive human behavior, and the values it promotes are mainly distrust, patriarchy, and intolerance. Within this ideology, masculinity is associated with violence, and action is often substituted for the democratic processes of deliberation and debate. Militarization as an ideology is about the rule of force and the expansion of repressive state power. In fact, democracy appears as an excess in this logic and is often condemned as being a weak system of government. Echoes of this antidemocratic sentiment can be found in the passages of the Patriot Act with its violation of civil liberties, in the rancorous patriotism that equates dissent with treason, and in the discourse of public commentators who, caught in the fervor of a militarized culture, fan the flames of hatred and intolerance. One example that has become all too typical emerged after the September 11 attacks. Columnist Ann Coulter, in calling for a holy war on Muslims, wrote, "We should invade their countries, kill their leaders and convert them to Christianity. We weren't punctilious about locating and punishing only Hitler and his top officers. We carpet-bombed German cities; we killed civilians. That's war. And this is war."[53] Although this statement does not reflect mainstream American opinion, the uncritical and chauvinistic patriotism and intolerance that inform it have become standard fare among many conservative radio hosts in the United States and these are increasingly produced and legitimated in a wide number of cultural venues. As militarization spreads through American culture, it produces policies that rely more on force than on dialogue and compassion; it offers up modes of identification that undermine democratic values and tarnish civil liberties; and it makes the production of both symbolic and material violence a central feature of everyday life. As Kevin Baker points out, we are quickly becoming a nation that "substitute[s] military solutions for almost everything, including international alliances, diplomacy, effective intelligence agencies, democratic institutions—even national security."[54] By blurring the lines between military and civilian functions, militarization deforms our language, debases democratic values, celebrates fascist modes of control, defines citizens as soldiers, appropriates popular culture as a form of symbolic violence, and diminishes our ability as a nation to uphold international law and support a democratic global public sphere. Unless militarization is systemically exposed and resisted at every place where it appears in the culture, it will undermine the meaning of critical citizenship and do great harm to those institutions that are central to a democratic society. At stake here is the recognition that militarization has become a form of public pedagogy working its values and assumptions through a wide range of media, popular, and cultural sites.

As militarization spreads its influence both at home and abroad, a culture of fear is mobilized to put into place a massive police state intent on controlling and manipulating public speech while making each individual a terrorist suspect subject to surveillance, fingerprinting, and other forms of "electronic tattooing." But the increasing danger of militarization is also evident in the attempt by the corporate–military–media complex to create the ideological and pedagogical conditions in which people either become convinced that the power of the commanding institutions of the state should no longer be held accountable or believe that they are powerless to challenge the new reign of state terrorism. As militarization spreads its values and power throughout American society and the globe, it eliminates the public spaces necessary for imagining an inclusive democratic global society. Militarization and the culture of fear that legitimates it have redefined the very nature of the political and, in doing so, have devalued speech and agency as central categories of democratic public life. Therefore it is to be opposed precisely as a particular ideology and cultural politics.

As the forces of militarization are ratcheted up within multiple spaces in the body politic, they increasingly begin to produce the political currency of fascism in the United States. Exposing and resisting such an ideology should be one of the primary responsibilities of intellectuals, activists, parents, youth, community members, and others concerned about the fate of democracy on a global scale. Working both within and outside of traditional public spheres such as the media, churches, schools, and universities, individuals and groups can expose the dangers the ideology of militarization in all its diversity holds and its potential to turn the United States into a military state while undermining crucial social programs, constitutional liberties, and valuable public spaces. Such intellectual work should be done across nation-states among researchers, academics, intellectuals, and others who produce ideas in the service of social justice, promoting indignation at and collective resistance to the ideology of militarization. This is the pedagogical task that must confront the politics and ideology of militarization. The spreading militarization both at home and abroad demands a new politics of resistance that expands the relationship between politics and everyday life. According to Arundhati Roy, this new politics of resistance requires

[F]ighting to win back the minds and hearts of people. … It means keeping an eagle eye on public institutions and demanding accountability. It means putting your ear to the ground and listening to the whispering of the truly powerless. It means giving a forum to the myriad voices from the hundreds of resistance movements across the country which are speaking about *real* things—about bonded labor, marital rape, sexual preferences, women's wages, uranium dumping, unsustainable mining, weavers' woes, farmers' suicides. It means fighting displacement and dispossession and the relentless, everyday violence of abject poverty. Fighting it also means not allowing your newspaper columns and prime-time TV spots to be hijacked by their spurious passions and their staged theatrics, which are designed to divert attention from everything else.[55]

At the same time, progressives everywhere have to reinvent the possibility of an engaged politics and real strategies of resistance. This suggests that collective struggle is not only working through traditional spheres of political contestation, such as elections or union struggles or various means of education, but also combining the tasks of a radical public pedagogy with massive acts of nonviolent collective disobedience. Such acts can serve to educate, to mobilize, and to remind people of the power of alliances, demonstrations, long-term commitments, and of the importance of struggles that change both ideas and relations of power. By making militarization visible through the force of images, words, and peaceful resistance, politics can become both meaningful and possible as a contested site through which people can challenge both locally and within international alliances the obscene accumulation of power symptomatic of the increasing militarization of public space as well as the creeping fascism that is spreading throughout the United States and across the globe. Arundhati Roy is right in her incessant and courageous call to globalize dissent, but if dissent is to work, it must have a focus that cuts across empires, nation-states, and local space, a focus that cuts to the heart of a clear and present danger to democracy and social justice. Challenging militarization in all its expressions is a direct strike at the heart of a policy that has exceeded its usefulness for democracy and has now formed a dreadful pact with a dangerous authoritarianism. We find ourselves in the midst of a war globally; it is not simply a war against terrorism, but a war against democratic solidarity, a war in which a democratic future both at home and abroad hangs in the balance.

NOTES

1. Susan Buck-Morss, *Thinking past terror: Islamism and critical theory on the left* (New York/London: Verso, 2003), p. 33.
2. Andrew J. Bacevich, *The new American militarism* (New York: Oxford University Press, 2005), p. 1.
3. Ibid., p. 2.
4. Tony Judt, The new world order, *The New York Review of Books* LII(12) (July 14, 2005), p. 16.
5. John R. Gillis, ed., *The militarization of the Western world* (New Brunswick, NJ: Rutgers University Press, 1989). On the militarization of urban space, see Mike Davis, *City of quartz* (New York: Vintage, 1992) and Kenneth Saltman and David Gabbard, eds.,_*Education as enforcement: The militarization and corporatization of schools* (New York: Routledge, 2003). For the current neoconservative influence on militarizing American foreign policy, see Donald Kagan and Gary Schmidt, *Rebuilding America's defenses*, one of many reports outlining such an issue and developed under the auspices of The Project for the New American Century (http://www.newamericancentury.org).
6. Catherine Lutz, Making war at home in the United States: Militarization and the current crisis, *American Anthropologist* 104(3) (September 2003), p. 723.
7. Jorge Mariscal, "Lethal and compassionate": The militarization of U.S. culture, *CounterPunch* (May 5, 2003) (http://www.counterpunch.org/mariscal05052003.html).
8. Richard Falk, *Will the empire be fascist?* (http://www.transnational.org/forum/meet/2003/Falk_FascistEmpire.html).
9. George Monbiot, States of war, *The Guardian/UK* (October 14, 2003) (http://www.commondreams.org/views03/1014-09.htm).
10. Mariscal, op. cit.
11. David Harvey, *The new imperialism* (New York: Oxford University Press, 2005), p. 192.

12. Kevin Baker, We're in the Army now: The G.O.P.'s plan to militarize our culture, *Harper's Magazine* (October 2003), p. 38.

13. Ibid., p. 37.

14. Ibid.

15. Ruth Rosen, Politics of fear, *San Francisco Chronicle* (December 30, 2003) (http://www.commondreams.org/views02/1230-02,htm).

16. Ibid.

17. Fox News's and MSNBC's Iraq war coverage was named by *Time Magazine*, no less, in its "The Year in Culture" section as "the worst display of patriotism" for 2003. See *Time Magazine* (January 5, 2004), p. 151.

18. Richard H. Kohn, Using the military at home: Yesterday, today, and tomorrow, *Chicago Journal of International Law* 94(1) (Spring 2003), pp. 174–175.

19. Ibid.

20. Kelly Field, Colleges that ban military recruiters would lose additional funds under new legislation, *Chronicle of Higher Education*, Daily News Online (October 11, 2004) (http://chronicle.com/cgi 2-bin/printible.cgi?article=http://chronicle.com). Also see print article, Kelly Field, Colleges risk losing more funds for banning military recruiters, *Chronicle of Higher Education* 51(9), p. A36.

21. David Goodman, Covertly recruiting kids, *Baltimore Sun* (September 29, 2003) (http://www.commondreams.org/views03/1001-11.htm).

22. Gail R. Chaddock, Safe schools at a price, *Christian Science Monitor* (August 25, 1999), p. 15.

23. Tamar Lewin, Raid at high school leads to racial divide, not drugs, *New York Times* (December 9, 2003), p. A16.

24. Sandra Rimer, Unruly students facing arrest, not detention, *New York Times* (January 2, 2004), p. 15.

25. Ibid.

26. Randall Beger, Expansion of police power in the public schools and the vanishing rights of students, *Social Justice* 29(1&2) (2002), p. 124.

27. David Garland, cited in Melange, men and jewelry; prison as exile: Unifying laughter and darkness, *Chronicle of Higher Education* (July 6, 2001), p. B4.

28. Peter B. Kraska, The military-criminal justice blur: An introduction, in *Militarizing the American Criminal Justice System*, Peter B. Kraska, ed. (Boston: Northeastern University Press, 2001), p. 3.

29. See Christian Parenti, *Lockdown America: Police and prisons in the age of crisis* (London: Verso Press, 1999).

30. Kraska, op. cit., p. 10.

31. Jonathan Simon, Sacrificing Private Ryan: The military model and the new penology, in *Militarizing the American Criminal Justice System*, Kraska, ed., op. cit., p. 113.

32. Sanho Tree, The war at home, *Sojourner's Magazine* (May–June, 2003), p. 5.

33. Cited in David Barsamian, Interview with Angela Davis, *The Progressive* (February 2001), p. 35.

34. Carl Chery, U.S. Army targets black hip-hop fans. *The Wire/Daily Hip-Hop News* (October 21, 2003) (http://www.sohh.com/article_print.php?content_ID=5162).

35. Ibid.

36. Mariscal, op. cit.

37. For a list of such "toys," see Nicholas Turse, Have yourself a Pentagon Xmas, *The Nation* (January 5, 2004), p. 8. For a more extensive list, see http://www.tomdispatch.com

38. Matt Slagle, Military recruits video-game makers, *Chicago Tribune* (October 8, 2003), p. 4.

39. Nick Turse, The Pentagon invades your X box, *Dissident Voice* (December 15, 2003) (http://www.dissidentvoice.org/Articles9/Turse_Pentagon-Video-Games.htm).

40. R. Lee Sullivan, Firefight on floppy disk, *Forbes Magazine* (May 20, 1996), pp. 39–40.

41. Gloria Goodale, Video game offers young recruits a peek at military life, *The Christian Science Monitor* (May 31, 2003), p. 18.

42. Wayne Woolley, From "An army of one" to army of fun: Online video game helps build ranks, *Times-Picayune* (September 7, 2003), p. 26.

43. Clive Thompson, The making of an X box warrior, *New York Times Sunday Magazine* (August 22, 2004), p. 35.

44. Ibid., pp. 34–37.

45. This description comes from *Gaming News* (October 2003) (http://www.gamerstemple.com/news/1003/100331.asp).

46. Ibid.

47. Turse, "Pentagon Invades."

48. Maureen Tkacik, Military toys spark conflict on home front, *Wall Street Journal* (March 31, 2003), p. B1.

49. Amy C. Sims, Just child's play, Fox News Channel (August 21, 2003) (http://www.wmsa.net/news./Fox News/fn-030822_childs_play.htm)

50. Mike Conklin, Selling war at retail, *Chicago Tribune* (May 1, 2003), p. 1.

51. Both quotes are from Cathy Horyn, Macho America storms Europe's runways, *New York Times* (July 3, 2003), p. A1.

52. Umberto Eco, Eternal fascism: Fourteen ways of looking at a Blackshirt, *New York Review of Books* (November–December 1995), p. 13.

53. This quotation by Coulter has been cited extensively. See http://www.coulterwatch.com/files/BW_2-003-bin_Coulter.pdf

54. Baker, op. cit., p. 38.

55. Arundhati Roy, *War talk* (Cambridge, MA: South End, 2003), pp. 37–38.

CHAPTER FOUR

Reappraising Critical Perspectives IN Popular Culture AND Education

ZVI BEKERMAN

"With the full deployment of capitalism, especially today's 'late capitalism' it is the predominant 'normal' life itself that, in a way, gets 'carnivalized,' with its constant self-revolutionizing, its reversal, crises, reinventions, so that it is the critique of capitalism, for a 'stable' ethical position, that more and more appears today as an exception. How, then, are we to revolutionize an order whose very principle is constant self revolutionizing? Perhaps, this is the question today" (Zizek, 2004).

This chapter is my opportunity to think about some troubles with popular culture and education philosophy. I make no attempt to provide a thorough review of the literature, for I see this chapter as an effort to clarify to myself the ways I have related through the years to these concepts in their complex relations. I do hope, however, that my thinking can help other readers think through their own positions regarding these issues.

A long time ago I used to share what seemed to be the accepted truth that education and popular culture are true opposites—the first is dedicated to shaping the mind of good moral citizens and; the second, at its best, offers solace from difficult educational processes, or at its worst feeds, provides comfort to the minds of those who will never make it in education.

By the way, in a paradoxical sense, what I sensed then remains true even today when I hold to this logic from a more critical perspective. Acknowledging this position's truth value does not mean that I agree with it. It only means that in the meantime I have lived many more years and experienced/researched more of what we call education. It also means that, in spite of the accumulation of knowledge in a variety of theoretical realms (education and cultural studies and whatever else the reader's theoretical background encourages him/her to add to these disciplines) and the efforts of goodwilled theorists in pedagogy and literacy, to this day, if you get a good education you might get into the ivory tower and if you have exposure only to popular culture, whether critically or not, you end up having difficulties making a living.

I do not want to engage with the interpretative analyses conducted on popular culture by scholars working within cultural studies traditions; theirs will keep finding intellectual pirouettes that, for the most part, stay in the realm of the abstract and the inconsequential. My writing seeks to question the work done by those who seem to believe that popular culture and its use within educational settings have the potential of embellishing the educational scene and/or bettering the lot of those failed by the educational system: mostly minorities.

Unfortunately I have given up thinking that a change in education or a sharpening of the senses through education (and/or student empowerment) can bring about any radical change (individual/particular changes there have always been and will always be, but I doubt whether my radical colleagues hope for these) in the one variable that best foretells school success—the socioeconomic status of the family.

This rather simple fact keeps me alert and asking whether those involved in trying to theorize about ways to emancipate humanity through education can truly contribute anything at all to the world, a world that seems to allow the theorizing to be heard but at the same time allows for nothing, or at best only a little, to change.

Today, "popular culture and education research" is one of those fussy fields that holds to the rhetoric of emancipation (for a recent review see Dolby 2003). What has the current critical discourse on popular culture to offer? In its present form and after the thoughtful revolutions of the discursive turn—postmodernism, post-structuralism, and as many other "isims" as you may see fit—this discourse still seems to be struggling, and through its struggle, to accommodate and at times ironically affirm the very dichotomies that it negates.

We are at times encouraged by these theoreticians to pay specific attention to the ways we conceptualize popular culture and the intersections between popular culture and education (Dyson, 1997; McLaren, 1995; Willis, 1990). We are told that paying attention to the particular ways in which youth manages both realms will enlighten our understanding of the way in which youth participate in the democratic sphere (Miller, 1998). Moreover, they say, if we as educators become better informed about popular culture, we will realize its significance for a political and pedagogical world, in the realm of education (Buckingham, 2003; Giroux, 1994). We are told that we need to adopt a less protectionist approach; we are told that the young can be mobilized as critical citizens within the consumerism represented/replicated in popular culture and its practices to change the democratic space that today seems to fail many, but mostly the indigent. Popular culture theorists have joined the redemptive discourse of other multiculturalists and literacy experts of sorts in their belief that educational settings can, when properly handled, be mobilized to bring about change toward a more just and equitable society.

Still, although theoretically this discourse is sustainable and might be correct, it seems at times to be lacking a realistic understanding of the limitations of educational theorizing. Thus I want to try illuminate a couple of issues that might seem trivial but that I suggest, although known in educational theorizing circles, are insufficiently accounted for in the popular culture and education discussions. Specifically I refer to the history of schooling and its closely related allies, identity and culture.

Popular culture is ill defined; however, when reading through the texts that attempt to interpret it and put it to work for the noble cause of redeeming the outcasts, one gets the impression that what is under examination belongs to the outcasts' cultural production or to the cultural products offered by hegemonic powers to gratify the cheap needs of the pariahs who, unable to find a place or holding to a place of low esteem in the normative world, use the dreams and nightmares offered by popular culture (theirs or others) as a palliative to their miserable existence. Yet, for whatever popular culture is said to be, it is always positioned outside the realm of canonical school texts. My last move, from the language of education to the language of schooling (mass education) is one of the central issues that I raise in this short chapter.

The move seems to me to be of importance, because I find that this ongoing overlapping of education and schooling an impediment to progress/change (defined here as the possibility of critical academics to influence the world for the better). I believe we urgently need to detach education from schooling in our discourse, first, because when doing so we will not fall into the trap that the hegemonic powers have so elegantly devised for us in recent history, and second (and maybe more important), because we might stop tilting at windmills, along with Don Quixote, and start to reconsider what we seek; we also can revisit what we can offer the indigent we say we care about.

In this respect, it is worth remembering that there is a close connection between schooling and high culture. In school rhetoric, schools are expected to deliver high culture against which popular culture is defined. Arnold's definition of culture as "the best that has been taught and said …" (Arnold, 1869; Bloom, 1987) sets the boundaries between aristocratic/middle-class culture and that of the uncivilized masses in need of schooling for their progress along the evolutionary path.

These perspectives have been upheld and are not likely to disappear in spite of the efforts of critical theorists who, although theoretically right, seem never to be able to amass the power needed to do away with the current well-adapted (for some) structures. For those acquainted with the American scene, the names of Hirsch, Bloom, and others (Bloom, 1987; Hirsch, 1987) come easily to mind as Arnold's heirs, and although these streams of thought gain loud voices only at a few historical moments, they are well and alive even in silence, negotiating their power through the consent of those they subordinate.

Moreover, popular cultural theorists remind us that we are not dopes, that there is no deterministic relation between the "message delivered" and the interpretations we accord them (Radway, 1984). They tell us that although we are shaped by communicational turns, we partake as well in their shaping. Identities from this perspective are not essential but constructed, and popular culture has the potential to add interpretative shades to the calibration of our students' self-definition and understanding, if only we put popular culture well to use. Again, it is worth remembering that identity and mass education are intricately connected in modernity. There is a long history that connects the development of the nation-state and the reification of culture and identity. The increasing tendency to conceptualize processes as if they were unchanging objects is closely connected to the struggle for power between the old aristocracy and the rising middle class. In the nation formation period in Europe, culture and identity served initially as collective images justified by general humanist and moral values geared toward a better future; they were then redirected, in the process of national development, toward a particularistic past tied to a specific ancestry and a peculiar nation's heritage (Elias, 1998; Porter, 1997).

Identity and culture are both revealed in the background/foreground of the modern nation-state, and although the nation-state seems at times to be withdrawing (I suggest we wait a little before reaching a final judgment), its power still seems to be alive and well enough to be accounted for. Even when considering globalization and multinationals, as an emerging phenomenon, it is not yet clear whether these changes represent radical changes in identity shaping or in the cultural valuing of the past.

Coming from sociohistorical perspectives, as I presume many of the readers of this volume do, I assume we all would agree that it is not the names of the constructs we deal with that count but the practices through which they get constructed and sustained. Most practices of globalization are not yet sufficiently clear, but even the few that have a little clarity show no signs of a radical break with traditional practices, excepting those concerning the "lucky" few, who are well-cybered in fluctuating spaces.

I would like to unravel these intricate connections. I do believe them to be representatives of an erroneous epistemology, but, given the present configuration of world politics and economy, I doubt whether teaching/learning right epistemologies can do any good. I feel that we need to get as many indigent as possible go through the system in the best way possible to better their lot. We have little chance to come out victorious in our struggles to better our schools, and the indigent have little to gain from our small progress. They need tools to struggle and survive better within the system. I suggest we stop defending them for the sake of our own theoretical truths, as rightful as these paradigmatic perspectives and epistemological positions may be, and help them to improve their future.

It seems that to do this we need to continuously remind ourselves that we are all born with a particular potential to learn. In this sense learning, the active and only meaningful side of education, is a biological "fact" and an inherent factor in human life; it has nothing to do with schooling, nor with education in its narrow and traditional sense. We all develop through participation in cultural environments while being influenced by biological abilities. This path affects most elements of our development, including our identity (Rogoff, 2003).

In opposition to this naturality, the powerful machinery developed by the nation-state, mostly in the shape of massive educational efforts that market universal (anonymous) literacy, has been successful in making seem natural or banal, as Billig (1995) would have it, the detailed practices through which nation-states become almost invisible settings in which we "mistakenly" hold a sense of individuality—an individuality always measured against a contingent other (Laclau, 1990) and the modern court of human appeal: the "high" culture of the nation-state (Williams, 1961).

Theoreticians have identified the national structure as one of the cruelest systems on the historical scene (Bhabha, 1990; Mann, 2004). For the community to be imagined in its national oneness (Anderson, 1991; Hobsbawm, 1983), borders had to be widened and groups lumped together through homogenizing efforts; culture had to be reified, and the individual and his or her relation to the authority of the sovereign, strengthened to undermine the power of smaller communal identifications. Concealed behind the promise of universal equality is the sovereign authority's demand to have no one other than an individual, stripped of any group affiliation, under its rod (Mendus, 1989).

The development of mass education, through schooling, is closely related to the Industrial Revolution and the development of the nation-state (Bekerman and Silverman, 2003; Gellner, 1983; Smith, 1998). Both needed to recruit masses in their service—masses with basic cognitive and behavioral skills that could serve the needs of the nation-state and its economic structures. Thus, as we all well know, schools are in no way disinterested arenas within which neutral knowledge or skills are transmitted from the minds of specialists to those of passive individuals. In the modern era, schools have been the primary means by which the sovereign authorities have unified the varied local groups inhabiting the areas they were successful in subordinating to their power, under one flag, one language, and one narrative. If we bear this in mind, it is surprising that emancipation-searching elements in society have chosen school-like educational structures to secure their emancipatory aims. Yet it could be argued that although existing structures are adopted, educators turn them into structures that serve their purposes and not just the authority under which they reside.

We should remember, however, that the central linchpin of formal schooling's success is its structure and its functionality—both based on, and expressive of, a particular paradigmatic perspective that, we doubt, can benefit the destitute. Schools are the central conduit for the transmission of two interrelated beliefs of the modern Western world: the first is the belief in the individual self; and the second is the outside existence of knowledge that this self can absorb, if properly guided.

These above-mentioned elements have been in the making for centuries in the functioning of schools. Over 5,000 years ago, when the first schools were created to produce a cast of scribes able to sustain the bureaucratic needs of growing, powerful, centralized, urban, economic human enterprises, they developed the three central characteristics that hold to this day (Cole, 1990; Goody, 1987):

1.   The student was trained by strangers, separated from kin and family;
2.   The knowledge slated for transmission was differentiated and compartmentalized into fields of specialization; and
3.   Learning took place outside of the contexts of its intended implementation, that is, students rehearsed knowledge "out of context."

If the goals of critical educators in society are indeed to promote emancipatory trends that are able to offer a variety of answers to real present socio-cultural-political issues, institutional educational structures and their foundational practices may not be the setting in which to achieve these aims. More doubtful is whether, given present conditions, schools will adopt/embrace any strategies/practices that will empower individuals or their identities; and if, as many believe, popular culture carries these powers, I doubt it will ever become part of the school curriculum. In cases in which it does, it is likely to become a tool, which, similar to multiculturalism as practiced today (for the most part), serves to justify and perpetuate the ongoing suffering of minorities, now recognized but with their structural subordination left fully intact (Bekerman, 2003; Bekerman and Tatar, 2005).

We need to become serious about our own theorizing. Contemporary social theory acknowledges complexity, specifically the complex interdependency of multiple contexts, each a part of wider—and even more complex—networks. When acknowledging complexity we need to realize—if we do not want to fall into the trap of educational reformers who seem to prefer short cuts, linear and causal, and who are not concerned if the reform does not bring about change, and all has to be reformed again after the lapse of five to ten years at best—that change is difficult and no curricular piece, however creative and culturally popular, can alone propel it. Schools might not be the right places in which to start processes of change. They have been part of the evolutionary process for too long; they have been central to it and too well adapted to its context for us to believe they can be flexible enough (weak enough) to become receptive to change or even worthwhile of consideration for starting change processes. Moreover, schools have been such a successful socializing agent that they will always be well guarded by the empowered—who in no small measure owe their power to them—for them to allow for easy cracks in the system. The fact that we work in education in our chosen academic fields does not necessarily mean that we need to ponder on schools; rather, it might mean considering how to overcome them, if this is at all possible.

Still, if we believe we must work in education (narrowly understood as schooling), it might be of greater benefit if we search for ways to get more of the school population successfully through the system. What can this mean?

The population that we hope will benefit by the introduction of popular culture into the educational sphere inhabits integrated schools or almost segregated ones in low-to middle-income urban areas. For the most part, these schools are governed by members of the majority group unable or at times unwilling to understand the deep cultural bases of learning, as present educational theorizing has been able to demonstrate thoroughly. Moreover, integrated or partially integrated schools function through similar paradigmatic perspectives. The central paradigmatic features that guide them will not allow the system to be reformed and thereby to benefit those wishing to sustain a level of independence to compete in the interpretative work that takes place when shaping the world they inhabit. These paradigmatic features, to which I have hinted above, are what modernity has come to call "universal cultural values" and their appointed recipients, "autonomous individuals" and their assumed identities (Bekerman, 2001; Bekerman and Silverman, 2000).

This is not the place to expound on a full-fledged critique of these paradigmatic Western bases, but suffice it to say that both culture, as a reified identifiable cast of behaviors and beliefs, and the individual as autonomous and universal, have been the focus of a long and wide theoretical controversy within a high and postmodernity culture discourse that has successfully demonstrated the link between these features and many of the world's current maladies (Giddens, 1991; Sampson, 1993; Taylor, 1994).

It is worth mentioning that these theoretical developments have pointed inter alia at two central issues related to our present understanding of culture and individual identity that are relevant to education. The first is that culture must be understood as a verb and not a noun; as something that grows, evolves, and intermittently becomes when executed to be promptly dissolved again into the doings of human activity that might, or might not, be able to reproduce it again in similar or different ways (Bauman, 1999). Second, individual identity must be conceived as a similar dialogic (verblike) process of becoming and shaping, mostly through the use of the most human of human tools—language (Harre and Gillett, 1995; Holland, Lachicotte, Skinner, and Cain, 1998). Thus, both culture and individual identity have come to be conceptualized as evolving processes widely dependent on language (Maturana, 1991; Wittgenstein, 1953).

These ruling paradigms of a reified individual's identity and culture, together with the practices through which these paradigmatic perspectives are framed and constructed within school-like educational initiatives, have long been exposed; but their exposure has not brought about change, again because these paradigmatic perspectives are adaptive to the hegemonic realm of school it so faithfully serves.

I have recently considered what has come to be called postpositivist realism (Bekerman and Tatar, 2005). This view, although acknowledging poststructuralist critiques, recognizes that goods and resources are still distributed according to identity categories. It recognizes that theoretical conceptualizations, although they are valid, might not influence the world as much as the constructed perspectives of hegemonies. All our high/postmodern "isms" might be theoretically right, that is, they might offer a good description of an empirical world, but they are not stronger than the powerfully "constructed" reality of a consequential hegemony that significantly affects our lives and sets the limits on where we can live, whom we can marry, and what educational and employment opportunities are available to us (Mohanty, 1997). If so, acknowledging reality (nation-state and its invented identities and culture)—although epistemologically wrong—might be the best way to start. The one thing of which we might want to be careful is not to allow this reality to confuse the educational aim. This in itself is a serious problem we must confront.

Perhaps what we need is less emancipation (through culture or other) at this point and more normalization, but this time one that acknowledges and implements efficient instructional pedagogic and communicative means (i.e., means culturally rooted in the recognized trusted sphere of the participants) that will positively affect the social and cognitive existence of the participating community.

Although this normalization might be confused with an acknowledgment of essentialist identity perspectives, it is worth remembering that these perspectives although theoretically wrong, might be the right path (at least at first) toward political resistance. True, schools are sites of negotiations—children are no dopes and they do partake in the construction of their realities. But it is also true, as much of recent research has powerfully shown (Varenne and McDermott, 1998), that although kids indeed negotiate their presents and futures in schools, if they belong to the caste of the destitute, they do so generally against their own advantage (Willis, 1977).

We could consider informal educational initiatives and/or after-school programs as ways to channel what has been thought of as positive educational options in popular culture, but again these settings have been shown to be progressively contributing to adult encroachment (Nocon and Cole, 2006) on low-income children's already limited ownership of their lives. It was believed that the traditionally open and tenuously institutionalized nature of informal educational settings would allow low-income and immigrant children access to safe, flexible, and responsive educational programming and provide opportunities for participation in problem solving, self-regulation, and learning that goes beyond rigid standards and limited basic content. However, recent research has shown that schooling, which colonized at first the lives of children and their families during what had previously been hours devoted to work, play, or other activities, is furthering its colonializing process and has slowly invaded after-school and informal settings through the professionalization, standardization, and rationalization of their activity (Halpern, 2002; Heath, 2000).

Some might say contemporary curriculum and educational policy, armed with the discourses of hybridity, diversity, multiculturalism (and popular culture), are not living up to their emancipatory goals or even to their increasing rhetoric of achievements. Additional theorizing of culture and identity through any of the above perspectives might promote academic positions but not the future of those we care about.

Acknowledging the existence of these identities in the real world helps us to offer resistance to domination by improving now the immediate future of participants; there is always time later to further the struggle until we all understand that, identity as a representation of self, and state as a representation of community, are the constructs from which we need to emancipate ourselves.

Freire clearly understood the need to relate to the common and the popular in his literacy campaign. However, we need to recognize that his struggle was never successful or at least not sustainable. Nonetheless, until the future is organized to allow for Freire's emancipatory educational insights to flourish, there is something I want to rescue from his teachings.

Freire (Freire, 1970; Freire and Macedo, 1995) argued that critical education or *concientizacao* entails learning "to perceive social, political and economic contradictions and to take action against the oppressive elements of reality." It is worth noting that Freire's call is not only for cognitive alertness but also for practical activity, seeking to overcome the educational institutions' traditional inclination to abstract knowledge from reality, that is, segregate knowledge from social activity. It is clear from the above that I am not too optimistic about the possibility of reforming schools' abstract inclinations, but we might try to limit our own inclinations toward abstraction. Popular culture theorizing, like other ideological/theoretical analysis, lacks connection to lived experience and as such risks becoming mightily irrelevant. Academic life replicates social forces to the same extent as do schools. We need to emancipate ourselves, and we might stand a better chance of doing it than young needy students in educational institutions who are still to acquire higher education. Emancipation implies, as Freire suggested, not only intellectual alertness, the lack of which we do not suffer (as it is the basis of our livelihood) but also practical activity. Perhaps becoming more practical in our activity and directing our practices to the political sphere will help more than any old–new twist of the rhetorical educational theoretical turn. If we strongly believe in the redeeming powers of popular culture, especially the products of the needy who find in it relief, perhaps our political activity should be directed to support them in the hope that more open spaces will be created for exhibition and consumption. Children are not dopes, indeed, and like us who, after receiving the best of high culture, have been able to come and appreciate critical thought, they will to be able to benefit from the redeeming power of popular culture.

Unfortunately, the needy need no promise of emancipation through manipulating popular culture; they need high culture only achievable in a trustful local cultural context to make it in the world. We would do well to remember that in the end, it is concrete political/structural changes that help to end human suffering.

POSTSCRIPT

A couple of weeks ago I saw an excellent Spanish film, *The Tongue of the Butterfly*. It is an amalgamation of three short stories by Manuel Rivas, a Galician author, that have been translated into cinema by Jose Luis Cuerda (director) and Rafael Azcona (screenwriter). The film is set in the late winter of 1936 in a small Galician village where Moncho, a boy of eight, is about to begin school. Moncho's father, Ramon, is a tailor and a Republican (Liberal-Democratic Socialist of that time in

Spain), who struggles with his leftist political leanings, being too timid to profess them openly, in part, at least, because his pious wife has no desire to be seen as a rebel. Don Gregorio is the elderly loving teacher who opens worlds of knowledge to Moncho's insatiable desire to learn. On July 18, 1936, the world caves in on them. The military uprising is successful, and Gregorio, the Republican, much-loved schoolteacher, is arrested along with other Republican sympathizers. Rosa, Moncho's mother, seized with anguish, makes sure her husband destroys all the Republican newspapers and magazines previously in his keeping, not to mention the party card. She is also careful to remind her children that their father never had a bad word to say about any priest and to never mention that he had engaged in the task of making a suit for the schoolmaster.

In the movie, Gregorio's arrest is preceded by a party in honor of his retirement. Don Gregorio austerely says in his farewell, "If we can raise in Spain only one generation which will grow free, no one will ever be able to eradicate liberty from them; no one will ever be able to take that treasure from them" (my translation).

But, as fate would have it, the schoolmaster, sporting the very suit made for him by Ramon is the last person to get on the truck that is taking the unfortunate prisoners to their execution, along with about a dozen Republicans. The entire village turns out to witness their departure. Rosa, afraid of the fate that might befall her husband, urges him to join in the insults being hurled at the prisoners. A desperate Ramon eventually complies, as does his elder son, Andrés. Moncho, in tears that scarcely allow him to be heard among his sobs, shouts: "Atheist! Red! Nightingale! Devil! ButterflyTongue!" Like all the other little boys present, Moncho proceeds to toss stones at the lorry as it inches away into the distance.

Popular culture, in this instance in the form of a movie, is indeed a powerful tool. In this specific case it plays out two of the issues raised in this chapter. First, education even when in the hands of emancipatory forces (Don Gregorio, the anticlerical and Republican Spaniard) fails to provide the tools for emancipation, given the wider political context. Second, liberals (intellectuals or others) may, given similar political contexts, betray the cause. As suggested, we would serve the emancipatory cause better if we realize the school is not the domain within which to battle the hegemonic structures (though it reproduces them) and turn our efforts instead to the political/practical arena. As for schools, given their present configurations, the best that we can hope for is that they will provide the indigent with equal access to the tools that will allow them to succeed within the present system, and it is toward this goal that we should turn our efforts.

REFERENCES

Anderson, B. (1991). *Imagined communities*. London: Verso.

Arnold, M. (1869). *Culture and anarchy: An essay in political and social criticism*. London: Smith, Elder and Co.

Bauman, Z. (1999). *Culture as praxis*. London: Sage.

Bekerman, Z. (2003). Hidden dangers in multicultural discourse. *Race Equality and Teaching* (formerly *MCT—Multicultural Teaching*), 21(3): 36–42.

Bekerman, Z. (2005). Complex contexts and ideologies: Bilingual education in conflict ridden areas. *Journal of Language Identity and Education,* 4(1), 1–20.

Bekerman, Z., and M. Silverman (2000). The liberal Jewish discourse on culture and Jewish continuity. *Cultural education in a multicultural society* (vol. 9, pp. 183–192). Jerusalem: The Hebrew University (in Hebrew).

Bekerman, Z., and M. Silverman. (2003). The corruption of culture and education by the nation state: The case of liberal Jews' discourse on Jewish continuity. *Journal of Modern Jewish Studies*, 2(1): 19–34.

Bekerman, Z., and M. Tatar (2005). Overcoming modern-postmodern dichotomies: Some possible benefits for the counselling profession. *British Journal of Guidance and Counselling*, 33, 411–421.

Bhabha, H.K. (1990). DissemiNation: Time, narrative, and the margins of the modern nation. *Nation and narration*. London: Routledge.

Billig, M. (1995). *Banal nationalism*. London: Sage.

Bloom, A. (1987). *The closing of the American mind*. New York: Simon & Schuster.

Buckingham, D. (2003). Media education and the end of the critical consumer. *Harvard Educational Review*, 73(3): 309–327.

Cole, M. (1990). Cognitive development and formal schooling: The evidence from cross-cultural research. *Vygotsky and education: Instructional implications and applications of sociohistorical psychology* (L.C. Moll, ed.). New York: Cambridge University Press, 89–110.

Dolby, N. (2003). Popular culture and democratic practice. *Harvard Educational Review*, 73(3): 258–284.

Dyson, A.H. (1997). *Writing superheroes: Contemporary childhood, popular culture, and classroom literacy*. New York: Teachers College Press.

Elias, N. (1998). Civilization, culture, identity: "Civilization" and "culture": Nationalism and nation state formation: Extract from *The Germans*. *Classical readings in culture and civilization* (pp. 225–240) (J. Rundell and S. Mennell, eds.). New York: Routledge.

Freire, P. (1970). *Pedagogy of the oppressed*. New York: Seabury.

Freire, P., and D.P. Macedo. (1995). A dialogue: Culture, language and race. *Harvard Educational Review*, 65: 377–403.

Gellner, E. (1983). *Nations and nationalism*. Oxford: Basic Blackwell.

Giddens, A. (1991). *Modernity and self identity: Self and society in the late modern age*. Palo Alto, CA: Stanford University Press.

Giroux, H.A. (1994). *Disturbing pleasures: Learning popular culture*. New York: Routledge.

Goody, J. (1987). *The interface between the written and the oral*. Cambridge, UK: Cambridge University Press.

Halpern, R. (2002). A different kind of child development institution: The history of after-school programs for low-income children. *Teachers College Record*, 104(2): 178–211.

Harre, R., and G. Gillett. (1995). *The discursive mind*. London: Sage.

Heath, S.B. (2000). Risks, rules, and roles. *Zeitschrift für Erziehungswissenschaft*, 3: 61–80.

Hirsch, E.D. (1987). *Cultural literacy: What every American needs to know.* Boston: Houghton Mifflin.

Hobsbawm, E.J. (1983). The invention of tradition. *The invention of tradition* (pp. 1–14) (E.J. Hobsbawm and T. Ranger, eds.). Cambridge, UK: Cambridge University Press.

Holland, D., W. Lachicotte, D. Skinner, and C. Cain (1998). *Identity and agency in cultural worlds.* Cambridge, MA: Harvard University Press.

Laclau, E. (1990). *New reflections on the revolution of our time.* London: Verso.

Mann, M. (2004). *The colonial darkside of democracy.* Cambridge, UK: Cambridge University Press.

Maturana, H. (1991). Response to Berman's critique of the *Tree of Knowledge. Journal of Humanistic Psychology,* 31(2): 88–97.

McLaren, P. (1995). *Rethinking media literacy: A critical theory of representation.* New York: Peter Lang.

Mendus, S. (1989). *Toleration and the limits of liberalism.* New York: Macmillan.

Miller, T. (1998). *Technologies of truth: Cultural citizenship and the popular culture.* Minneapolis: University of Minnesota Press.

Mohanty, S.P. (1997). *Literary theory and the claims of history: Postmodernism, objectivity, multicultural politics.* Ithaca, NY: Cornell University Press.

Nocon, H., and M. Cole (2006). School's invation of "after school": Colonialization, rationalization, and expansion of access? In Z. Bekerman, N. Burbules, and D. Silberman Keller (Eds.), *Learning in Places: The informal educational reader* (pp. 99–122). New York, NY: Peter Lang.

Porter, R. (1997). Introduction. *Rewriting the self: Histories from the Renaissance to the present* (pp. 1–17) (R. Porter, ed.). London: Routledge.

Radway, J. (1984). *Reading the romance: Women, patriarchy, and popular literature.* Chapel Hill: University of North Carolina Press.

Rogoff, B. (2003). *The cultural nature of human development.* Oxford: Oxford University Press.

Sampson, E.E. (1993). *Celebrating the other: A dialogic account of human nature.* Hertfordshire, UK: Harvester Wheatsheaf.

Smith, A.D. (1998). *Nationalism and modernism.* London: Routledge.

Taylor, C. (1994). The politics of recognition. *Multiculturalism: A critical reader* (pp. 75–106) (D.T. Goldberg, ed.). Oxford: Blackwell.

Varenne, H., and R. McDermott (1998). *Successful failure: The schools America builds.* Colorado: Westview Press.

Williams, R. (1961). *Culture and society, 1780–1950.* Hardmondsworth, UK: Penguin Books.

Willis, P. (1977). *Learning to labor: How working class lads get working class jobs.* New York: Columbia University Press.

Willis, P. (1990). *Common culture: Symbolic work at play in the everyday cultures of the young.* London: Milton Keynes England: Open University Press.

Wittgenstein, L. (1953). *Philosophical investigations.* Oxford: Blackwell.

Zizek, S. (2004). *Organs without bodies: On Deleuze and consequences.* New York and London: Routledge.

CHAPTER FIVE

Education AND Popular Culture: Chiasmatic Reflections IN Almodóvar's *Bad Education* AND Tarantino's *Kill Bill**

DIANA SILBERMAN-KELLER

I
Education, popular culture, and cultural construction in Almodóvar's *Bad Education* and Tarantino's *Kill Bill*

From a formal consideration of education and popular culture, as exposed in a plethora of popular culture productions (film, comics, pop music, photo romances, detective and pornographic literature), the two types of projectors, mixers and screens participate in a conversation about what ought to be a culture or a society, a well of knowledge and, of course, an education. I approach the figuration of the two types in Quentin Tarantino's *Kill Bill (KB)* and Pedro Almodóvar's *Bad Education (BE)*.

Skirting pragmatic justifications for scholarly writing in education, I withdraw from advising immediate practical applications, such as revising the application of popular culture in education and vice versa (Cheung, 2001; Lambirth, 2003), to study the mutual chiasmic effects in these two films. The study's importance lies in the opportunity it offers to observe some modalities of cultural construction in process.

By thematically centering on the conversation between popular culture and education, Tarantino's fourth and Almodóvar's sixteenth films invite consideration of the formal and aesthetic configuration of this thematic cluster even if not from the vantage point of professional educational philosophy (Dimitriadis, 2001; Giroux and Simon, 1989).

Yet the "education" and "popular culture" figurations in *KB* and *BE* deserve being studied as intrinsic to these artistic creations, and the wide public debate waged over education and popular culture at the beginning of the twenty-first century. This is especially so as school education is threatened by the rapid development of alternative knowledge resources, the widespread influence of media developments, and globalization (Burbules and Callister, 2001; Burbules and Torres, 2000; Popkiewitz and Fendler, 1999).

This study is part of a research project intended to observe formal education systems from the fringes of the central activities (Bekerman, Burbules, and Silberman-Keller, 2005) in order to create the possibility of an "oblique gaze." One side of this oblique gaze opens opportunities to problematize the centrality of formal educational systems as educational agents; its other side proposes broadening the conversation about education and pedagogy toward the margins of canonic educational activities.

Graziana Ramsden (2003) has evaluated Almodóvar as an artist whose work creates a "redemptive reevaluation of a shared mass and popular culture." I assume that it is possible to include Tarantino in this evaluation and to consider education as part of what is reevaluated in each of their films in a specific way. Reevaluation and redemption in *BE* and *KB* are not the outcomes of the movement of cause and effect but a multidirectional positioning of possible alternative reflections on education and popular culture, positioning one about the other in multiple poses. This multiple positioning is what evades representation of one clear stance or evaluation. Instead, as in "real life," my purpose is to observe education and popular culture participating in their mutual construction in the two works.

Problematization of the mutual relations of education and popular culture is not, of course, exclusive to these two films; the process has accompanied the two terms along their differing movement over time as indicating two opposing institutions: the first as the carrier of "high" culture and the latter as "infected space," invaded by the masses and not something to be studied or researched but only understood in term of the extent to which they manipulate people (Adorno, 1991; Ortega y Gasset, 1964).

Alternative positions have been embraced, for instance, by Walter Benjamin (1969) and Lenin (Chanan, 1985). A notorious list of thinkers and scholars followed Benjamin's recommendation to practicize "theoretical productive and subversive readings of the highest spiritual products of a culture alongside its common, prosaic, worldly products" (Zizek, 1991).

Mixing the two "types" of culture was and still is opposed to the Enlightment project; essentialist and new essentialist educational and cultural epistemologies have found as menacing the possibility of creating "cultural milestones" to be inculcated in people for the purpose of helping them becoming "educated human beings" (Hirsh, 2002). Postmodern critics and art critics, such as Hutcheon (1989), have approached this problem by evading the popularly differentiated "high" and "low" categorizations. They have developed "transcontextualization" as a mechanism that makes possible imitation encompassing critical distance, or the repetition of conventions of both high and low cultural materials while simultaneously investing them with a subversive meaning that works as a critique of as well as a tribute to the parodied text.

This explanation, very much based on the notion of "low culture as redeemed" in "high culture," preserves the initial asymmetrical difference that initially caused the movement of the transcontextualization of the presumed low culture "up" to high culture, not the other way around.

KB and *BE* are films distributed for mass consumption through the usual film industry channels; as such, alongside their artistic valuation, they are culturally situated inside popular culture's territorial boundaries. The directors of both films are not only aware of this but became film directors from inside popular culture, which they love and study profoundly (de Zengotita, 2004; Triana-Toribio, 1996). If their work has redemptive effects, these effects are based on the fact that blurring the borders between high and low culture has become one of the central thematic clusters in their films. Thus, it might be that they not only "redeem" popular cultural in their films, they may also create the utopical and heterotopical (Foucault, 1986) spaces where an open conversation about culture is at all possible.

We are thus dealing with two films that not only do not elevate popular culture by a redemptive gesture toward normative educative (high culture) content but, instead, flexibly elaborate a movement of constant chiasm, with each con(founding) the other into a new thing. Taking the opportunity "to commit deicide" (Vargas Llosa, 1971), Tarantino and Almodóvar create "reality" by a chiasm that itself is a fictional reflection of culture construction, precisely the kind of construction through which boundaries between genres, positions inside and outside hierarchies, classifications, and differentiations are demarcated. In this sense, the two films veritably redeem at each new round of mixing and mixed traces not only popular culture but the entire (con)versation on cultural construction, education being a central content and institution that carries out and participates in cultural construction as part of its own *raison d'etre*. Hence, the two films practically mirror high culture and normative education within popular culture and vice versa, each time using different kinds of mirrors to create different chiasmic positions.

In its dictionary definition, "chiasmus" is considered to be "a figure of speech by which the order of the terms in the first of two parallel clauses is reversed in the second. This may involve a repetition of the same words ("Pleasure's a sin, and sometimes sin's a pleasure"—Byron) or just a reversed parallel between two corresponding pairs of ideas. It is named after the Greek letter *chi (x)*, indicating a "criss-cross arrangement of terms" (see www.chiasmus.com). In his essay, "The Law of Genre," Derrida (1980) defines the principle of this law, a notion that I find relevant to the study of chiasmatic space and functioning:

> It is precisely a principle of contamination, a law of impurity, a parasitical economy. In the code of set theories, if I may use it at least figuratively, I would speak of a sort of participation without belonging—a taking part in without being a part of, without having membership in an asset. With the inevitable dividing of the trait that marks membership, the boundary of the set comes to form, by invagination, an internal pocket larger than the whole; and the outcome of this division and of this abounding remains as singular as it is limitless.

Following Derrida, it is possible to conjure this "invaginated space" as the place of cultural production, the place where chiasmus is so extant that it is not even seen. This place includes an "internal division of the trait, impurity, corruption, contamination, decomposition, perversion, deformation, even cancerization, generous proliferation or degenerescence" (Derrida, 1980) and becomes, in effect, the place where the mirror puts into motion continuous invention, reproduction, reflection, projection, echoing, formation and de-formation, transversion, and transmission. Foucault (1986) considers the mirror a place of mixed, joint experience of utopia (as a nonspace) and heterotopia (as a counterspace). In alluding to this chiasmic criss-cross, Foucault conjectures that in every culture, in every civilization, there are real/unreal places that do exist having been formed during the very founding of society. These are like countersites, a kind of effectively enacted utopia in which real sites—that is, all the other real sites that can be found in a culture—are simultaneously represented, contested, and inverted (Foucault, 1986):

> The mirror is, after all, a utopia, since it is a placeless place. In the mirror, I see myself there where I am not, in an unreal, virtual space that opens up behind the surface; I am over there, there where I am not, a sort of shadow that gives my own visibility to myself, that enables me to see myself there where I am absent: such is the utopia of the mirror. But it is also the heterotopia in so far as the mirror does exist in reality, where it exerts a sort of counteraction on the position I occupy. From the standpoint of the mirror I discover my absence from the place where I am since I see myself

over there. Starting from this gaze that is, as it were, directed toward me, from the ground of this virtual space that is on the other side of the glass, I come back toward myself; I begin again to direct my eyes toward myself and to reconstitute myself there where I am. The mirror functions as a heterotopia in this respect: It makes this place that I occupy at the moment when I look at myself in the glass at once absolutely real, connected with all the space that surrounds it, and absolutely unreal, since in order to be perceived it has to pass through this virtual point which is over there.

As Merleau-Ponty remarks, the most familiar technique of the visible body, of this enigmatic seeing-being seen, is the mirror. Noting that "every technique is a 'technique of the body'," he states that the mirror "outlines and amplifies the metaphysical structure of our flesh" (1968, p. 33). Almost as confirmation of Merleau-Ponty's phenomenology of sight in the mirror, it has been discovered that mirrors exist not only as physical objects, in humanly constructed mirrors, but that mirrors are part of the human (animal) body, as demonstrated by the mirror neurons discovery by Rizzolati and others in 1997 in Parma, Italy (Ramachandran, 2000). Mirror neurons are specific cells that ignite when we (animals) perform an action, such as pulling or pushing something. Different neurons ignite for different actions, tempting us to believe they could be a type of motor neuron. However, these neurons also ignite when we see others perform a task, even if we are at rest. This phenomenon is, most likely, what enables us to foresee, read, or even understand others' intentions and actions (Ramachandran, 2000).

Going back to Linnaeus, quoted by Agamben (2004) as having a "weakness for apes" and who defined "homo" as the animal that *is* only if it recognizes that which *is not* [italics in the original], situates Linnaeus' optical machine very close to the important findings about the human (animal) brain as containing mirror neurons that ignite not only when an imitation is performed but also when humans recognize themselves in the performances of others. Would it be too much of an exaggeration to translate these insights on mirrors as being linked to animal or human brains to the study of culture (or popular culture and education, too)? Derrida, Foucault, and Merleau-Ponty, to name a few, have contested the Cartesian separation between the seer and what is seen. These contestations have actually been confirmed by the stated recent neurophysiological research and findings, according to which a mirror and all its action variations are inseparable parts of the human (animal) body.

Staying in a "what if" format, could it be possible to think that people, the creatures who construct cultures, as having a mirror and chiasmus, their most basic technique, function, and effect, implies that a swallowed recognition and imitation do participate in human cultural creations? And, so being, do created things carry inscribed upon themselves the seeing gesture through which they, by means of cultural creations as humans reflections, "see" and "are seen" as well? This could mean that mimesis takes place not only between "reality" and its representations but also within reality's very representations and that this specific movement is an inseparable part of cultural construction. Could it not be that the Hitchcockian technique of alternating the subjective view of the approaching object (house) and an objective shot of the subject in motion (Zizek, 1991), as performed in *Psycho* when a woman approaches Norman's house and the house "looks" at her, is an example of this idea. The director's eye has discerned exactly this: Humans are seers and seen; their creations (Norman's house, metaphorically speaking) reflects this very human mechanism. Is this posture not a way of surmounting the physically limited and *limiting* position of the eyes in the human body (compare with Zizek 1991, pp. 126–127)? Studying education and popular culture in *KB* and *BE* according to their mutual chiasmic effects allows us to perceive the act of seeing, as if high or low culture could see one another, as composed by mutual presences and absences, the one participating in the other according to its own performative figurations by, among other things, blurring hierarchies and orders but by no means abolishing them yet but, instead, considering the way projections and reflections operate as cultural creators/destroyers in the "making of a world."

Filmmaking, or the making of a world, is a central thematic cluster in the two films not only as the depiction of "a human world charged with meaning" (Culler, 1975) but also as a created world whose most vital and constant movement conceals and unconceals the practical devices of filmmaking and the making of a world.

This praxis is installed as the salient "plot" in *BE* by including the making of a film within the film, which becomes a surprising echo of the "hall of mirrors" in which plots and characters, including those of the audience, exchange roles as seers, seen and reflected figures. *BE*'s melted real-fictional world includes verisimilitudes' connotators, which blur the possibility of discerning where the movie finishes and reality begins.

In *KB I* as in the sequel, this effect is created by demarcating the "film-made world" by its almost pristine chirurgic construction, made complete by stressing "artifice" and eradicating almost every trace of a "natural" world. Film and reality are then completely equated for in the film reality, there is neither apposition nor questioning between the film as a high cultural product and popular culture. "Education" in *KB* then is completely seen and reflected from the vantage point of popular culture.

What mobilizes the plots in the constructed worlds of *BE* and *KB* is revenge. As in many classic tragedies and myths, this motif activates plot generation, development, and dénouement. Revenge (or vengeance) consists of retaliation against a person or group in response to perceived wrongdoing. Although many aspects of revenge echo the concept of making things equal, revenge usually has a more destructive than constructive goal. The vengeful wish is to make the other experience what they went through or make sure that their target will never be able to repeat that action again.

Revenge in *KB* and *BE* is created and reflected by a chiasmic criss-cross movement intended to wound the teacher/father for, first and foremost, having wounded the daughter/child. Protection and care were not exactly what Beatrix Kiddo or Ignacio found in "educational institutions," which became instead menacing shadowy places where common significations linked to pedagogies and educations were inverted in *KB*. Not surprisingly, each film poses pedophilia and extermination as extreme possibilities in teacher/pupil father/daughter relationships.

Revenge in *KB* and *BE* is not based on symmetrical forces or possibilities but on the "leaping" out of "reality," on excess. The outstandingly redeeming act is performed by the *femme fatale* (Beatrix Kiddo, Zahara, and Juan) the singularly wounded avenger who literally breaks the father's (teacher's) heart for the sake of possibly installing a shout of protest, resistance and negation within the chains of mastery (compare Ronell's introduction to Solanas, SCUM, 2004).

But negation or protest against what? I find Avital Ronell's answer to Schirmacher's question in her lecture "Testing Your Love, or, Breaking Up" (2002) as illuminating the pedagogical figure by indicating the need for the disciples to in some way "digest" the teacher's roles:

Schirmacher:	… Being noble means you have to be noble from the beginning, that you're just not built to be a follower—you can love, appreciate and admire, but you'll never be somebody else's servant, not even when you're young and ignorant. So is this not the condition of a noble traitor, that you have never been, from the beginning, someone who has been taken in?
Ronell:	I wish I could have gone over with you the extreme masochistic submission that he [Nietzsche–DSK] performed for Wagner, the notes that Wagner shot to him which said *Do the Christmas shopping for me, and I want the packages here a few days early, and while you're downtown, get me some underwear and while you're at it rewrite "Schopenhauer as Educator" because it's fucked-up, my name isn't in there.* So, Nietzsche's submission was so severe that this would not be an issue for us. Once I took a walk with Gadamer, who said to me: *"You have to totally submit yourself to a master, otherwise you'll never understand what thinking is".* So the question of pedagogy that you raise, when Lacan says: "language is a body," where does this body enter your body? Where does pedagogy begin or end? Let's say learning can only be accomplished, if it's ever accomplished, through trauma. Then something has to really, severely risk and threaten the subject. A devastation and destruction has to be risked if

> we're following the Nietzsche channel here … If you're already broken up
> before you enter the body of the other, then you're not risking your own
> disillusion and destruction. You know how you treat the kids, Wolfgang,
> there is something very brutal, devastating and threatening before even
> the break-up can be considered. The break-up was never desired, it's
> something that had to happen; it remains ambivalent and complicated.
> If you think you were built to break up, then what's the big deal? This
> guy was not built to break up, which is why he had a breakdown.

The revenge journeys of teachers and students, masters and disciples found in *BE* and *KB* do not submit an exclusive response to the "loving or breaking up" question, but they do exhibit trauma at the edge of suffering. That excessively figured trauma allows life's cathartic mourning for all the masters and knowledge bodies lost or on their way to be lost, represented by Kiddo's and Ignacio's/ Zahara's melancholy. Film noir, to which we will return in the third part of this article, takes on the color of mourning in *BE* and *KB* in campy, installed blonde femme fatales brimming with the excesses of transversion (Ignacio/Zahara) or violence (Beatrix Kiddo), loving and breaking up with their masters.

II
Bad Education: Education and Popular Culture Poses

FILM SYNOPSIS

Madrid 1980: Enrique Goded is a young film director in need of inspiration for his next project. Unexpectedly, Ignacio, a figure from the past, reenters his life. Ignacio is now a struggling actor in need of a job. One option would be for Enrique to adapt Ignacio's mostly autobiographical short story, "The Visit." At first reluctant to rekindle the old friendship, Enrique starts reading the short story, which brings a flurry of buried emotions to the surface.

Enrique is transported back in time to his boyhood at the Catholic school where he had met Ignacio—then a beautiful boy endowed with a rich singing voice. In the short story, the two boys discover love, sex, and the movies, but their affair is cut short by the jealous Father Manolo, who is madly in love with the angelic Ignacio. Years later, Ignacio, now the transvestite Zahara, returns to blackmail the pedophilic priest. Why? Zahara needs money to have a sex-change operation.

Enrique decides to make a film out of the gripping short story. He invites Father Manolo to view part of its shooting. Now known as Señor Berenger—the priest left the church in favor of becoming the managing editor of a book-publishing house—Manolo appears at the studio making *La Visita* and discovers Juan once more. At this moment, the audience viewing Almodóvar's *BE* becomes aware that Ignacio, having earlier discovered Sr. Berenger, has blackmailed him in order to pay for his drug habit and the cost of his sex-change surgeries. Juan convinces Sr. Berenger to kill Ignacio, thereby putting an end to his role of Ignacio as involved in a love affair with Enrique.

BE'S MIRRORS OF EDUCATION AND POPULAR CULTURE

> *I also like to consider the screen as a*
> *mirror to the future …*
>
> PEDRO ALMODÓVAR

Catoptromancy as divination in mirrors requires that by staring fixedly in a mirror or any other bright object, mediums put themselves into the kind of trance that enables them to see past, present, and future. Through these visions—which frequently include an auditory component—mediums try to bridge the gap between their limited knowledge and the wisdom available to their ancestors (Pendergrast, 2003). In *BE*, catoptromancy proceeds by superimposition of plots and characters, each of which continues the plot line of the story in some respects and changes it in others by switching actors and point of views while implicitly rendering the invocation: "Mirror, mirror on the wall." This invocation, expressed by each character in turn, is what advances and obstructs the possibility of an univocal clear-cut divination of *BE*, a film noir that portrays the quest for knowledge and the failure of obtaining it. Past and present, memories, reality and actuality, film world and real world intertwine to the point where truth is nowhere and everywhere.

It should not be difficult to identify the title *BE* with a seemingly simple story that judges Catholic education and the Fascist regime in Spain until the 1960s to be the major causes for the "incredible and shocking events" to which—taken from a simplistic and conservative point of view—we are exposed as film viewers. Meaning, *BE* is, at the very least, the cause of pedophilia, homosexuality, sexual transversion, murder, lying, theft, and betrayal, to name only a few of the film's central themes that can be considered as "bad." But, *mal educado* also means badly educated; therefore, *BE* in Spanish refers to someone who has bad manners. Yet bad manners are easy to treat by applying *good education.*

This double meaning of *BE* liberates the oxymoronic stress on the literal meaning of the film's title, leaving it as a pretext that can absorb different meanings and plots, if not the possibility to finish watching the film, and asks, "What is education and what does the film have to do with it?"

BE's general plot structure is produced by the folding, unfolding and refolding of plots, by actors playing different roles, by similar roles played by different actors, by meshing different "historical" epochs in a way that any inquiry into the specific relationship between education and popular culture responds to this procedure. Its results allow the possibility for identifying each in different and differing figural situations.

Pure education: A "noncontaminated" panoramic gaze

The first educational figure in the film makes possible discernment of a supposedly objective gaze, describing routines in a religious school in 1960s Spain. The scene is observed from a bird's eye view, transmitting a picture of the entire class during a gymnastics lesson. The scene seems quite ordinary, just a class of boys in gym uniforms, exercising discipline and body development in a quasi-military way. This scene mimetizes, condensates, and stresses the usual educational practices: The teacher sits in front of the busy class, which moves uniformly according to the rhythm dictated by the teacher. Yet, the teacher's position puts us in doubt of what we are observing: Are these children exercising, exposing their backs to the teacher's inspection, or perhaps saluting authority? The children do not have individual identities; on the contrary, they are represented as if part of a disciplined uniformed group that functions as one body. This scene represents a field where "pure" school education takes place, without intercession of any kind, a situation that becomes rarer in the progressing educational landscape of *BE*, for it is, ultimately, the only "school" scene in the film.

Education and popular culture (con)fusion

The second image of education, which leads to its (con)fusion with popular culture, takes its departure from the same scene, now in close-up, focusing on teacher-pupil relations. This shot reveals a space that, while apparently innocent, betrays sexual molestation, love, admiration, and fear in its shadows. These scenes, beginning in the schoolyard, take place during festivities that transmit cheerfulness, clarity, normality, and bright colors on the one hand but obscures secrets and abuse on the other. These two effects are meshed in the film's cheerful moments, for instance, during a football game when priests are photographed in quasi-comic situations, jumping and running with their cassocks in the air, an effect that erases any clear-cut masculinity and assigns them a maternal/paternal chiasmatic semblance.

An even closer gaze focuses on nonformal moments, such as when Father Manolo, the school principal and literature teacher, induces Ignacio to sing during a class expedition by a river. In the first song scene Ignacio sings a Spanish translation of "Moon River," whose lyrics about turbulent and dark waters contrast sharply with the figures seen on the screen; we see pupils jumping into the river, with the bright rays of the sun on the water and the pupils' bodies reflecting the purity of baptism and initiation. This brightness blurs the difference between what is seen and what is suspected as really taking place. The idyllic scene of informal educational activities at school acquires at least one double meaning, not only hinting that "all that glitters is not gold" (from the Spanish idiom *no todo lo que brilla es oro*), suggested by the suspicious black shadows that appear on the rivers' border, but also of the "covert," intimated by the dusty bamboo plants that negate the idyllic nature of the scene by alluding to the "dark" (noir) events taking place behind the scenes.

In the second song scene, "Sorrento"—"Jardinero" in Spanish—is sung by Ignacio, who has been invited (forced) to sing at Father Manolo's birthday party. The song describes the gardener's (teacher's) power over his flowers (pupils), which gives them life and color. What should be a carefree scene nevertheless configures an ambiance saturated with Ignacio's fear and Padre Manolo uncontrollable desire. It is at this moment that the teacher's educational ideas, transformed into the lyrics of a popular song, present the common image of education as agricultural work, according to which pupils are seeds, plants or flowers, and teachers are gardeners or farmers that use water and fertilizers in order to develop knowledge in their pupils' heads and hearts (Silberman-Keller, 1994). Yet, a second level of interpretation can be added to this obvious layer; this level refers to the erotic relationship existing between teacher and pupil, what is usually referred to in the Western culture tradition as characterizing knowledge transmission. This song's frame of reference—a catholic school for boys where teachers are men—adds to the image of the teacher as gardener and students as flowers needing care, a pornographic contour, "the gardener," being one of the most popular narratives in porno films. Eros transformed into pornography and abuse is one of the critical positions of *BE*, elaborated through commonly known figures of popular culture and education. Chiasming educational philosophies, transmitted into popular songs that reflect education in addition to Popular Culture, creates an amalgam, a figure that includes both, not simply an equalization of the two but a confounding of which is which and who is who into an indissoluble entity. Character couples: Sarita Montiel and Father Manolo; institutional couples: the cinema building and the residential religious school building; the couple confirmed by the sainted as well as the impure: angelic scenes of white voices singing during religious services, with the same voice singing to satisfy their teachers' desires; finally, the couple Ignacio and Enrique, lovers who reflect each other while populating and animating an anamorphic figure. Education in this case includes all that has been experienced in childhood. The (con)fusion between the "El Olympo" Theater where Ignacio and Enrique together watched Sarita Montiel, the famous Spanish star in *Esa Mujer*, echoing the *Ecce Homo* while creating its feminine counterpart, and the church where Ignacio has robed and disrobed Father Manolo for religious services and sung angelic songs and prayers, equates scenes as might Genet, by blurring the differences between sacred and profane spaces (see Sartre, 1983), those where either gods or goddesses might find rest. This criss-cross movement between Jesus and Sarita Montiel feminizes Jesus and masculinizes Sarita Montiel; the fusions between school, church and cinema create the ultimate venue for enactment of the spectacle as a "fatalist thriller that happens in the territory of *The Law of Desire.* An arid, visceral, wealthy in secrets place, where all the characters endanger themselves without fear of consequences and that is inhabited mostly by masculine characters, like in war films" (Almodóvar, 2004).

Apprenticeship: Folding and unfolding identities

Presenting himself as Ignacio, Juan, eager to become a lead actor in *La Visita*, transforms himself into Zahara, a composition that includes Sara Montiel together with traces of many other artists and actors. Ignacio's conversion into Zahara occurs during a gradual process of self-education during which he serves as the apprentice to a drag queen nightclub actor who specializes in playing Sarita Montiel singing her best-known hits. Ignacio will become an imitation of Zahara in three turns, through three paired conversions and transversions: From Juan to Ignacio, from Sarita Montiel to the drag queen and from Ignacio to Zahara. This process unfolds the stances taken when adopting a personality, a gender, a body, and mannerisms in order to play a role. This is role-playing conducted by chiasmic interchanges reflecting, recognizing and projecting the desired image. The last instance of this transversive movement is that of Zahara, the *femme fatale* (not an essential but definitely representative character) who, as defined by Almodóvar (2004), is a woman utterly aware of her seductive power. She is so hypotensive that she is not easily agitated. She has lost her scruples and is unwilling to relocate them. Sex to her is not a source of pleasure but of pain for others. In *La mala educación*, the *femme fatale* is an *enfant terrible* who appears in many forms and layers, maximized by her figuration in Zahara. The role played by Gael García Bernal puts into practice elements taken from Barbara Stanwyck, Jane Greer, Jean Simmons (*Angel Face*), Joan Bennett (*Scarlet Street*), Ann Dvorak, Marie Windsor, Lisabeth Scott, Veronica Lake and many other women who have cast womanly spells in film. Education here adopts the definition of transformation, a process of becoming "a composed other." We find essentially the same scene, in different guise, presented in *All About My Mother*, when Amparo relates the cost of her body construction to the audience attending a play. Becoming a "composed other" includes obtaining another body, other clothes, and different body language. Moreover, this "composed" other unfolds through its similarities with art and pop culture, the traces of which allow us to recognize the different folds of Zahara's composition and her singularity in uncovering most of them.

Juan transverts into Zahara during his apprenticeship by exercising keen observation (Rogoff, 2003), imitation enacted as in front of a mirror, and by taking care to meticulously study every detail of her behavior. He demonstrates how an actor learns her roles and, ultimately, how people imitate different characters in the process of becoming themselves. In one scene Zahara wears a Jean-Paul Gautier suit. The suit, representing a naked female body, recalls Magritte's paintings *Homage to Mack Sennett* as well as *Philosophy in the Bedroom* (Paquet, 1992). At the center of the suit in their works, both Magritte and Gautier mark breasts and pubic hair in a way that confounds fabric with skin, body, and dress. Identity, so they seem to say, is something one can wear. But, more than characterizing a specific woman (or man), it confounds woman and snake, dress and skin, appearance and nature, man and woman. Thus, an identity is obtained through a self-learning apprenticeship that includes not only growing a physical body and knowledge corpus, it also includes transversion as integral to metamorphosis. Once obtained, this identity includes the (con)fusion of what has been culturally defined as opposite positions, generated by celestial and infernal gestures.

The characters in *BE* interchange roles, acts that blur the cinematic tradition of marking consistently "good" and "bad" guys. Doing so throws spectators into a situation where Education and Popular Culture, as assimilated in the film world, appear in at least four different figures, each nostalgically caressing albeit simultaneously criticizing—ironically and radically—the two arenas.

III

kill bill synopsis

> *… although the Pagan fables are not believed, yet we forget ourselves*
> *continually, and make inferences*
> *from them as existing realities …*

Edgar Allan Poe, The Purloined Letter

KB I and *II* are films composed around one fundamental plot that relates to Beatrix Kiddo's revenge itinerary on her journey to kill Bill, her lover, for having cancelled the possibility of abandoning her former life as a killer in favor of motherhood. Other plot twists reveal, synchronically and diachronically, the biographical details, instructional processes and personalized weapon production undergone by Beatrix and her enemies; all this information coherently supports Beatrix Kiddo vengeance carrier albeit using forward and reverse movements.

THE MAKING OF A MYTH

In a dialogue conducted between Beatrix Kiddo and Bill, her lover, boss, father, daughters' father, friend, and enemy, seems to converse with Umberto Eco's (1984) "The Myth of Superman." Superman is considered a singular figure. He did not become Superman; he was born Superman. When Superman wakes up in the morning, he is Superman. Clark Kent is his alter ego and his outfit with the large red S is the blanket he was wrapped in as a baby when the "Kents" found him. Those are his clothes, which are part of his body. The Clark Kent costume includes glasses and a business suit. Superman blends with us by means of his costume. So, Clark Kent is how Superman views us. Clark Kent is weak, unsure of himself: He is a coward. Bill concludes: "Clark Kent is Superman's critique on the whole human race …"

The relationship traced between Superman and *KB* by one of the film's characters, Bill himself, adds a popular myth constructed by ramified sets of ancient and modern mythic traditions, reframed in a new playing space: *KB*. This mythic space includes Tarantinos' own oeuvre and allegorically goes to and fro between many of the parricides, revivals, revenges, instructions, births, rebirths, live burials, loves, wars and contests for power ensconced in myths as they appear in high/low cultural, textual, iconographic, cinematic, audible productions in an endless number of versions.

Bill's allusion to Superman, seen as a kind of superheroes' comparative analysis, situates Beatrix's question to Bill regarding whether she is a superheroine in the context of a new mythology. In this mythic production, she and all the other main *KB* characters are in some way linked not only by blood (or bloody) relationships, but also by interchangeable roles as teachers and students, masters and disciples, instructors and apprentices in a hierarchy that precisely points to Beatrix's superiority over each of the other characters.

Bill's response to Beatrix about her being a superheroine is negative; instead, she is characterized as a "natural born killer," alluding to another script written by Tarantino, a work that may provide a definition of being human according to Tarantino. Nevertheless, Bill's reading of the Superman myth, Beatrix's question and Bill's answer open the door to Beatrix's character like that of any other fictional character, to that of a dramatic potential veering toward its possible mythical development inside and outside the film but also through time as a superheroine.

"The Deadly Viper Assassination Squad" composed by Beatrix Kiddo (aka The Bride, Black Mamba, Arlene Plimpton and Mommi), Elle Driver (aka California Mountain Snake), O-Ren Ishii (aka Cotton Mouth), Vernita Green (aka Copperhead), Budd (aka Sidewinder) and Sofie Fatale, one of Bill's lovers and O-Ren's lawyer, are all tied to Bill (aka Snake Charmer) as an oligarchic group composed of the mythical characters making up the "Kill Bill Saga." Renaming these characters with code names borrowed from the viper world has suggestive mythical and psychological implications for the personages' characterizations as well as their figural roles. After all, it is the Snake Charmer, Bill, the group leader or symbolic father, who plays the flute that exerts some magical effect on the snakes' rearing and domination until the moment when his power is contested by Beatrix.

The Deadly Viper Assassination Squad is indeed a clan; abbreviating their titles as "DiVAS" implies that they are a group of flamboyant females. The DiVAS are an allusion to a mixture of woman, snakes, temptation, curiosity in addition to the means and costs incurred when obtaining knowledge, a combination stipulated in the biblical narrative of Eve as well as its repeated and transverted versions, up to and including these colorful women, together with Bill and Budd. Bill and Budd are brothers who grew up without a father. O-Ren Ishii was left an orphan after her parents were killed by Japanese crime boss Matsumoto for unknown reasons. The origins of the other three assassins are unknown. Bill is known to have had affairs—or at the least sexual relations—with The Bride in addition to Elle Driver and possibly Sofie Fatale, too. The Bride, Beatrix, is the only one of his lovers who will become the mother of his child, a daughter.

Although never explicitly said, it was widely held that Black Mamba was the most lethal and skilled of the DiVAS after Bill himself, making her the deadliest woman (*femme fatale*) on the planet. But Black Mamba is strong not only for being a deadly woman; she has been re-born twice, once after a coma that has lasted for four years (much like Almodóvar's sleeping girl in *Talk to Her*), allegorically recalling the tale of Sleeping Beauty and a scene where the same actress, Uma Thurman, awakens from a cocaine overdose in Tarantinos' *Pulp Fiction*. The second rebirth occurs after she has been buried alive, like Sophocles' Antigone. But unlike Antigone, Beatrix does not accept her destiny; she breaks out of her coffin to walk out of Paula Shultz's grave (resembling the fictitious Elke Sommer character from the 1968 *The Wicked Dreams of Paula Schultz*, directed by George E. Marshall). To revive and emerge from a tomb clears the way for the birth of a new super heroine that, like Paula is able to jump over the divide between West and East to create a unique cinematic figure–the Blonde–literally a *femme fatale* who in her vengeance-wreaking career grows up to become a member of a cinematic pantheon. Beatrix's lethal power, rooted in her fierce desire to kill Bill, develops in part from her numerous revivals and grows from duel to duel with her enemies and enemies' friends, each a performance of self-control, professionalism and discipline.

Bill, The Bride, and Elle Driver were trained by Pai Mei, a Chinese martial arts master. Pai Mei agrees to train Beatrix at Bill's request. Far from the camera, Bill is supposed to have obtained a personal reminder of Pai Mei's capacities, an experience representing the organizing principle behind the hierarchies found in the DiVAS, an act indicating that Bill not less that Beatrix is Pai Mei's disciple.

In addition to their training in the martial arts, the DiVAS were also fluent in several languages, well versed in the use of firearms, and skilled in various assassination, espionage, surveillance, and weapon combat techniques. In one of the film's final scenes, Bill asks Beatrix if her adversaries were good. The question's positive response is Beatrix's Olympian recognition of those qualities taught to and learnt by all the DiVAS, with Beatrix retaining her position among the best.

Teachers and students, masters and disciples, instructors and apprentices have a profound sense of mutual respect that honors the singular powers each has developed. Nevertheless, when conflict arises, no nostalgic memories of camaraderie will interrupt the inevitable course of one's tragic destiny. Hattori Hanzo makes a sword at Beatrix's request, breaking his 28-year-old oath while honoring Bill's destiny. Esteban, the pimp who brought up Bill, delivers Bill's address to Beatrix, knowing of her intentions to kill Bill. Budd recognizes that Beatrix deserves revenge and that they, the wedding rehearsal assassins, deserve to die. Part of the killing is done symbolically: Although Budd is killed by a "real" black mamba (Beatrix's pseudonym), brought by Elle inside a suitcase carrying Budd's payment for supposedly having killed Beatrix, it is suggested that the bloody round of destiny initiated by the call for revenge will never stop.

Not far from ancient mythologies, the *KB* myth is charged with a sense of tragedy whose core stresses that women and men cannot escape their destiny, that family affairs are characterized, a la Mauriac, by vipers' knots, that love is far from consummation, as suggested by Beatrix's name: the saintly woman and objective of courtly love.

If Clark Kent is, according to Bill, Superman's critique of human nature, Beatrix's conversion into a superheroine represents the quest for strength, self-confidence, and bravery. Beatrix's quest is therefore a radical critique of woman's (and man's) condition and an ultimate act of resistance. Seen in this way, *KB* is a colored sad tale about the human condition, plastically constructed on the paraphrase and citation of low/high culture that determine the "plot" of a critical narrative (Johnson, 1988). The possibilities for redemption in the *KB* Saga are thus left open and ambiguous, unlike those of Superman: "… the figure who switches identities in a telephone booth. A telecommunication specialist par excellence, Superman becomes what he is by literally ascending beyond himself, rising above the journalistic persona that suffers a still more heavily weighted temporality than the one guiding the flying rumor, faster than a bullet or any train of thought …" (Ronell, 1998). Yet, like Superman, Beatrix Kiddo literally ascends and descends as part of her individual carrier and quest, not due to any Kryptonian radiation but to self-determination and training.

B.B. (Beatrix's and Bill's daughter and Brigitte Bardot's famous sobriquet, another trace found in *KB*) has her first killing experience when playacting the shooting of her father and mother. This act circularly closes the *KB* tale by literally performing the lyrics of the Nancy Sinatra song: "My baby shot me down." Her leaving the stage raises a twofold question: Is B.B. to become a killer? Will Beatrix, the heroine who changed her own destiny, be able to change that of her daughter, too? The answers to these questions are crucial not only for viewing *KB* as a critique of human nature but also as a cinematic developing myth. In this sense it is worth asking if the films, games and comics inspired by the *KB Saga* will be able to sublimate the cinematic maternal superego as describe by Zizek (1991) in relation to Hitchcock's three films: *North by Northwest, Psycho* and *The Birds*. According to Zizek, these three films illustrate the "dead end of the modern American family" or, in other words, "the deficient paternal ego ideal makes the law 'regress' toward a ferocious maternal superego, affecting sexual enjoyment, the decisive trait of the libidinal structure of 'pathological narcissism.'"

The Hitchcockian possibility delineated by Zizek could be problematized, as already alluded to in *KB*, by adding a close reading of Butler's (2000) "Antigone's Claim: Kinship Between Life and Death." Beatrix's likeness to Antigone is suggested by a partial comparability between *KB* personalities and those found in the classic tragedy. Budd (Creon is Oedipus's brother-in-law), Bill's (Oedipus) brother, buries Beatrix (Antigone) alive for trying to change her destiny and disobeying Bill (the law). Beatrix, by walking out of the grave, indeed creates an alternative to her destined tragic death as planned by Bill. In this sense, as suggested by Butler and in part by Tarantino, Beatrix's reaction could be considered a call for the reconsideration of Kinship through actual situations, a remodeling of the very idea of family in these times of divorce, remarriage, exile, migration, displacement, multiple or single parenthood as well as step, gay and blended families. *KB III*, the adjacent comics and games inspired by *KB I* and *II*, will surely answer these questions in some form.

BEATRIX BECOMES A SUPERHEROINE

As a mythic saga, *KB* provides the background for Beatrix Kiddo's conversion into a superheroine. In contrast to Superman, Beatrix's past and family records are potential data for apprehending her outstanding development yet remain outside her myth's figuration. A short and unique scene shows Beatrix in her childhood, at school, where her name's origin is rectified as descending from the past. Every attempt at discovering Beatrix's origins is blurred yet, in *KB I*, stressed by beeping each time her name is pronunciated. Alternatively, as seen in the wedding ceremony rehearsal, she has friends and a mysterious past.

Beatrix Kiddo's figuration as a superheroine is initiated by a plot configured by her desire of revenge for being allowed to be a mother and change her lifestyle. This figuration is attained through a long carrier of training and tests she has to endure while gradually achieving her objectives. Translated into Freudian and Lacanian imaginary, to "kill" Bill means to annul the origins of the law for the relationship between Bill and Kiddo is a multilayered and (con)founding father-daughter, loved and loving, master and disciple, owner and owned couple relationship. This kind of relationship is allegorically recalled when Bill appears in the wedding rehearsal scene and presents himself as Kiddo's father.

Such a relationship is not an easy one to annul but is destroyed by contesting her supposed "brothers" and allies, with each figured not less trained, intelligent, strong and fast as she is. These actions eliminate the ring supporting Bill and prepare Beatrix to face him, partly disarmed yet knowing that his fate is sealed.

Beatrix Kiddo's construction as a super heroine is thus accomplished by a continuous hyperbolic movement of successive long tests, a carrier composed of training, weapons preparations and periodic retesting. Beatrix Kiddo, more than Superman, becomes "inconsumable" the more she is "consumed" (Eco, 1984) not only because she is twice reborn but because each of her encounters with her enemies stresses, by their deaths, her vitality as a survivor. This vitality is also intensively inscribed by her potential for giving birth.

Beatrix's most important trainer is Bill himself. He is the one who knows her best and who valuates her capacities and powers. He is also the one unwilling to give up on her even though he, as her test carrier witness, portends his own end. He is informed about every step she takes and knows every one of her test results. Bill's participation as Kiddo master and instructor is mostly swallowed and assumed to happen behind the scenes yet it is Bill who honors Kiddo by bringing her to Pai Mei, the world's greatest master of Martial Arts. The film's tale of Pai Mei, a man of infinite power, is the magnificent measure of the tests Beatrix will endure under the Master's instruction. Knowledge transition during Kiddo's training by Pai Mei is in itself a test during which the disciple admits the master's superiority with humbleness and obedience. Training is a transformative process that includes gaining or conquering discipline, modesty, pain, suffering, self-control, dominion, openness, physical hard work and endurance. A good education a la Pai Mei is the possibility of gaining dominion over the body by using mind control. As observed by Aaron Anderson (2005), "throughout the long training sequence with Pai Mei, martial ability is deliberately linked to 'power'." Training sequences in most action films do the same. Pai Mei effortlessly avoids Kiddo's attack and fights without using a weapon or even taking his hands from behind his back. His ease visually demonstrates their respective power by making clear the degree to which he overmatches Kiddo. Prolonged training sequences permit us to view characters voluntarily suffering physical pain and thus judge the strength of their inner desire. The way Kiddo suffers humiliation without overt complaint suggests her deep inner resilience and personal fortitude. Movement and other cues—such as blood and pain—highlight the characters' relative power. Pai Mei effortlessly plucks out Elle's eye, which shows he has absolute mastery not only over his own body but also over Elle's. The fact that Elle could not bear the pain and humiliation of training as well as Kiddo did also suggests something lacking in Elle's character. When Kiddo plucks out Elle's remaining eye, we see Kiddo exercising a power similar to Pai Mei's, who seemed almost a demigod.

Beatrix Kiddo's power will be contested several times. Each one of her confrontations with her "stepsisters" is a repetition that adds elements to vary and magnify Kiddo's powers and diminish those of Bill's and his defenders. Beatrix therefore leads the battle out of the "family" through contests with all her powerful relatives. As we follow this long journey, we see Kiddo testing her mental and physical powers during periods of interrupted capacities. She is able to own her physical autonomy after it has been removed from her control by her four-year coma; once in control again, she is able to walk away from paralysis to movement. Once she has the power to move, it is through movement from one site of the globe to another. Together with controlling her body and mind, she gradually approaches a situation in which each repetitive diminuendo—such as the Budd and Elle confrontations—become moments building up to a crescendo in Kiddo's powers.

School, contrasting instruction and self-development, appears in *KB* three times. The first, during the oxymoronic scene in which the interior of the house where Beatrix Kiddo and Vernita are fighting allows us to view Vernitas' daughter coming home from school, a scene that opposes inside and out, normal/peaceful and criminal/violent reality. The second time that school appears is when Beatrix Kiddo's name is called out by her teacher; in this way we became acquainted with the idea that this is her "original" name. The third allusion to school occurs when Gogo Yubari dresses as a Japanese schoolgirl (the costume is also a popular sexual fetish). Gogo's violent behavior directly challenges traditional gender roles, captured in her appearance as a schoolgirl. Her capacity for extreme violence, which empowers female characters including Elle and O-Ren Ishii, stimulates Kiddo's own heroic development. School, in *KB*, is another of those public places—for instance, a church, bar, and the like—that function as the film's ecological habitat connotators. These three scenes configure school as disconnected from "real" life, as a place where one's name and presence are checked and where pupils are not always what they seem (as may be the case in school generally). Information and knowledge, then, are available not only in school but also in volatile places; consider Elle's reading a text about the Black Mamba's characteristics and poisonous effects, obtained from the Internet, to the dying Budd.

Education and training in *KB* are therefore intimate processes that take place voluntarily. They are carried out in couples or pairs composed of master and disciple or, alternatively, through self-learning motivated by mind, power and dominion.

CONCLUDING REMARKS: THE BLONDE, CAMP AND FILM NOIR

Specialists in Almodóvar and in Tarantino have widely tracked films, motives, sound tracks and characters homaged and quoted in *BE* and in *KB*. These two directors' work have indeed created "contextual conventions, precautions, and protocols in the mode of reiterations" (Derrida, 1980) of "high" and "low" culture in their work.

These two films stress the "love of the unnatural, of artifice and exaggeration" (Sontag, 1964). *KB* is a violent, bloody film that studies the construction of violence in Westerns, kung fu, and spaghetti Westerns, whereas *BE* builds upon the exaggerations of film noir and melodrama. Each film is constructed as new signs in the stylistic esthetics developed by their respective directors in previous films.

The two films are impressive for being highly stylized in the construction of artifice and exaggeration; from this point of view they are campy in peculiar ways. Nevertheless, the apolitical attitude attributed to camp by Sontag (1964) is replaced in these films for a space of cultural construction, situated at the margins; witness, among other things, the construction of the films' personages as transvestites or androgynous beings. These constructions open spaces of severely transgressive political considerations about the relationship between the center and the margin, between high and low culture. What is politically important in camp's discursive space is not any specific answer to questions about "low" and "high" culture but the existence of a space where questions about the difference between them is openly raised.

In *KB* and *BE*, film noir's mysterious ambience, accompanied by gloom, is left unrelated to the anguish caused by redemptive pictures of unknown yet possible worlds or reality's black holes (Zizek, 1991). On the contrary, "the image of this world" is what does not function in the two films. School is not a safe place, fathers kill daughters, teachers molest students, knowledge is not exactly what is so labeled, and sometimes obtaining knowledge literally means losing every possibility for redemption: brothers kill brothers, friends kill friends, mothers and daughters can also be killers. In the midst of the most cherished expectations of normative life, something is always decomposing; more than being linked to Freud's concept of the uncanny, the *noir* effect of this decomposition reflects sadness and tragedy.

In the forefront of this blackness, Almodóvar and Tarantino give birth to the Blonde. Tarantino's revives Beatrix Kiddo from the grave of a personage from a 1968 B movie starring Elke Sommer (The Wicked Dreams of Paula Schultz) thereby reviving and renewing the ultimate *femme fatale*. Zahara, as described, unfolds many cinematic blondes. The two blondes contain folds from other personages and come to know themselves the experience of how their (Kiddo and Zahara) world backgrounds were constructed. Their role is to reveal that: "An oeuvre in the old sense (again in art, but also in life) is not possible. Only fragments are possible … Clearly, different standards apply here than to traditional high culture. Something is good not because it is achieved, but because another kind of truth about the human situation, another experience of what it is to be human—in short, another valid sensibility—is being revealed" (Sontag, 1964). The apparition of the blonde *femme fatale* as an alternative "Truth purveyor" in the middle of the scene is what kills Bill and breaks Father Manuel's (Sr. Berenger) heart. The film noir ambience, the camp sensibility and the blonde *femme fatale* might be, together with all the enjoyable components of *KB* and *BE*, a most politically transversive lesson about the chiasming conversation about the (con)fusion of "education and popular culture" yet to appear.

The conversation and mutual reflection of popular culture and education conducted by Almodóvar and Tarantino by means of these personages give birth to new versions of all the changing roles undertaken by the personages as "educated" people in the invaginated space of cultural construction occupying the worlds of *BE* and *KB*. These educated people, embody the (con)fusion of traces of all kinds of "high" and "low" culture. Sr. Berenger's remark as he leaves the movies, that "all the movies seemed to talk about us" may perhaps be an echo of indefiniteness not only as a result of some sense of identification aroused by the film, but also as a reminder of the *bildung* narrative, according to which the possibility of a "sterilized" place (school, for instance) where education takes place devoid of most high and low feelings; "high" and "low" culture is a fictional place.

In this sense *BE* and *KB*, two films representing an oblique gaze toward canonical cinematic and cultural bodies, offer by the cathartic effects caused by transversion and exaggeration unusual opportunities for considering education and popular culture not as hierarchically qualified poles but as differences in cultural construction that work chiasmatically. These constructions operate reflectively and project each other as seers and seen, which might indicate that not only movies "seem to talk about us" but that all the cultural and educational figures in which we take part as seers or seen talk to us and about us and sometimes with us.

This archive, the archive of all the cultural participations, expositions, regressions, and progressions in which we take part, is what allows recognition, a la Linnaeus, of what we are not as the limit that blurs between backward, forward, and multilateral movements but between realities and potentialities of being and not being.

The last reflection invites us to consider education and popular culture in a more flexible and permissive way, as elements in an array of actual educational practices.

REFERENCES

Adorno, T. (1991). Culture industry reconsidered. *The culture industry: Selected essays on mass culture.* London: Routledge.

Agamben, G. (2004). *The open: Man and animal* (K. Attell, Trans.). Palo Alto, CA: Stanford University Press.

Almodóvar, P. (2004). *Bad Education* official site: Autointerview. http://www.clubcultura.com/clubcine/clubcineastas/Almodóvar/malaeducacion/autoentrevista_eng.htm

Anderson, A. (2005). Mindful violence: The visibility of power and inner life in *Kill Bill. Jump Cut: A Review of Contemporary Media, 47.* http://www.ejumpcut.org/currentissue/KillBill/index.html

Bekerman, Z., Burbules, N.C., and Silberman-Keller, D. (eds.). (2005). *Learning in places: The informal education reader.* New York: Peter Lang.

Benjamin, W. (1969). The work of art in the age of mechanical reproduction, in H. Arendt (ed.), *Illuminations* (pp. 217–251). New York: Schocken.

Burbules, N.C., and Callister, Th. A. (2001). Watch IT! *The risks and promises of information technologies for education.* Boulder, CO, and Oxford: Westview Press.

Burbules, N.C., and Torres, C.A. (eds.). (2000). *Globalization and education: Critical perspectives.* New York and London: Routledge.

Butler, J. (2000). *Antigone's claim: Kinship between life and death.* Wellek Library Lecture, University of California, Irvine. New York: Columbia University Press.

Chanan, M. (1985). *The Cuban image: Cinema and culture politics in Cuba.* London: BFI Publishing.

Cheung, C.K. (2001). The use of popular culture as a stimulus to motivate secondary students' English learning in Hong Kong. *ELT Journal, 55*(1): 55–61.

Culler, J. (1975). *Structuralist poetics.* London: Routledge and Kegan Paul.

Derrida, J. (1980). The law of genre (A. Ronell, trans.). *Critical Inquiry, 7*(1): 55–81.

De Zengotita, T. (2004). She'll *Kill Bill* while you chill. http://www.wie.org/j26/kill-bill.asp?ifr=rm

Dimitriadis, G. (2001). Pedagogy and performance in black popular culture. *Cultural Studies Critical Methodologies*, 1(1): 164–172.

Eco, U. (1984). *The role of the reader: Explorations in the semiotics of text* (pp. 107–124). Bloomington: Indiana University Press.

Foucault, M. (1986). Text/Context of other spaces (J. Miskowiec, trans.). *Diacritics 16*(1): 22–27.

Giroux, H.A., and. Simon, R.I. (1989). *Popular culture, schooling, and everyday life.* Critical studies in education series. Granby, MA: Bergin and Garvey.

Hirsch, E.D., Kett, J.F., and Trefil, J. (2002). *The new dictionary of cultural literacy, 3rd ed.* Boston: Houghton Mifflin.

Hutcheon, L. (1988). *A poetics of postmodernism: History, theory, fiction.* New York: Routledge.

Johnson, B. (1988). The frame of reference: Poe, Lacan, Derrida, in J.P. Muller and W.J. Richardson (eds.), *The purloined Poe: Lacan, Derrida and psychoanalytic reading* (pp. 213–251). Baltimore: Johns Hopkins University Press.

Keller, D. (1994). The text of educational ideologies: Toward the characterization of a genre. *Educational Theory*, 44(1): 27–42.

Lambirth, A. (2003). "They get enough of that at home": Understanding aversion to popular culture in schools. *Reading, Literacy and Language*, 37(1): 9–13.

Merelau-Ponty, M. (1968). *The visible and the invisible* (A. Lingis, trans.). Evanston, IL: Northwestern University Press.

Ortega y Gasset, J. (1964). *The revolt of the masses.* New York: Norton.

Paquet, M. (2000). *Rene Magritte 1898–1967: Thought rendered visible.* London and Los Angeles: Taschen.

Pendergrast, M. (2003). *Mirror: A history of the human love affair with reflection.* New York: Basic Books.

Popkewitz, T.S., and Fendler, L. (1999). *Critical theories in education: Changing terrains of knowledge and politics.* New York: Routledge.

Ramachandran, V.S. (2000). *Mirror neurons and imitation learning as the driving force behind "the great leap forward" in human evolution.* http://www.edge.org/3rd_culture/ramachandran/ramachandran_p1.html

Ramsden, G. (2003). Manuel Puig, Pedro Almodóvar and the politics of Camp. *The Mind's Eye* (Spring, 2003): 19–39.

Rogoff, B. (2003). *The cultural nature of human development.* Oxford and New York: Oxford University Press.

Ronell, A. (1994). *Finitude score: Essays for the end of the millenium.* Lincoln, NE, and London: University of Nebraska Press.

Ronell, A. (2002). *Testing your love, or, breaking up: A lecture by Avital Ronell.* http://www.egs.edu/faculty/sandystone.html

Sartre, J.P. (1983). *Saint Genet: Actor and martyr* (B. Frechtman, trans.). New York: Random House.

Solanas, V. (2004). *SCUM manifesto/Valerie Solanas, with an introduction by Avital Ronell* (pp. 1–34). London and New York: Verso.

Sontag, S. (1964). *Notes on camp.* http://pages.zoom.co.uk/leveridge/sontag.html

Triana-Toribio, N. (1996). Almodóvar's melodramatic mise-en-scène: Madrid as a site for melodrama. *Bulletin of Hispanic Studies*, 73: 179–189.

Vargas Llosa, M. (1971). *Garcia Marquez: Historia de un Decidio.* Barcelona, Barral Editores.

Zizek, S. (1991). *Looking awry: An introduction to Jacques Lacan through popular culture.* Boston: MIT Press.

CHAPTER SIX

Make A Point AND Score Ten Thousands: Learning FROM Serious Games

GONZALO FRASCA

If you walk into a game store you will get a glimpse into today's videogaming world. Even though this experience will provide you with a snapshot of most of the best-selling titles, there is much more to videogames than what you can read about in the average magazine. The world that I am referring to does not involve games created with million-dollar budgets, nonetheless it also has a substantial cultural impact on the players. The scene of casual games—such as those that can be bought online at Shockwave.com—offers independent videogames created by small teams with small budgets. Even though independence from big production houses does not necessarily guarantee originality, these games at least could potentially take more creative risks that those developed by teams of hundreds of people—sadly, they usually do not. Another flourishing game scene is *advergaming*—which marries advertising and videogaming. As more and more people spend a larger part of their spare time online, advertisers are investing more heavily in new online communication techniques. As revenues from traditional outlets such as television and magazines fade, companies create online games that showcase their products and services. Again, this field has the potential for promoting originality and experimentation (as it happens sometimes in the world of traditional advertising). Unlike regular videogames that simply attempt to provide some fun, *advergaming* has its own agenda: its main goal is to persuade players into buying a product or, at least, learning more about it. Somehow connected to *advergaming* is another game genre known as *political games*, which also seeks to persuade, even though the "products" it showcases are ideas. *Political games* can be created either by political organizations or by artists and amateur designers who have something to say and share it online.

In this chapter I analyze three different games from these offbeat game genres that do not receive as much attention as console superproductions. All three games have something in common: they try to be persuasive, and they try to make a point. In addition, they are all connected to reality. There are no gnomes, princes, or spaceships in these games. These games can be understood as being political in the broadest sense of the term: they deal with different aspects of human coexistence. The first explores technical work environments, the second is a recreation of a controversial regicide in the not-so-distant Camelot, and the third deals with the mechanics of war.

I personally believe that you do not need to be a total cynic to see the points in common shared by both education and persuasion. I am not arguing here that we should tailor our educational approaches with the language and ideology of advertising. However, I do claim that it may be worth a shot to take a look at these techniques because they illustrate how ideas are conveyed in videogames. This could be useful on two different levels. First, because it can deepen our understanding of games as such and therefore can provide us with better tools for analyzing them. The second reason is that it could help educators facing the task of creating or adapting a videogame for educational purposes by introducing them to some of the potential assets and pitfalls of the genre. This will be particularly true if the subject in question deals with humanities or social science.

In any case, I would like to warn against the hype about the educational potential of videogames. I am absolutely convinced that games, as simulations, provide us with tools for understanding the world in a way that traditional structures such as narratives cannot. In spite of this great potential, videogames are definitely not the one-size-fits-all solution for education. They can simply be one strong, powerful tool that complements other existing ones, but we should be careful not to expect games to deliver what they cannot. This caveat may sound strange coming from somebody who works on trying to bridge such dissimilar fields as gaming and politics. However, I have seen too many technologies been hyped as wonderful solutions only to be totally forgotten a couple of years later. This is why I think that we should definitively be excited about the potential of games for better understanding ourselves, but at the same time we should not forget about the limitations that games, as any other human endeavor, have. In other words, we should keep our heads dreaming up in the sky while leaving our feet on solid ground.

FROM CODE TO REALITY OR HOW INTEL
DISCOVERED WOMEN

Generally, game-programming code does not care about the color of your skin, your age, or your religious beliefs. When you program a computer character you are mainly interested in how it behaves. Characters can perform many behaviors such as walking, running, jumping, grabbing objects, or opening doors. It is quite common to start programming different characters from basic common characteristics like walking and then add up different behavioral features in order to set them apart from each other. In the game-programming world, virtual people are usually born equal by default, and it is only later that their differences are set by the programmer. Most of the time, the characters that you see walking down the streets of a game city may look totally different but still can share the exact behaviors. They may look diverse on the outside, but they are technically clones on the inside.

In April 2004 Intel Corporation launched a Web-based advergame called the "Intel IT Manager Game." It was targeted at IT managers—the people in charge of managing the computer technicians who provide support to employees in large institutions. The game allowed players to hire different employees and administrate their tasks. This Intel advergame was only available for a few hours: between the time it was launched till it was suddenly removed. The Web page where the game used to be hosted gave the following message:

> Your Interest in the IT Manager game is appreciated. Intel is currently making revisions to the game, please check back again in the end of May to test your IT Manager skills.

Based on this message, it was quite reasonable to assume that the game was pulled out because of some bug. Indeed, it did have some sort of compatibility problem even though it was not a technical one. Intel's game was not compatible with more than 50 percent of the world population: it did not allow players to hire female employees.

The "bug" was fixed a few weeks later and, if you play the game now, you will be able to hire both men and women. Still, the blunder did not go unnoticed and the news was distributed online through many Web logs. The anecdote is ironic: a huge corporation like Intel, with a million-dollar budget in public relations, tries to impress their clients by making a cool videogame. Instead, they made a huge faux pas by launching a product that totally ignores women.

The issue here is not merely political correctness. It would be very easy to dismiss this story with a "take it easy, it's just a game" sort of argument. I am afraid it is a bit more serious than that. It is quite common that commercial video games allow players to select the gender of their characters. Game designer Peter Molyneux explained at the European Game Developers Conference in 2004 that he intended to include male and female characters on his game *Fable*, but he finally decided to keep only the male ones because otherwise the would not have met the deadline. It is likely that many players—especially women—may have been disappointed at this, but nobody accused him of chauvinism. Unlike *Fable*, which is set in a fantasy world, Intel's game modeled a real-world work environment. In this real world of ours, gender discrimination at work is a reality. To make things worse for Intel, the IT industry is not particularly the most gender-equal trade.

I wonder how the Intel game "bug" went unnoticed until it was actually launched. I seriously doubt whether such an omission would have happened if the communication had been a printed or television advertisement. These media have a longer history and there are standards for reviewing them before they are released. Interestingly, the first edition of the game clearly featured racial diversity, so it is safe to think that the designers had given at least a thought at the issue of portraying a broad range of characters. I am only guessing here, but based on my experience as a game developer, this situation makes me think that not even a single woman did indeed play the game before it went public. Naturally, this scenario—if true—would not be very flattering for a major corporation.

As I explained before, computer game code is genderless by default. Actually, the updated version of the game now features female characters even though the mechanics of the game are exactly the same. This means that both male and female characters behave exactly the same because they share the same code. To put it in a different way, the game was "fixed" simply by adding new graphics: there was no need to implement new programming. Although I admit that I personally enjoy this story of a powerful corporation's clumsiness, the main goal of this example is not making fun of Intel. Unlike databases, videogames are not merely computer code and data: they are cultural products. As such, they are ruled by the same conventions as other forms of communication. Games may still be perceived as "just for fun," but they can be deadly serious, especially when you use them for such serious goals as corporate communication. Intel learned this the hard way.

As a side note, I would like to add that the Intel game was also victim of a videogame disease: realism for the sake of realism. The videogame industry always tries to push technology toward delivering graphics with the highest degree of photorealism. It is true that most players also demand better graphics, but there is also an economical reason behind this trend: it forces customers to regularly update their machines by buying expensive hardware. Yet games do not need photorealistic graphics to look good. Actually, photorealism can go against the realism of the character's behavior (Laurel, 1997). As we learn from Scott

McCloud's *Understanding Comics*, we can project much more of ourselves into abstractly represented characters. Intel would not have run into a problem if they had instead used abstract characters—stick figures, for example—in their game. Rest assured that I am not suggesting this technique as a way to avoid dealing with serious problems. Still, this event exemplifies the risks of translating what used to be a merely entertainment form into a communication strategy. If we are to exploit videogames' capability for modeling reality we should definitively draw from the knowledge gathered by the game industry over the past three decades. Nonetheless, we should also remember that industrial conventions may not work well outside the entertainment realm and this is why we cannot afford to accept them without giving them a second thought.

I KILLED JFK (AND I CAN DO IT AGAIN)

Who killed JFK? The official story is that he was killed by a lone shooter. Was Lee Harvey Oswald capable of taking those infamous shots from the bookstore window where he was allegedly located? In Oliver Stone's film (1991), the character played by Kevin Costner—Jim Garrison—tries to solve this political murder mystery. In a particular scene, Garrison travels to the actual spot from where Oswald supposedly shot Kennedy. With the help of a stopwatch and a rifle, he recreates the shootings. The actual scene provides him with information that may have seemed too trivial to include in a written report. For example, he notices that there is a tree that may have interfered with the aiming process. From the window, he realizes that it may have been easier to shoot Kennedy before his car made a turn. The simulation allows him to raise new questions, create hypotheses, and contest previous assumptions. This process is definitively something that he could have never achieved by sitting in his office desk. After all, reconstructing crimes at their scene is a quite common technique in criminology.

In 2004, a Scottish game development company created *JFK Reloaded*, a videogame that allowed players from all over the world to recreate Oswalds shots, just like how Garrison does in the movie—with the exception that it does not require to actually travel to Texas. Even though it may sound like an educational game, it can be better understood as one of the rare examples of docugames: videogames that aim to explore real events in the same way that film documentaries do. This particular game simulates the environment where Kennedy was shot. Buildings, streets, and trees are recreated in 3-D graphics. It also features the president's car moving at the same pace that it did the day the assassination happened. Oswald's rifle is also simulated and the game creators claim that they were able to model its ballistics with a high degree of realism. In Oliver Stone's film the audience has to trust Garrison's conclusions after he attempts to recreate the shootings. However, this videogame allows players to aim and shot themselves. You do not have to empathize with the Oswald character: you can actually see the world through his eyes (and through the scope of his rifle). Once the shooting is over, the game recreates the event in 3-D from different perspectives, including the one from which the famous Zapruder film was taken. The game is coded as a physics simulator that analyzes the ballistics of your virtual shots and compares them to the real impacts received by Kennedy.

As a piece of persuasive software, *JFK Reloaded* is quite convincing because it literally makes you share Oswald's point of view. You get a chance to judge by yourself how hard or easy it was to take those shots. The game creators argued on their Web site that their main goal was to prove that, indeed, it was possible for a lone gunman to kill the US president. Actually, they included a particular feature in the game: there was a cash reward of up to one hundred thousand dollars for whoever was able to get closer to replicating the actual shots. Instead of having a million monkeys randomly typing texts, they created a system where players from all over the world can shoot until they can match the real assassination.

Oliver Stone's film provides a lot of information, no matter whether you agree with it or not. However, the film could have never replicated the feeling that I experienced while playing the *JFK Reloaded*. Simulations can offer a first-hand experience that other representational genres such as narrative simply cannot. The game was clearly not a good format for delivering most of the facts, hypotheses, and doubts surrounding the event (this is something that the film was able to do without a problem). Each format has its own limitations and we are certainly much more familiar with the conventions of narrative, which have been perfected through the past thousands of years. For several reasons, it has been historically tempting for developers to try to mix games and stories (particularly when it comes to film narrative). In most cases, this created problematic hybrids that failed to capture the advantages of both genres. This temptation is also particularly strong in educational environments because teachers usually want to make sure that students receive a lot of facts and information. This is why it is quite easy to recognize bad educational games: the gameplay is constantly interrupted by tons of text and animations. *JFK Reloaded* creators were smart enough not to include all the information about that assassination case in the game. Because of this, the game perfectly complements Stone's film—even if the two are not affiliated—by providing an interactive first person experience that the film could not deliver. Similarly, educators should not expect videogames to be able to cover all the possible angles of a certain topic. That being said, it is technically possible—but also extremely difficult—to reach a good balance of information and gameplay within an educational game. My favorite example is the United Nations World Food Program's *Food Force,* an excellent game where information is delivered during the game through voice-overs that do not interrupt the gameplay. The game also includes plenty of animated sequences—known as cutscenes in videogame jargon. Unlike the—usually long and boring—cutscenes in commercial games, the ones in *Food Force* do not try to impress players with Hollywoodean angles and camera movements. Instead, they heavily borrow from the visual language of televised news in order to successfully deliver a lot of useful information in a very dynamic way.

Going back to *JFK Reloaded,* I must say that after playing it I realized that it was quite hard for me to kill Kennedy. However, other players have posted online that they were surprised by the exact opposite: it was quite easy for them. Unlike what we may assume, *JFK Reloaded* cannot really offer any sort of hard proof about the assassination. Obviously, it cannot prove if JFK was in fact killed by Oswald. It can neither necessarily prove if a single shooter could have been able to kill the president the way he was killed. This is because simulations are always biased. A simulation is always an abstraction, a simpler version of reality. Whoever creates the simulation must select which variables will be modeled and which should be discarded. Still, it is technically possible to create an accurate ballistic simulation. However, in this particular case the player does not have any access to the simulation's programming code, so she has no way to check the model for accuracy. In other words, she must trust the game programmers as much as a viewer has to trust the fact that Oliver Stone is not merely making things up. Without that sort of feedback, the simulation can never be considered as scientific. However, words such as "physics," "simulation," and "ballistics" still offer an aura of truth. The myth that "the computer cannot be wrong" still persists even if most people are now much more literate in informatics that what they used to be a few years ago. It may be packaged as being realistic but *JFK Reloaded* remains entertainment— albeit quite sophisticated. In any case, this game is an excellent example for discussing what it means for a simulation to be realistic. Media literacy students may learn how editing is used in order to provide the illusion of continuity in film documentaries. They know that documentaries are technically as much constructed as fiction films, even though certain parameters should be observed by filmmakers in order to offer a minimum degree of truth. So far, *JFK Reloaded* is as close as we have to a game documentary and, as such, it should be viewed as revolutionary. I have no doubt that it could certainly be used as a teaching tool. The fact that simulations, just like books or documentaries, carry their own bias does not necessarily make them ineligible for valid educational purposes. However, players should also be aware that computer code can be as partial as any other human product. Players already know that realistic games are not really "real." However, we are not yet so familiar with the conventions used by designers in order to induce the belief of realism. Simulation literacy may not seem essential when the educational videogames in question deal with abstract themes such as mathematics or physics. However, as videogames become more sophisticated, they increasingly explore issues dealing with politics, economy, history, psychology, or sociology. If videogames become more pervasive in educational environments—and I believe they will—this is why players should be offered more critical tools to better understand games' assumptions and limitations.

SEPTEMBER 12TH AND THE WAR ON ERRORS

I am quite familiar with the final example I analyze. The reason is that I created this game—along with Sofia Battegazzore and my other colleagues at the Newsgaming team. I always feel a bit awkward when my researcher and game developer agendas collide but the fact is that I see both activities as complementary. A game can also work as an academic essay and that was the main goal that I had in mind when I lead the team that launched the Newsgaming.com experiment.

I started playing around with the idea of newsgaming—games based on the news—when I was a journalist working at CNN. I always enjoyed the way political cartoons editorialize different subjects in newspapers and I wondered if a videogame equivalent could be created. In late 2003 we launched *September 12th*, a free online game that reflected on the US-led so-called War on Terror. It became a small online hit with well over one million unique players from all over the world.

The game features a Middle Eastern village populated with civilians and terrorists. The player controls a target that looks like the scope of a sniper rifle. However, when the player clicks no bullet is shot. Instead, a missile is launched. It does not take long to realize that the game cannot be won: it is almost impossible to kill terrorists without killing bystanding civilians and causing the so-called collateral damage. Once a civilian is killed, other civilians mourn him or her and they quickly turn into terrorists. The rules of the system show that the more you try to combat terrorism with bombs, the more terrorists you generate.

September 12th is usually described as part of the "political games" movement, a sort of online agitprop that gained momentum after hundreds of anti–Osama bin Laden games were published by amateur designers on the aftermath of the September 11 attacks. Other examples include the work of Italian group La Molleindustria, Australia's *Escape from Woomera*, and French artist Martin Le Chevallier's Vigilance 1.0. While these games are created by independent groups of artists, more and more political groups and organizations are also becoming interested in creating games to deliver their ideas. For instance, the U.S. Army is responsible for *America's Army*, a free and technically excellent game created to recruit new members. Hezbollah created *Special Force*, a commercial PC game where you fight the Israelis in Lebanon. There are even democratic uses of political videogames, as they are also being used for election campaigns. In late 2003, I created along with Ian Bogost the *Dean for Iowa Game*, the first official videogame ever commissioned for a US presidential election. What we are witnessing is the slow evolution of games into an acceptable form of speech, in the same way that in the past drama or television mutated from mere entertainment into a serious political tool.

Political videogames may be new but they have a much longer history. A clear example is *Monopoly*, one of the most popular board games in the world. The game was invented by an American woman—Lizzie J. Magie—in 1904 and was originally called *The Landlord's Game*. Magie was a follower of the economic ideas of a certain Henry George who supported a particular system of land taxation that aimed at discouraging speculation and fostering equal opportunity. Originally, *The Landlord's Game* was pretty much the opposite of what *Monopoly* was to become. It started as a critique of capitalism but later become one of its more powerful game symbols. It would be easy to disqualify Magie's attempt as a huge failure. After all, the political point of her game did not prevail and it actually pretty much became the exact opposite of what she was trying to argue. I would not be too harsh with her—after all she is probably one of the most successful game designers of the twentieth century even though her name is virtually unknown. One unsuccessful first try may not be enough to dismiss the potential of the whole genre. Still, it is true that political game designers can face the risk that the abstract mechanics behind their games could be used to model a totally different political point. *The Landlord's Game* should serve as a cautionary tale for political game designers about the dangers of games taking a life of their own.

The situation is a bit different if your main goal as a designer is not simply to make a point but rather encouraging discussion around it. Augusto Boal is a playwright and drama theorist who created a set of techniques that combine theater, games, and computerless simulations in order to foster critical debate around social, personal, and political issues. He named his work the *Theater of the Oppressed* because his ideas follow that of Brazilian pedagogue Paulo Freire. It is beyond the scope of this chapter to describe Boal's techniques, as I have already done that elsewhere (Frasca 2001, 2004). However, it should also be noticed that Boal is also a disciple of German playwright Bertolt Brecht. The "alienation effect" (*verfremdungseffekt*) is among Brecht's most famous techniques. Brecht believed that the Aristotelian suspension of disbelief had narcotic effects on the audience because it prevented them from making the connection between what was being staged and their everyday lives. This is why his plays constantly alienated the staging of his plays by reminding the public that what they are seeing is just a fabrication. This was achieved by showing all the gear that is usually hidden behind the scene, as well as by interrupting the action with written banners and other nonconventional effects.

Even though I have previously explored the possibility of creating Boalian videogames, *September 12th* certainly owes more to Brecht than to Boal. The game constantly attempts to break the player's immersion by reminding her that she is playing not with reality but with an artificial construct. One of the most basic game conventions is challenged: even though the game looks like winnable, the player can never reach victory. The basic rhetoric of games is that there is always a solution to the problem that is being introduced, but *September 12th* does not offer any answer at all. Unlike traditional shooting games, it takes a very long time in this game for the weapons to reload, forcing players to witness the consequence of their actions rather than mindlessly shooting at the targets. In addition to this, there is a delay between the moment that the player clicks to shoot and the moment that the missile is actually launched. This allows the scenario to change quite a bit making it more likely for a civilian to walk by the targeted area and becoming a victim of the attack. Through these techniques, I intended to introduce a computer equivalent of Brechtian alienation effects.

Even though the model behind *September 12th* clearly criticizes the futility of the Bush administration's strategies on the War on Terror, it was more important for me as a designer to prompt debates rather than making sure that players would simply agree with my point. I am convinced, as is Boal, that a good discussion can be better than a good solution—especially when dealing with questions that do not have obvious answers. The system seemed to have worked pretty well considering the amount of hate mail—as well as supporting mail—that I received. The game has been discussed both online and offline and, in my experience, most players start arguing about the game itself to later switch to the larger problems of international politics and terrorism. In that sense, I consider that the game fulfilled its main purpose even though its simplicity certainly sheds too much of a Manichean light into the subject.

I am definitively not arguing that Brechtian or Boalian videogames are the ultimate solution for game-based political expression. Just like in my game, I am not here in the business of selling solutions but rather exploring alternatives. Videogames have mutated quite a lot in the recent decades and, in spite of what huge gaming corporations may want us to believe, there is no determinism that forces all games to just be visually improved versions of previous products.

CONCLUSION: PLAY AGAIN

My main intention in this chapter was to provide a serious discussion of non-mainstream videogames. As I said before, I do believe that there is much that we can learn from commercial games—dismissing them would not only be unfair but also quite stupid. However, there is a broader spectrum of games from which inspiration can be drawn, specially if we are interested in exploring their application into fields such as education, training, art, or communication. Good games reveal their secrets only after a lot of work. This process may seem painful to an outside observer but can instead be a passionate, fulfilling activity to the player. If we want to unlock the mysteries of game rhetoric we must indeed work hard. Clues are everywhere: not just in other games but also in other disciplines. It does not even matter if we cannot achieve at putting all the pieces together since the main pleasure of play is starting again, over and over.

REFERENCES

Fortugno, Nick and Zimmerman. (2005). *Soapbox: Learning to play to learn. Lessons in educational game design*. Gamasutra. Available at <http://www.gamasutra.com/features/20050405/zimmerman_01.shtml> (free registration required).

Frasca, Gonzalo. (2001). *Video games of the oppressed*. Master's thesis, The Georgia Institute of Technology. Excerpted in *First person: New media as story, Performance, and game*, N. Wardrip-Fruin and P. Harrigan, eds. Cambridge, MA: MIT Press, 2004.

Laurel, B. (1993). *Computers as theater*. London: Addison Wesley.

McCloud, S. (1994). *Understanding comics*. New York: Harper.

Molyneux, P. (2004). *Fable*. Microsoft Game Studios.

Stone, O. (1991). *JFK*. Warner Home Video.

Walsh, T. (2004). *The playmakers: Amazing origins of timeless toys*. Sarasota, FL: Keys Publishing.

CHAPTER SEVEN

Critical Education
IN AN Interactive Age

KURT SQUIRE

Over the past few years, video games have transformed from the pariahs to darlings of academic, with a host of academic journals, conferences, and even entire organizations dedicated to the academic study of video games. Video games are now being taken seriously as art, culture, and commerce, as academics, industry, and government leaders recognize that video games are pushing the boundaries of interactive narrative, consumer-grade simulation, artificial intelligence, and cultural practices with technology. Educators have posited *economic* and *social/cultural* arguments for including video games in curricula, suggesting that ignoring video games and their role in society is akin to ignoring the impact of comics or films in the early twentieth century (Gee, 2003; Jenkins, 2006; Squire, 2003, 2004; Williams, 2004). This paper argues that video games are perhaps the quintessential site for changes in popular culture, suggesting how popular culture serves as a "leading activity" for participants whereby they have entrees into social practices that surpass those available in most schools (Squire and Giovanetto, in press; Steinkuehler, 2006; Steinkuehler and Chmiel, 2005).

Although video games are nodes in a Web of new media, technology, and social shifts, they are good sites for examining how popular culture is having an impact on contemporary social institutions. Video games are the "medium of choice" for the millennial (or Nintendo) generation and a critical site recruiting, even requiring, new literacies. Fan message forums, DYI (or do-it-yourself) media production, and blogs have many of these same characteristics, and indeed, are frequently core components of gaming practices. However, video games can be considered the prototypical site for studying such technologies because (1) they are built on a logic of simulation, which is core to the logic of the computer, as well as the postmodern age (Baudrillard, 1994; Squire, 2003), and (2) they have been the predominant popular art form of the computer over the past twenty-five years (Kent, 2000).

To date, arguments for using video games in classrooms have been framed as "arguments of opportunity" whereby video games hold untapped promise for engaging kids in meaningful learning activities (Prensky, 2001; Squire, 2002; Squire and Jenkins, 2003). As digital media becomes more pervasive in children's lives, this *opportunity* is becoming a *necessity*; while schools remained shackled to literacies of print, media like video games offer pedagogies of *interactivity*, where players can inhabit possible worlds and participate in vibrant learning communities with trajectories of participation far more consequential than those found in schools. Participation in today's popular culture—and video gaming in particular—is to participate in the design of one's social world. If we take the New London Group's manifesto—that education for the information age ought to be one where students learn to design their lifeworlds—then video games offer a powerful indictment of schools indeed (Gee, 2004; New London Group, 2000). The key question facing educators at the moment is not "are video games good or bad?" but who will gain access to these experiences? Sadly, equity questions to date have been framed around representations in media, with precious little investigation into what those who work with digital media make of it. I argue here for new critical studies, one that acknowledges how popular culture today is a powerful site for recruiting identities into sophisticated practices. These opportunities shift questions from merely *access* to technologies, or awareness of representations to understanding how participants have differential access to social networks and social practices.[1]

VIDEO GAMES AS INTERACTIVE SYSTEMS

For the generation raised on *Pong* (which is now over thirty years old, the same age as this author), advancements in video games and game technologies can be astonishing. Video games have evolved from primitive sports played on televisions or simplistic space-age battles into complex worlds. Today, most media scholars agree that games are capable of sophisticated expression, at least in the case of interactive fiction, the heir to traditional print fiction (Bolter and Grusin, 2000). Adventure video games from *Zork* onward have aspired to the dream of interactive fiction, a phenomenon that ten years ago was curious to many humanities scholars.

Jenkins and Fuller (1995) were among the first to note that role-playing adventure video games such as *Super Mario Brothers*, which have occasionally been critiqued as being vapid, in fact share much in quality with the tradition of travel narratives, a (currently) much more highly valued narrative genre (Provenzo, 1991). What early critics of video games missed is that games are not narratives, but *worlds* to explore and inhabit. Video games are constructed according to ideologies (ideologies in the sense of systematic ideas that govern how worlds operate), but these are not necessarily ideologies that gamers are inculcated into; they are ideological worlds that players play within, experience, and reflect upon. As such, game designers such as Shigeru Miyamoto, the genius behind *Mario and Zelda*, are less authors and more designers or landscape artists. Will Wright, designer of *SimCity* and *The Sims* draws connections between traditional Japanese gardening, which is an aesthetic of designed experience, and the worlds Miyamoto (who happens to be a gardener himself) creates.

As such, contemporary video games are truly global phenomena, drawing on artistic forms and traditions from Japan, Korea, and to a lesser extent China, as well as the United States and Europe. One of the most intriguing convergences spurred by gaming is the mixing of Japanese role playing video games such as *Dragon Quest* or *Final Fantasy* with American culture (for an excellent description of the phenomena, see Kohler, 2004). The narrative structure and internal logic of such games draw on both popular and traditional Japanese art forms and games (such as beetle collecting, a popular Japanese children's past time that became the basis for *Pokémon* [Tobin, 2004]). Although media franchises such as *Pokémon* are adapted for Western audiences (in the case of *Pokémon*, to create more defined "good guys" and "bad guys"), *Mario, Pokémon, Yi-Gi-Oh!, Final Fantasy,* and *Dragon Ball Z* are all Japanese media that bring non-Western assumptions with them, including assumptions about humanity's relationship with nature, ideas about "good" and "evil," and nonlinear plot structures. As communities of game, comic, and Anime translators flourish over the Internet, participation in these cultures also extends over cultural lines and frequently leads to opportunities for learning second and third languages (Black, 2005; Kohler, 2004).

As those who have "invested" in *Pokémon* cards, comics, and DVDs will attest, many contemporary video games are not "video games" in any isolated sense; they are transmedia properties (or worlds) designed with multiple points of entry, access, and *routes for expertise. Pokémon* and *Yu-Gi-Oh!* are constructed around an ethos of collecting, and as such remediate earlier forms, such as collecting cards and the comic book. *Pokémon* in particular (which designer Satoshi Tajiri modeled in part after his childhood fascination with insect collecting) is built on the logic of expertise.[2] To be a good *Pokémon* trainer (the child's role in the world) is to learn about *Pokémon* (including their names, types, and so on), and to develop an expert knowledge of them. *Pokémon* is an extreme example of this multimodal expertise, but far from the only one. *The Sims, RollerCoaster Tycoon,* and *Railroad Tycoon* are all video games that are akin to hobbies, rewarding the participant for insider knowledge and expertise within the domain.

Management simulation video games such as *Railroad Tycoon* come with a suite of *digital tools* and resources that allow players to try their hand at running a company. In fact, the sophistication of management simulation video games such as *Railroad Tycoon,* which include not just accurately modeled trains but realistic geographical maps, historically accurate scenarios, robust spreadsheet tools, complex charts and graphs, and even a stock market simulation where players can create dummy shell companies, frequently astonishes educators. *Railroad Tycoon* contains ships with historically accurate maps, scenarios, and of course, trains. The fact that teenagers willingly pay $50 for a game that allows them to relive the industrial era, building railways across the northeast United States should be of interest to educators, given that American History is routinely listed as the least favorite among thirty-two academic subjects for American high school students. As such, *Railroad Tycoon* poses an interesting challenge to educators: although we argue the role of spreadsheets or calculators in classrooms, outside of school kids (with access) can play with sophisticated simulations where they learn history by entering historical eras.

Video games (and, by extension, gaming cultures) are designed and organized around *functional epistemologies* of doing. By this, I mean that gamers learn about the game world literally through their controller, testing out what can be done in the gameworld. Watch any game player with a new game, and usually he or she will skim the manual briefly for an overview of the game (with the manual serving as a preorganizer of sorts), and then the gamer will proceed to press buttons, learning what the player can and cannot do, as well as the rules by which the world is constructed. In *America's Army,* for example, it is not uncommon for players to shoot their commander upon first receiving their rifle, which results in the player being sent to jail.[3] It is no wonder that Miyamoto (quoted in Sheff, 1994) describes his video games as being designed around verbs: what the player can do in the world, which stands in stark contrast to the organization of schools, which are organized around academic subjects as they were constructed in the medieval period (Shaffer, 2004; Squire, 2005). In a preliminary analysis of game FAQs, extensive guides written by gamers for gamers, Squire finds that many are unique designed around players' actions, designed as texts to augmented and enhance their experiences of the gaming world. Indeed, most all video games are constructed this way, with information provided just in time and on demand, in the service of (as opposed to preceding) the action.

As players learn by doing, they also learn through failure. In studies of students learning *Civilization III*, Squire (2004) describes how players learn through cycles of trial and error, as limitations in their understandings of history bump up against the rules of the game world. For mature gamers, failure conditions are learning opportunities, challenges to be overcome, which constitute opportunities for developing expertise. In fact, many video games—particularly strategy video games—record players' actions allowing players to chart performance over time and compare choices across video games. After a game of *Civilization*, it is common to pour over game logs, charts, and graphs looking for patterns in game play in order to improve performance in subsequent video games. Video games provide constant formative feedback so that players can improve. When they do not, they are panned as being too difficult.

If video games are constructed around players' actions, then game rule systems are designed through *cycles of choices and consequences* (Crawford, 1982; Salen and Zimmerman, 2004; Squire, 2006). In the game *Deus Ex* (released in 2000), for example, players are in the role of JC Denton, a government agent who comes to learn that his brother (a former agent himself) has left the government and is working for a group of terrorists who were formerly backed by the U.S. government. Through the course of the game (and particularly in the sequel *Deus Ex 2*), the player chooses particular events (such as whether to kill hostages or set them free) that create consequences in the game world. The game experience is designed to challenge the player to think about social allegiances, particularly whether he or she will align with family, nationalist, religious, or political groups. A core feature behind this and many other role-playing video games is that the player has opportunities to make significant choices that affect the unfolding of the world, which can be contrasted with the lack of effect that students have on the domains or "worlds" via participation in their classrooms Gee (2004).

Although video games have a reputation for being "mindless" button mashing, most video games require quite sophisticated, creative practices. In *Black & White*, the player is a god who trains a creature (using a curious combination of conditioning and social modeling), who interacts with people. The world evolves in response to the player's actions as a god, as well as the creature's interactions with the people. The entire world evolves in response to players' actions; the player literally designs how the flora, fauna, towns, and villages unfold via the video games rules. The *Tycoon* video games operate under a similar logic, allowing the player to design theme parks, malls, schools, ski resorts, and companies—almost any sort of social structure imaginable—albeit within a set of constraints (of varying realism). Many video games now ship with the tools by which they were made, allowing the player to design their own levels, characters, teams, or obstacles (Squire, 2003). Will Wright describes how for advanced players, *The Sims* and its accompanying

Web site, are essentially a story-generating engine. Players use the game's artwork and development tools as building blocks for creating stories.

The stereotypical image of "the gamer" is a lone teenager, sitting in his or her basement. In reality, video games are a highly social, collaborative exercise for many of their participants. "Violent" games such as *Quake* are highly competitive athletic endeavors with players competing for hundreds of thousands of dollars in cash prizes (Kushner, 2003; Squire, 2003). Most modern video games, such as *Counter-Strike* or *Battlefield 2* are both collaborative and competitive, with gamers joining teams (or clans or guilds). Although there are few existing ethnographies of game-playing communities, the few that do exist emphasize the social aspects of video games. Single-player video games such as *Zelda* are designed to be unsolvable by one person, leaving multiple hidden, unlockable features and paths of advancement, providing children something to look for onscreen and something to talk about on the playground.

In her studies of massively multiplayer video games, Steinkuehler (2004) argues that video games are new third spaces, spaces that are neither home nor school, allowing us to try on and inhabit new identities. Steinkuehler argues that such video games offer spaces for *retribalization*, spaces where players form lasting bonds and allegiances around social values in an effort to shape the virtual worlds that they inhabit (cf. Castronova, 2005; Jakobsson and Taylor, 2003). Persistent, online video games—video games that are available and online 24/7—offer alternative social systems for participants to inhabit, social systems that are built around social values of meritocracy. One might problematize gamers' notions of meritocracy, but as Steinkuehler argues, such games are possibility spaces for their participants, possibility spaces where physical looks, social class, or even national origin matter less than one's in-game behavior.[4]

The last quality of video games explored here are their qualities of rhythmic immersion. Video games are a deeply rhythmic medium, one where the precise timing of actions generally matter greatly, and where cycles of action build on one another to create complex practice. This phenomena may be best illustrated through today's action video games, where players begin learning through relatively simple actions (jumps, kicks, punches) that are ramped up to be complex multibutton sequences (Squire, 2005). The result is a game experience where players become immersed in the rhythm and pacing of the game, which is frequently managed (and communicated) through the arrangement of space. The most vivid example of this phenomenon may be *Harmonix Frequency*, a rhythm action music game where players manipulate controllers in order to capture notes as they fly by onscreen. In effect, the game turns the PlayStation controller into a musical instrument, as symbols on screen are matched to sounds and notes in the song. Lead designer Alex Rigopulous notes that gamers are adept at coordinating rapidly moving visual stimuli with fine motor control muscle movements with a high degree of precision—exactly the sort of skills that playing musical instruments requires. He views the game as an effort to build on gamers' skills but open up the world of music performance. Through the game's editor, players can also remix and republish songs for others to play.

In describing the impact of simulations, particularly *SimCity* on education, Paul Starr (1994) writes,

> For better or worse, simulation is no mere fad. Indeed, to think of simulation video games as mere entertainment or even as teaching tools is to underestimate them. They represent a major addition to the intellectual repertoire that will increasingly shape how we communicate ideas and think through problems…We shall be working and thinking in *SimCity* for a long time. Moreover, as computer video games become more elaborate and widely used, their sheer multiplication and increasing plasticity may promote a healthy skepticism about their predictive power. Playing with simulation is one way to see its limits as well as its possibilities.

Writing a full decade before the blossoming of the Serious Games movement, Starr paints a vivid portrait of the impact that computer and video games might have on our thinking. Today's video games offer more than just an untapped resource for educators; they represent a powerful new medium, the entertainment medium of the computer, which is shaping (and being recursively shaped by) popular culture.

Achievements in game design over the past decade illustrate how video games fundamentally are about *simulation*, possibility spaces where we can explore ideas, including who we are and who we want to become. However, part of what makes video games so successful is how they organize our experience through trajectories of participation that usher players from novices to expert. Will Wright describes how, from the moment the player picks up a game box, the game designer is building a model of the game in the player's head. Video games do more than just create a cognitive model, however; opening cut scenes depict compelling situations the player will be in. Voiceovers challenge the player or ask who it is that she will become. Everything about the experience of playing a game—from the moment a player picks up the box to the moment she logs out is tailored for immersion. As such, video games are much more than just simulations; they are worlds that provide *designed experiences.*

As designed experiences, video games employ features that modern learning scientists have theorized to be important in learning but have often struggled to realize in curricular enactments (Gee, 2003; Shaffer, Squire, Gee, and Halverson, 2005; Squire, 2003). Learning is driven by personal quests for meaning. Learning is a deeply embodied experience, arising through doing with complex digital tools. Knowledge that is presented on time and in demand functions as a tool for doing.

Learning occurs through cycles of choices and consequences, and failure is an occasion for preparation for future learning. Learning itself is deeply social, occurring through participation in global media networks. Finally, and perhaps most critically, competence means to act creatively within the boundary conditions and parameters set by the game system.

These game systems—or *ideological worlds*—are complete rules and systems of thinking set up for players to inhabit. *Grand Theft Auto: San Andreas (GTA: SA)* is exciting to kids not just because of its content, but because it sets up an entire world based on 1990s hip-hop popular culture that kids can inhabit and make their own. Studies of *GTA: SA* game players suggest that what is interesting to most players is not the content per se, but what the game allows them to do with it. *GTA: SA* allows for the pastiching of an array of cultural representations—from the leftist radio talk shows to "pimp my ride" automobile customization opportunities. "Literate" game play, from this perspective, is performance, having a deep enough understanding of the game system to act creatively within its constraints (Squire, 2006; in press). What counts as "expert" gaming performance is of course, socially constructed, varying according to one's values, goals, and systems of taste; whereas a Christian gaming guild might emphasize one's ability to recruit (and convert) members (a surprisingly common goal of guilds of all sorts), others might emphasize competitive performance by a set of fixed game rules (such as honor points in *World of Warcraft*).

Games cultures (as reflective of contemporary popular culture) are sites where we develop competence in specific domains and self-organize into affinity groups where that expertise is valued and developed. To be proficient in today's gaming culture is to develop a design-type knowledge of game systems. More importantly, affinity spaces within popular culture—some of which operate as self-organized learning communities—present trajectories of participation where people can not only develop skills but engage in social practices and take on leadership roles in organizations with consequences that extend beyond the gaming context. The following section examines one such community, Apolyton University, in depth, using it as a context for theorizing changes in contemporary popular culture and suggesting their implications for schooling.

INTERACTIVE LEARNING SYSTEMS

Contemporary technologies (and routes for participation in popular culture) offer an implicit critique of the traditional organization of schooling. Any student with a $100 cell phone can not only access, but contribute to, knowledge forums like Wikipedia. Whereas schools have traditionally been set up around a model where expertise is funneled to students through secondary texts and teachers, technologies like Google Earth, print, and video make the world's texts and communities widely available. Within a few years, these technologies will be available on portable computing devices, making them nearly ubiquitous as students use communication technologies to connect with their friends or access popular culture (i.e., downloading videos, reading news, or playing games).

Today's popular culture, driven by entertainment technologies, has made information cheap and access ubiquitous. What are less ubiquitous are the conceptual understandings to make sense of that information, and access to the socio-technical networks that open trajectories of experience for broader participation in complex, socially valued practices. In other words, every student may have a cell phone, but a student's ability to make sense of the information on screen differs wildly, as does the types of contacts in that phone book. These technologies and issues reframe equity issues from ones of access to information to access to socio-technical networks. Just because every student has access to *SimCity* does not mean that every student has the background of literacies to make sense of the interpretations on screen, or access to the social networks (parents, peers, experts) that turn an interest in *SimCity* into an interest in programming, urban planning, or complex systems theory.

AFFINITY SPACES: SOCIOTECHNICAL NETWORKS FOR AN INTERACTIVE AGE

If we are to design educational systems appropriate to the digital age, it is critical that we understand both the technologies that fuel them and the modes of social organization that accompany them. Restated, if digital games are an emerging medium ushering in an array of emerging literacy practices, then one strategy for understanding the design of educational systems for the interactive age is to study how learning systems are indigenous to the digital age function. Just as cognitive psychologists and ethnographers have studied traditional tailors, Alcoholics Anonymous, or Weight Watchers communities to understand how learning occurs through participation in communities of practice, researchers are studying digital learning communities to build models of how digitally mediated learning communities function. The argument is that educators might seek to discover what a learning system for the interactive age looks like by studying how such communities function in popular culture.

Gee (2004) argues that social systems in the digital age are organized into affinity spaces, spaces where learners of any background or skill level can explore areas of interest and develop expertise. Forums, Wikis, and blogs are not just technologies, but *sociotechnical networks* that carry with them particular values. In the case of affinity spaces such as the Web sites built around games like *Rise of Nations*, these values include accessibility and democratic authorship, and individual customization. Participants can contribute to any forum regardless of age, gender, or national origin. Nine-year-old American children interested in American and Roman history contribute as readily as European graduate students in computer science with an interest in computer-gaming artificial intelligence. In practice, the discourses that emerge from such spaces is not always democratic, but compared to other forms of social organization, affinity spaces are marked by their accessibility regardless of geography, social class, and ethnic cultural/background. Rules for participation are not only unusually open but are also made transparent. Many communities actively solicit moderators or leaders and make explicit the qualities of good posts and participation.

Such affinity spaces have permeable boundaries not just in terms of membership but also in terms of their relation to other social structures. In *Next: The Future Just Happened*, Michael Lewis (2001) documents several high-profile cases where teenagers participated in online spaces, giving legal advice, making financial decisions, or programming software, showing how today's popular culture is deeply *participatory* when compared to the popular culture of the past. Lewis documents how the Internet and its accompanying social structures are blurring insider/outsider status, making it possible for any highly motivated person to participate in a variety of social practices and industries.

For what it is worth, I owe some of the success in my own career to this emerging social model. While teaching a course on video games at Indiana University, Jon Goodwin and I noted a lack of good games journalism and critical game discussion, leading us to start a Web site Joystick101.org, dedicated to the "in-depth" study of games culture. A few months after the site's launch, I wrote an article chronicling my experiences trying to purchase a PlayStation2 on launch day, closing with a few late-night observations about games culture and its relationship to broader social issues.[5] This article, written by a graduate student, was picked up and linked by Slashdot.org, drawing 120,000 readers. Eventually Wired.com linked to the article, drawing thousands more readers (Manjoo, 2001). At last count, the article had about 250,000 hits, making it by far the most widely read piece this academic has written.

Whereas classrooms are notoriously "cleaved" from other social processes, erecting tall boundaries between practices occurring within them and the outside world, affinity spaces (not limited to, but typical of games) increasingly blur them, providing opportunities for participation in social practices far beyond what is otherwise possible. The proliferation of sites like Slashdot makes it possible for anyone with Internet access to participate in journalism practices that lead to participation in mainstream journalistic practices. Sites like Wired function as facilitators of this boundary crossing providing exposure, legitimacy, and professional experiences to bloggers and amateur experts. In the political realm, Ana Marie Cox (Wonkette), Marcos Zuniga (dailykos.com), and John Aravosis (Ameriblog) have parlayed their Web writing into opportunities inside and outside of journalism. Within gaming, this kind of practice is somewhat commonplace; bloggers such as "Lum the Mad" and "Old Man Murray" are among the most respected commentators and journalists. At Joystick101.org, for example, Kyle Orland, a high school student when he started writing, became one of our most popular writers (and had several pieces Slashdotted), and parlayed his experience in writing through sites like Joystick101.org into a freelance career including publications such as *Electronic Gaming Monthly*, *Gamespot*, *The Escapist*, *Next Generation*, *Happy Puppy*, and *GameCritics*, as well as becoming a founding member of the International Game Journalists Association.

The examples of Kyle, Joystick101.org, or other bloggers suggest that today's popular culture provides opportunities not only for developing expertise but also for participating in practices with broader social significance. In the case of Joystick101.org, writers like myself designed, promoted, and used Joystick101.org to connect with academics like Henry Jenkins (from MIT Comparative Media Studies), game designers like Raph Koster (*Star Wars Galaxies*), or industry leaders like Nolan Bushnell (the founder of Atari). It is instructive to think of the case of Kyle Orland, who as an undergraduate is writing papers simultaneously for English classes and the World Wide Web, knowing full well that his English paper at best will lead to an "A" and maybe a letter of recommendation, whereas a good gaming piece could lead to more readers, prestige, and perhaps some pocket change. In my case, interviewing academics like Henry Jenkins led to a career in game studies.

As suggested by the New London Group (2000), these examples suggest that literacy within this kind of media context means designing one's environment for personal gains. In other words, it is not just that students know how to access or navigate such affinity spaces—the real value results in their knowing how to leverage them for personal ends. Just as a generation of parents took their kids to libraries and museums in past generations, we can imagine a generation of parents teaching their children to use popular culture wisely, seeking out affinity spaces that draw on their children's interest in popular culture and allowing them to extend their expertise into new domains. Such a stance toward popular culture signals a very different stance toward popular culture for critical educators. It suggests not a "prohibitionist" stance toward popular culture but one where children are encouraged to seek out arenas where they can develop expertise, and then redesigning those spaces in accordance with their goals for learning.

SELF-ORGANIZED LEARNING SYSTEMS
IN APOLYTON UNIVERSITY

One of the most potentially powerful forms of online learning connected to games and popular culture are self-organizing learning systems, learning organizations created by and for users to learn more about a particular phenomenon. In many respects, Joystick101.org can be thought of as a self-organizing learning community in the sense that participants intentionally designed a community for the purpose of studying games culture. Such sites are commonplace on the Web, most commonly occurring around rapidly evolving topics such as technology, news, and the media (Wiley and Edwards, 2002). Many such communities have arisen around gaming cultures, which is perhaps not surprising given the interactive nature of games; if games are worlds for performance, exploration, and developing expertise, perhaps it is not unusual that communities surrounding them have a particular emphasis on learning.

Over the past year, Levi Giovanetto and I have been conducting a cognitive ethnography of one such community, Apolyton University (AU), an online, self-organizing community of game players forming around Civilization III (Squire and Giovanetto, in press). AU is a subset (or subcommunity) of Apolyton.net, an affinity group of strategy game players. AU currently consists of twenty-five courses designed to help players hone strategies while simultaneously perfecting the core game. Each course is based around players who share a common game, play through the game and take detailed notes on their progress. Several times throughout the game, players gather these notes into "During Action Reports," which are detailed, think-aloud protocols of their game play that they subsequently post on the AU Web site.

The "meat" of the course is the During Action Reports, detailed conversations about the game, where players examine one another's thought process and make suggestions on their game. The typical DAR exchange starts with a one- to three-page explanation of one's game, including a discussion of how the player is interpreting the state of the game (or simulation), what future plans the player has, and what questions he or she has about future steps. Other players contribute their posts, sometimes reframing how their game ought to be read, calling out data in the game the player was not attending to, and reframing players' questions so as to be "better" questions. For many students, a highlight of AU was one thread when Soren Johnson, the lead artificial intelligence programmer, joined the discussion to challenge the communities' understanding of a particular game mechanic. Through these interactions, more and more sophisticated readings of the game space emerge. Players contribute their readings based on their particular expertise; whereas some players may be experts in military conflict, others are masters of the game's economic system. The end result is a type of *design knowledge* of the simulation, a flexible knowledge of the game system as a simulation, where players understand the game system as more than just a particular set of strategies and as a coherent rule system with particular emergent properties (and biases).

How such a university materialized may be something of a mystery. One participant posted the following piece, describing his interest in creating AU.

> For several reasons I want to get a lot sharper at *CivIII*. First, I just enjoy it. Second, I've really liked some of the tourney and tournament discussions, have learned a bunch, and have been waaay impressed by some of the strategies and tactics employed. Third, multiplayer is coming and while I never participate in that way, I intend to this time around.
>
> Also, although I still enjoy playing the stock game, it definitely could be more of a challenge.

Several themes in this post illustrate the unique nature of high-end participation in gaming cultures. First, learning and pleasure are closely connected, with many players believing that learning is naturally fun, and learning enhances the gaming experience. Second, learning is (and gaming) intrinsically a social experience. This player both enjoyed learning from other players and wanted to play more players. In this way, learning was tied to a particular goal—a desire to play competitively with other players. Finally, the player enjoyed the "stock" game but wanted more of a challenge. As many educators studying games culture have noticed, a particularly curious nature of gamers is that they desire challenges, becoming frustrated or bored with games that are overly simplistic or "dumbed down."

The player ended the post by acknowledging the social nature of learning, writing, "So what I want is a combination boot camp and war college leveraging a varied group of players and a variety of techniques, to polish collective skills." For this player, learning is inherently a social process consisting of two equally important parts: first is the "boot camp" aspect, suggesting the desire for being enculturated into a particular community of practice to hone specific gaming skills. The space this player desired demands a consistently high level of interaction toward honing game skills, unlike affinity spaces (such as the encompassing Apolyton site) where players are free to enter and participate at whatever level they choose. Second, the player desired a "war college" type of community where players could develop new skills, exploring cutting-edge techniques. In this case, the community functions more like a research community than a traditional classroom. It is particularly interesting that this player valued a diverse set of play skills in order to improve a *collective* end.

Here, the player is expressing a desire not just to improve his own skills but to improve his skills as part of a collective body, one that brings together diverse backgrounds and perspectives toward creating an improved collective. This phenomenon of "collective intelligence" is common among Web communities, a phenomenon that Henry Jenkins (2006) ties to Pierre Lévy's (1999) notion of collective intelligence. The core idea here is that it matters less what any one individual person knows, but rather what the community as a whole can do. In today's networked, interactive age, it matters less what any one person can do, but more of what someone can do when situated within a community. A mark of intelligence, then, is knowing how and when to leverage participation in such communities (including designing them) in order to achieve one's ends. These communities are common in gaming, but as Jenkins (2006) describes, they are part and parcel of today's media landscape and can be found among television, film, and other fan communities.

As a self-organizing community, participation in AU routinely waxed and waned, eventually dying down to a mere trickle. As we observed this dying off, we asked a variety of participants why they were withdrawing, and we heard a variety of responses. Some had learned all that they needed to learn. A few moved on to other games. One participant, the dean, wanted to resign because he felt that the role of a dean—providing direction and making decisions was sufficiently being conducted by the community itself, and he was redundant. Analysis of forum posts revealed that a large lurking community still existed at AU and was accessing the forums much as one that would access course notes.

Indeed, as it turns out, participation in AU did not end entirely, but Soren Johnson, the artificial intelligence programmer, had begun using the community as a testbed for the next installment of the game, *Civilization IV*. Johnson had been so impressed with the sophistication of discourse at AU that he recruited key members to make the next installment a better-designed game. Although this case is somewhat unique (how often are hundreds of fans recruited to contribute to the sequel to a popular media franchise?), it does mirror the kinds of phenomena described in affinity spaces more generally; participation in spaces such as AU allows for the development of expertise and trajectories for participating in social systems transcend the game space and have an impact beyond particular game communities. As such, AU serves as a powerful model of a self-organizing learning system indigenous to the interactive age of simulation. Driven by participants' desire to learn as a natural extension of pleasurable play, participation in AU requires "students" to start thinking like designers. In fact, writ large, participation in AU is to participate in a culture of a design, and as such, an informative example of how contemporary popular culture operates.

CONCLUSIONS

In this chapter, I have used the lens of gaming cultures to argue that the nature of today's popular culture requires a new kind of critical approach to education. In the past, popular culture has been somewhat polarizing, putting critical educators in the uncomfortable bind of having to acknowledge and understand popular culture as the "people's culture" and those concerned with the hegemonic effects of popular media (Giroux, 1996). Distinctions between high and low art have largely been acknowledged to being little more than issues of social class, concerns still prevail that video games perpetuate oppressive ideologies (cf. Provenzo, 1991). Games do in fact carry ideologies with them, but as I argued here, these are not narratives as much they are as ideological worlds—worlds build according to particular rules that come together into world views.[6] It is critical that educators see beyond simply the representations in games (or on box covers) and examine how game worlds themselves are experienced. This chapter and others emerging discussing game studies suggest the importance of a critical analysis based not just on the text but on interpretations of players' experiences and the modes of production as well.

To date, concerns about the "bad effects" of games have perhaps caused educators to miss the real message behind the medium. Core to the logic of games is that they are far from simulations of the world—they are spaces designed to provide specific forms of experience. Games, as an interactive medium, create ideological worlds, possibility spaces for their players, spaces where they can learn via cycles of choices and consequences; we have the opportunity to develop skills, engage in creative practices, participate in virtual organizations, and otherwise explore identities unavailable to them other places, such as in schools. As such, games offer a deeply experiential form of learning, a form of learning that occurs through thinking, doing, and *being* in a space.

There are many qualities of these experiences that should be of interest to educators. I want to briefly retouch on one of those qualities here: that of popular culture in general (and games in particular) as spaces for valuing and developing expertise. It is interesting that amidst all the concerns about *Pokémon* as wasting children's time, promoting competitivism, consumerism, or even causing epileptic seizures, most critics failed to comment on the underlying logic of the game world: it is through becoming an expert *Pokémon* collector and caregiver that one develops status within both the *Pokémon* game and within *Pokémon* fan communities (cf. Tobin, 2004). From the moment the player creates a character (or *Pokémon* trainer) and meets the "professor" (one of the many games where PhDs and professors are positioned as heroes and/or sages) to the final battle, expertise and knowledge of the gameworld are given a premium. For all of the concern about games as a competitive medium (as if our children would graduate from schools into a "noncompetitive global economy," we seem to have ignored the potentially positive flipside: children have a space to hone and value expertise, having a place to become "little experts" in areas of personal value.[7]

If contemporary popular culture is indeed built around "building expertise" then critical educators face a whole new set of questions about the value and role of popular culture in education. In short, if popular culture is offering opportunities to develop, hone, and extend expertise in complex areas, then we need to take popular culture seriously (cf. Johnson, 2005). Perhaps more critically, if popular media like games offers opportunities for legitimate participation in social systems that transcend the classroom, then we may need to rethink the organization of schools, lest they become even less relevant to students than they already are. Popular media increasingly allows us not only to develop specialized skills but to participate in practices that have a real impact on the world.

Today's popular media landscape raises new critical questions of equity for educators as well. Whereas some students have the past resources, experiences, and self-efficacy to leverage these technologies and media for personal and professional development, others may not, raising new equity questions particular to the digital age. First, issues arise as to who has both the traditional literacy skills to survive in such an environment. Such communities are potentially democratizing in that they create new demands and new niches where expertise can flourish, but they may also be limiting as networks; they tend to follow power laws where hubs and nodes have inordinate influence, which one might anticipate carry with them their own inequities. Second, they reframe questions of access from ones of technological access to sociotechnical access. Just because a student has access to the Web does not mean that he or she has access to the right affinity spaces—or even that looking for the right affinity spaces to leverage is what one ought to do.

Although sites such as Slashdot.org, Joystick101.org or AU do not exclude participants on the surface level, they do exist as discourses that effectively privilege some ways of knowing while excluding others. The importance of such communities has scarcely been recognized, let alone studied, but Slashdot at least has a well-deserved reputation for privileging a combative, male-gendered discourse with a technoutopian libertarian bent. Such affinity spaces may act as accelerators for participants with the propensity for such discourses while systematically excluding those without such affiliations. If gaming discourses are in fact valuable for their ability to engage their players in academic practices, then educators might be well served to design alternative programs and spaces that with discourses might attract a broader array of participants. Given the nature of games as a male-gendered play space, women in particular may be systematically shut out of new media literacies.

NOTES

1. These ideas were developed in conversation with James Paul Gee and Constance Steinkuehler, to whom I'm indebted for their insights on social learning practices.
2. For a description of the Pokemon universe and the design ideas behind it, see http://pokedream. com/pokemon/infocenter/tajiri.php For a good introduction into the Pokemon universe, see Tobin (2004). Gee (2004) makes a similar argument to that provided here.
3. In what has been generally hailed as a brilliant design move, the game actually does not end there; the player will sit in a jailcell (free to move about) until he or she decides to hit escape and restart the game.
4. This is not to suggest that race, gender, and ethnicity are not played out and remediated online, both through the iconography and representations in game systems, as well as through player generated content and talk. It is to say, however, that most gaming cultures are deeply committed to these notions and that *for their participant*s, they tend to function as such meritocratic spaces.
5. http://web.archive.org/web/20010412205321/http://www.joystick101.org/?op=display story&sid=2000/10/26/4840/38766.
6. While games certainly demand more critical study then they are currently given, most serious critiques of games as ideological worlds have resulted in accounts of games that are far more sophisticated and nuanced than perhaps most educators have thusfar given them credit for. Examples of this include games such as Deus Ex, described in this paper, or the ironic commentary on capitalism that can be found in The Sims.
7. As educators, we might wish that children focused this desire for expertise in areas that aligned more closely with our own, whether they be literature, mathematics, or science. However, as literacy scholars (c.f. Gee, 2003; Steinkuehler, 2005) point out, the literacy tasks alone demanded by such forms of popular culture are far from trivial; in the case of Massively Multiplayer Gaming, they actually recruit and require skills that meet, if not exceed national literacy standards. As Steinkuehler argues, what the emerging popular culture teaches us is that it is not whether kids are reading that concerns parents; it is *what* they are reading. While these concerns may indeed pose some merit,it is worth also considering the prevalence of these concerns across the history of media—from the early comics onwards, which Jenkins (1999) and others have argued relates much more to one generation seeking to impose its morals and tastes on another than any qualitative difference in "quality" of media.

REFERENCES

Baudrillard, J. (1994). *Simulacra and simulation*. S.F. Glaser, trans. Ann Arbor, University of Michigan Press.

Black, R.W. (2005). Access and affiliation, The literacy and composition practices of English language learners in an online fanfiction community. *Journal of Adolescent* and *Adult Literacy*, *49*(2), 118–128.

Bolter, J.D., and Grusin, R. (2000). *Remediation, understanding new media*. Cambridge, MA, MIT Press.

Castronova, T. (2005). *Synthetic worlds, the culture and business of online games*. Chicago, IL, University of Chicago Press.

Crawford, C. (1982). *The art of computer game design*. Vancouver, WA, Washington State University. Retrieved January 24, 2006 from, http,//www.vancouver.wsu.edu/fac/peabody/game-book/ Coverpage.html

Gee, J.P. (2003). *What video games have to teach us about learning and literacy.* New York, Palgrave Macmillan.

Gee, J.P. (2004). *Language, learning, and gaming. A critique of traditional schooling.* New York, Routledge.

Giroux, H. (1996). *Fugitive cultures, race, violence, and youth.* New York, Routledge.

Jakobsson, M., and Taylor, T.L. (2003). *The Sopranos* meets *EverQuest*, socialization processes in massively multiuser games, in *Digital Arts and Culture (DAC) 2003 Streaming Wor(l)ds Conference Proceedings*, Melbourne, Australia, May.

Jenkins, H. (2006) *Convergence culture, where old and new media collid.* New York, New York University Press.

Jenkins, H., and Fuller, M. (1995) Nintendo and new world travel writing, a dialogue. In S. Jones (Ed.), *Cybersociety, Computer-mediated communication and community* (pp. 57-72). Thousand Oaks, CA, Sage Publications.

Johnson, S. (2005). *Why everything bad is good for you.* New York, Riverhead.

Kent, S. (2000). The first quarter, A 25-year history of video games. Bothell, WA, BWD Press.

Kohler, C. (2004). *Power-up, how Japanese video games gave the world an extra life.* Indianapolis, IN, Brady Games.

Kushner, D. (2003). *Masters of doom.* New York, Random House.

Levy, P. and Collective intelligence. *Collective intelligence, mankind's emerging world in cyberspace.* New York, Perseus.

Lewis, M. (2001). *Next, the future just happened.* New York, Norton.

Manjoo, F. (2001). PS2, I'm not sure I love you. *Wired*, January 1, 2001, Retrieved January 24, 2006 from http,//www.wired.com/news/business/0,1367,41012,00.html

New London Group. (2000). A pedagogy of multiliteracies, designing social futures. In B. Cope and M. Kalantzis (Eds.), *Multiliteracies, literacy learning and the design of social futures* (pp. 9-37). New York, Routledge.

Prensky, M. (2001). *Digital game-based learning.* New York, McGraw Hill.

Provenzo, E.F. (1991). *Video kids, making sense of Nintendo.* Cambridge, MA, Harvard University Press.

Salen K., and Zimmerman, E. (2004). *The rules of play.* Cambridge, MA, MIT Press.

Shaffer, D.W. (2004). Pedagogical praxis, the professions as models for post-industrial education. *Teachers College Record, 106*(7), 1401–1421.

Shaffer, D.W., Squire, K. A., Halverson, R., and Gee, J. P. (2005). Video games and the future of learning. *Phi Delta Kappan, 87*(2), 104–111.

Sheff, D. (1994). *Game over, how Nintendo conquered the world.* London, Vintage.

Squire, K., and Jenkins, H. (2003). Harnessing the power of games in education. *INSIGHT 3*(5), 5–33.

Squire, K.D. (2000). *PS2 launches, Word from the str*eet. Joystick101.org October 28, 2000. Retrieved January 24, 2006 from http://web.archive.org/web/20010412205321/http://www.joystick101. org/?op=displaystoryandsid=2000/10/26/4840/3876

Squire, K.D. (2002). Rethinking the role of games in education. *Game Studies, 2*(1). (http,//gamestudies. org/0201/Squire/)

Squire, K.D. (2003). Video games in education. *International Journal of Intelligent Simulations and Gaming,* (2)1. Retrieved November 1, 2003, from http://www.scit.wlv.ac.uk/~cm1822/ijkurt.pdf sively multiplayer online games.

Squire, K.D. (2004). *Replaying history, learning world history through playing Civilization III.* Accessed October 13, 2007 from http,//website.education.wisc.edu/kdsquire/dissertation.html

Squire, K.D. (2005). Educating the fighter, buttonmashing, seeing, being. *On the Horizon, The Strategic Planning Resource for Education Professionals, 13*(2), 75–88.

Squire, K.D. (2006). Games as designed experiences. *Educational Researcher.*

Squire, K.D. (in press). Video game literacy, A literacy of expertise. In D. Leu, J. Coiro, C. Lankshear, and M. Knobel (Eds.), *Handbook of research on new literacies.* Mahwah, NJ, Lawrence Erlbaum Associates.

Squire, K.D., and Giovanetto, L. (in press). The higher education of gaming. *E-learning.*

Starr, P. (1994). Seductions of Sim, policy as a simulation game. *The American Prospect, 5*(17), 19–29.

Steinkuehler, C.A. (2004a). Emergent play. Informal essay for "culture of play" panel at the State of Play Conference, New York University Law School, New York, October 28–31. Retrieved June 29, 2005 from http://website.education.wisc.edu/steinkuehler/papers/SteinkuehlerSoP2004.pdf

Steinkuehler, C. A. (2006). Massively multiplayer online videogaming as participation in a Discourse. *Mind, Culture, and Activity, 13*(1), 38–52.

Steinkuehler, C.A., and Chmiel, M. (2005). *Gendered talk in massively multiplayer online games.* Paper presented at the 14th World Congress of Applied Linguistics (AILA), Madison WI, July 25–29.

Tobin, J. (ed.) (2004). *Pikachu's global adventure, the rise and fall of Pokémon.* Durham, NC, Duke University Press.

Wiley, D.A., and Edwards, E.K. (2002). Online self-organizing social systems, the decentralized future of online learning. *Quarterly Review of Distance Education, 3*(1), 33–46.

Williams, D. (2003). The video game lightning rod, constructions of a new media technology, 1970-2000. *Information, Communication* and *Society, 6*(4), 523–550.

CHAPTER EIGHT

Convergence AND Divergence, Informal Learning IN Online Fanfiction Communities AND Formal Writing Pedagogy

REBECCA WARD BLACK

In recent years, the marked proliferation of new forms of information and communication technologies (ICTs) and online "centers of learning" (Purves, 1998) has led to extensive consideration of the dubious boundaries between the real and the virtual, teaching and learning, and official and unofficial forms of knowledge. Bekerman and Silberman-Keller (2004) addressed such changes by arguing how, in light of widespread "failures of formal education" (p. 50) and the rapid processes of globalization and technological change that are giving rise to alternative, transnational learning communities, there is a growing need for research that challenges the "image of stark differentiation" (p. 50) between informal and formal approaches to instruction. Moreover, such challenges can be presented in ways that might encourage practitioners and policy makers in formal education settings to consider the potential benefits of adopting more informal approaches to teaching and learning (Bekerman and Silberman-Keller, 2004). In such a spirit, this chapter explores the points of convergence and divergence between the literacy and informal learning practices of an online fanfiction writing–based site and those of formal writing instruction in school spaces. Through such a comparison, the chapter considers the many shifting boundaries of this informal "center of learning"—between different languages and cultures, print and electronic text, official and unofficial forms of knowledge, teaching and learning—that youth, particularly English Language Learners (ELLs), successfully navigate in this interactive networked site. Such considerations are crucial if we are to design meaningful and effective literacy curricula for new generations of youth that are and/or will be expected to navigate such media, ICTs, and transnational learning spaces in social, academic, and career-related endeavors.

The expanded reach of new ICTs and mass media makes it nearly impossible to overlook the centrality of pop cultural and media texts in adolescents' lives. However, Giroux and Simon (1989) point out that, in the past, educational theorists have "almost completely ignored the importance of popular culture both for developing a critical understanding of student experience and for examining pedagogy in a critical and theoretically expanded fashion" (p. 2). In recent years, very little scholarship has emerged that recognizes the sophisticated forms of literacy (Lam, 2000; Steinkuehler (2006), self-directed learning (Squire and Jenkins, 2003), and online learning spaces (Black, 2005b; Gee, 2004; Stone, 2005) that are developing around forms of popular culture. Nonetheless, the relationship between popular culture and schooling is still problematic at best, as most schools and administrators steadfastly continue to dismiss popular culture and media as frivolous, potentially harmful, and as a distraction from more important (e.g., formal) learning endeavors. This chapter addresses this relationship and such indictments by exploring how engagement with popular culture through online fanfiction writing provides a means for fans to take up knowledgeable social roles, enact more powerful identities, and participate in a range of creative literate, learning, and social interactions around their respective fandoms of choice.

CONTEXT

The term fanfiction encompasses an array of texts, ranging from uncommissioned sequels to Jane Austen's work (Super Cat, 1999) to love stories written by Star Trek fans about Captain Kirk and Mr. Spock (Jenkins, 1992). Scholars have detailed some of the many creative forms that fan texts take, such as politically oriented pastiche; "slash" and "femmeslash" fiction, which features same sex romantic pairings (such as Kirk/Spock or Buffy the Vampire Slayer/Willow); and "shipper" or relationship-based fictions, which often offer powerful social commentary on gender roles and sexuality.

Online fanfiction sites provide a unique context for study in that they incorporate an interplay of officially sanctioned forms of knowledge, such as traditional writing conventions and genres, and unofficial forms of knowledge, such as intimate knowledge of the characters and settings of television series, popular books, and video games. Fanfiction.net, one of the largest fanfiction archives on the Web, houses hundreds of thousands of fan texts. In this chapter, I focus on an Anime or Japanese animation-based subsection of this archive featuring 16,000 *Card Captor Sakura (CCS)* fictions (as of January 15, 2005). *CCS* is an Anime series chronicling the adventures of Sakura Kinomoto, a young Japanese girl with magical powers, and this section of the site primarily attracts adolescent females from a number of countries, including Canada, the United States, Philippines, Mexico, and the United Kingdom, to name just a few. Native and nonnative English-speaking fans meet up in this space, not only to write *CCS* fanfictions but also to read and peer review each others' fictions while socializing, debating, and discussing the finer points of the Anime series.

This chapter draws from the *CCS* fanfiction texts of one participant in an ongoing ethnographic research project aimed at exploring the social, literate, and learning-related activities of ELLs in the broader online fanfiction community. Over a two-year period, this participant, Nanako,[1] a now sixteen-year-old native Mandarin Chinese speaker, posted more than fifty pieces of fiction and received an impressive 6,000 reviews from readers on fanfiction.net. Interviews with Nanako coupled with discourse analytic analyses of her texts and public posts on the site have helped me focus on her perspectives and meaning-making practices as she writes, interacts, and uses the varied resources in this space. In addition, through participant observation, I have been able to gain a nuanced understanding of how language and discourse shape and are shaped by the social practices, artifacts, and context of the community (Hine, 2000; Spradley, 1980).

LITERACY, LEARNING, AND IDENTITY

Work within the New Literacy Studies (NLS) tradition emphasizes a practice-based approach to literacy research (New London Group, 1996; Street, 1984). In this spirit, NLS researchers have emphasized the social nature of being and becoming literate through dynamic meaning-making processes that are acquired and embedded in specific social, historical, and material contexts (Gee, 1999; Heath, 1983; Scribner and Cole, 1981) and are tied to particular socially situated identities (Gee, 2002). Such research has recently included a notable focus on popular culture as a resource that adolescents draw on as they enact certain identities through their literacy practices outside school (Alvermann and Hagood, 2000; Lankshear and Knobel, 2003) and in school spaces (Chandler-Olcott and Mahar, 2003a; Dyson, 1997). This chapter suggests that popular culture and media technologies are not only resources for but also integral components of the literacy and sense-making practices in the daily lives of contemporary youth. As Giroux (1996) points out, "Educators need to understand how different identities among youth are being produced in spheres generally ignored by schools" (p. 75) and to develop an understanding of how language, culture, and identity are implicated in relations and negotiations of power within these spaces.

With his notion of "big D Discourses," Gee (1999) establishes an analytical construct that recognizes how language and identity are crucially tied to authentic social practice and interaction. This notion of Discourse emphasizes how different ways of reading, writing, and being literate are "accepted as instantiations of particular roles (or 'types of people') by specific *groups of people*" (Gee 1999, p. viii). Such a notion of language in use is crucial to understanding how, through their literate practices, ELLs are able to construct and enact identities that are recognized and valued within the fanfiction site. According to Gee, the process of learning and taking on new Discourses is a matter of "changing patterns of participation in specific social practices" (2004, p. 38). From this perspective, the informal learning space of fanfiction.net provides an apt context for answering the following questions: *What specific patterns of participation do adolescents find manageable, meaningful, and motivating in their writing and language learning activities in this site? How do these patterns converge and diverge with participation in formal learning spaces such as schools? What aspects of this site make it possible for a female adolescent EL, not only learn English composition skill, but also to take on and enact an identity as a knowledgeable fan and a powerful and accomplished English writer that may depart significantly from the one that has been constructed for her in the ESL classroom?*

ACTIVITY THEORY

An activity theoretical framework is a particularly apt means of conceptualizing how possibilities for discursively constructing identity and choices for writing and participation differ between the informal practices of writing online fanfiction and composing in school (Chandler-Olcott and Mahar, 2003b). L.S. Vygotsky's (1978) work has been instrumental in the development of present-day Cultural-Historical Activity Theory. Vygotsky's notion of activity theory has been used within Second Language Acquisition (SLA) research to understand how social context and scaffolding influence second-language (L2) learning (Aljaafreh and Lantolf, 1994; Ohta, 2000). For the purposes of this study, the organizing principles of an activity theoretical approach are "triangulated" with discourse analytic analysis to emphasize how the patterns of participation for fan authors in affinity spaces and for students in school spaces differ. Specifically, these activities involve mediation by different linguistic, cultural, and technological tools, and participation in these spaces is shaped by distinct community norms and values and learning objectives.

From an activity theoretical perspective, the common organizing elements of a system of activity include the *object* or *objective* (which can be abstract such as creating a plan or tangible such as creating a book), *subject* (individual or collective), *mediating artifacts* (e.g., signs, tools, genres), *rules* (official and unofficial), *community*, and *division of labor* (Engeström and Miettinen, 1999). Central to this approach is understanding how mediating artifacts in an activity (e.g., genres, Discourses, computers) are historically formed and both shape and constrain the actions of individuals within a system. As individuals make use of existing artifacts, tensions develop between the constraints of the existing tools and individual goals. It is these tensions and contradictions that drive change within and across systems as individuals adapt and adopt new artifacts and tools (e.g., media, genres, technology) to serve their purposes at the local level (Barab, Barnett, Yamagata-Lynch, Squire, and Keating, 2002). From such a perspective, qualitative analysis of short-term individual activities must take into account the ways in which these activities are embedded in, linked to, and discursively shape historical, cultural, and institutional systems, thus providing a means of bridging the micro and macro levels of analysis (Nardi, 1996).

LEARNING TO WRITE IN SCHOOL SPACES

Of late, contemporary writing instruction has taken a turn toward expressivist and process-centered pedagogies such as Writing Workshop, with the belief that these approaches are effective for both improving struggling writers' abilities and increasing their engagement with writing (Moje, Willes, and Fassio, 2001). Workshops are designed to give students "ownership" of their learning by creating a literate environment and classroom community in which students have the time and freedom to explore self-selected topics, to write from their own experience, to question conventions and strategies before adapting them to their own purposes, and to engage in authentic discourse with peers and expert others about writing (Atwell, 1998). Pedagogies such as Writer's Workshop are designed to be responsive to student experiences and are based on effective research and theories of writing as an expressive, socially situated, and recursive process (Atwell, 1998; Calkins, 1994); however, it has been suggested that when introduced in classroom spaces, such pedagogies can serve as normalizing practices that privilege certain texts, literacies, and mainstream experiences (Moje et al., 2001). In the following section, I discuss components of Writer's Workshop in relation to the central tenets of activity theory as a means of structuring a theoretical comparison of the different opportunities for patterns of participation in the fanfiction site and those promoted via formal instruction in school spaces. In so doing, this chapter draws attention to the potential that popular culture and networked computer environments might offer for developing classroom writing activities that are responsive to the sort of literacy practices that adolescents find engaging, meaningful, and helpful for developing written communication skills.

The typical instructional components of process-based writing activities such as Writer's Workshop include planning or prewriting, drafting, peer review, revising, editing, and publishing or sharing. Although the components are aimed at scaffolding students into participation in all stages of the writing process, such activities still have an end goal—production of the *object* of student texts with the *objective* of scaffolding students into officially sanctioned forms of discourse and writing. The production of these texts is *mediated* through artifacts such as academically valued genres of writing—grammatical, orthographic, and print-based conventions—as well as more tangible tools such as writing and drawing utensils, paper, and sometimes the computer. A result of this mediation is that texts produced in the classroom are artifacts of a print-based culture and reflect the conventions of print as well as the constraints of academic genres and writing.

Text production is also mediated through the expertise and knowledge of the teacher. In Writer's Workshop, the teacher's role is meant to be that of facilitator, mentor, and co-writer (Atwell, 1998). The teacher writes, shares his or her own writing process with the class, and helps students identify strategies they could use to solve problems they are struggling with. The teacher also acts as a listener and observer, identifying areas where the class needs help, and then conducting minilessons in these areas. This means that as artifacts the texts both reflect and reproduce an array of sociohistorical composition practices that are rooted in a print-based rather than a digital "mindset" (Lankshear and Knobel, 2003) and are mediated both through human and nonhuman means.

Process and expressivist writing activities, although intended to build on individual student's abilities and life experiences, are also constrained by sets of formal and informal *rules* that can act as normalizing measures in classrooms. For example, although formal orthographic and grammatical conventions are not the main emphasis of the Workshops, they are threaded through all the activities, and mastery is an underlying curricular focus in classrooms. For example, teachers conduct minilessons at the beginning of Workshop to introduce the strategies and/or conventions that are to be emphasized in the day's activities. Writing process-related rules also shape students' possibilities for participation: There are guidelines for peer-review sessions, rules for helping other students to revise and/or edit their papers, as well as official rules and unofficial norms that shape what are considered valuable and acceptable topics to write about. Also significant in shaping the dynamics of a classroom-based activity is the *division of labor*. Although the teacher's role in Workshop is intended to be that of a co-writer and facilitator, by virtue of his or her role as an evaluator, the teacher remains an authority figure who both enforces the classroom rules and influences the sort of abilities, literacy practices, and forms of participation that are recognized, valued, and allowed in the classroom space.

LEARNING TO WRITE IN FANFICTION SPACES

While long-time proponents of Writer's Workshop (Atwell, 1998; Calkins, 1994) and experts on adolescent literacy instruction (Alvermann and Phelps, 2002) foreground the importance of building on student experience and the social in teaching young adults, within the institution of school there are official rules and unofficial norms shaping the extent to which student interests and the social may come into play in learning activities. In one interview, Nanako speaks directly to this sort of constraint in school-based writing activities when she explains that "on fanfic.net..u can rite anything u want..but in skool..they always like assign u stuff to rite abt n mark u based on it n me dun like dat ..." (2005). Nanako's words illustrate how writing in the fanfiction.net site differs from composing in school on several fundamental levels. First, as Nanako points out, many school-based composition activities rely on writing prompts, topics selected by the teacher, or goals and themes determined by the curriculum. Although contemporary approaches to teaching writing emphasize the importance of allowing students to choose their own topics, this is often overlooked in the pursuit of content area and curricular goals. In addition, owing to the enormous pressure that educators are under to meet curricular goals, in a great deal of classroom writing the primary object of activity is producing textual products, with the objective or desired outcome being to develop specific writing skills that are mandated through the curriculum and driven by the imposition of state testing standards. As a result, student texts are evaluated primarily according to form and conventions, whereas the content or meaning value of their texts takes a back seat.

For fanfiction.net, all instances of activity also center on the object of producing fan texts; however, the objective of this activity is participation in a specific fandom (Anime and *Card Captor Sakura*)—the desired outcome of such activity being to affiliate with other fans and to produce texts that are directly related to these young authors' and readers' life experiences and/or knowledge of popular culture. Thus, the writing and associated literate interactions (e.g., peer review, metadiscussion of genre, elements of composition) on the fanfiction site also are directed toward discussing common interests, sharing various forms of knowledge about writing and popular culture, and forming social relationships. The objective of the activity thus is significant for scaffolding ELLs' participation and interaction in that all members of the community enjoy reading Anime fanfiction have voluntarily decided to participate in this space, have a point of affiliation with other members, and have a means of participating and demonstrating expertise in the realm of popular culture in multiple ways.

HYBRID FORMS OF PARTICIPATION

From what we know about best practice in teaching writing and ESL, it is crucial to recognize and build on students' cultural and linguistic backgrounds, as well as non-language based abilities, in order to help ELLs fully participate in classroom activities while they develop proficiency in an L2 (Atwell, 1998; Freeman and Freeman, 2001). Because the objective of participation in the fanfiction site is to affiliate around a particular fandom, ELLs are able to work on their English writing skills, while at the same time displaying affiliation and enacting their identities as Anime fans in other ways. For example, technologically adept fans are able to put up links to homepages and personal fan Web sites where the digital medium allows for easy incorporation of elements such as images, sound, color, and shape that can be integrated with text to convey meaning. Such links also enable ELLs to showcase their expertise in areas such as fan art, Web design, and video production, while at the same time facilitating communication with other members of the site. Thus, the objective of activity is also consequential for ELLs in that they can be recognized as legitimate Anime fans by virtue of such skills that are not wholly dependent on English proficiency, writing skills, and print-based forms of standard language (Black, 2005a). Moreover, they are able to garner respect and recognition within this space via proficiency in what Fiske (2002) calls the "unofficial capital" of popular culture and fandom.

Although fanfictions are wholly innovative in many respects, they are derivative in the sense that their design is mediated through fans' understandings or interpretations of forms of media and popular culture that the fictions are based on. While fans in the *CCS* site draw primarily from the plot and characters of the Japanese animation, when the constraints of this interferes with an author's individual goals, design of their texts can be mediated through other media as well. In the fanfiction community, the term *crossover* is used to describe mixed-genre texts in which the fiction "crosses over" from one fandom or media form to another. For instance, Nanako sometimes composes what are known as *songfics* (songfictions) and *moviefics* (moviefictions), which are stories based on the lyrics of songs and elements of movies respectively (Fanfiction Glossary, 2005). As an ELL who is learning to write in English, the intertextual presence of multiple media texts in crossovers supports Nanako's composition and helps her to negotiate the tensions of composing in an L2 in many ways.

First, the song provides a textual model for her writing, as she is able to emulate the rhyming stanza format of the lyrics to create many parts of her text. And, because she drew from a popular song that was played on the radio, she was better able to convey emotional elements of her fiction by drawing on the emotions evinced by the well-known song. Second, crossovers such as moviefics provide writers with alternative frameworks to draw on and then creatively extend through their own writing. Having a preexisting setting or cast of characters to choose from makes it easier to focus on developing elements of the plot, and vice versa. In addition, if spelling and grammatical errors are significant enough to impede comprehension, readers can still follow the plot if they are somewhat familiar with the original media productions (Black, 2005a). In spite of the derivative nature of such texts, the fictions are also highly creative, as Nanako crafts an entirely new setting and develops new characters for the story. As such, ELLs are able to draw from other media in varying degrees to support their composition as they develop writing skills. This in turn enables them to create more sophisticated fan texts, develop an audience of readers, and construct identities as successful authors within the community (Black, 2005a).

With regard to formal instruction in classroom composition, there is a clear point of divergence here. One of the primary goals of English Language Arts is to immerse students in academic genres of writing so that they are better able to reproduce them. It is not my intention to in any way downplay the importance of providing ELLs with access to and practice with the sort of powerful academic forms of writing that are valued in schools, but rather to point out that with the curricular demands and time constraints that many teachers are working under, there is little time or opportunity for students to actively experiment with and/or transform language forms. In classrooms, students are rewarded for producing texts within genres that are recognizable in the state curriculum standards; whereas fanfiction authors are rewarded for challenging and extending the constraints of genres by creating hybrid texts such as crossovers—as evidenced by the 1,700 reader reviews that Nanako received on her highly popular moviefic. Moreover, I would argue that through their active processes of redesigning and combining different genres and semiotic texts (e.g., movies, the social registers or Discourses of fanfiction.net and *CCS*, music, images, screenplays, books) to convey messages to a broad readership, fans are developing the sort of meta-awareness of Discourse (Gee, 2002) that will help them make informed decisions about how to use different forms of language and representation to achieve certain purposes, with specific audiences, in different contexts of use.

SELF-DIRECTED LEARNING

Like many fanfiction.net authors, Nanako begins each of her chapters with what is known within the fanfiction community as an Author's Note (A/N), which essentially is commentary to readers that the writer inserts before, after, or within the text itself. The following A/N from an introduction to one of Nanako's chapters is useful for understanding one of the many ways that she uses language to discursively construct and work toward maintaining the identity of a knowledgeable and successful writer within this Anime-based site. It also illustrates how Nanako negotiates the tensions between her own needs as an author and her readers' expectations. More specifically, she does this by leveraging tools available in the networked writing space as she artfully uses the Discourse of *CCS* fanfiction to play a part in shaping her own learning experience and the sort of interactions she will have with her peer reviewers.

> A/N: Konnichiwa minna-san! This is my new story ☺. Please excuse my grammar and spelling mistakes. Because English is my second language. Also, I'm still trying to improve my writing skills..........so this story might be really sucks.........;

Nanako begins this Author's Note with romanized Japanese as a means of signaling her insider status in the realm of Anime. It is interesting to note that she addresses readers with the Japanese title *san* to signal respect, and then follows with an emoticon for a smiley face (☺). Both the emoticon and the title, which could loosely be translated as "esteemed readers," are cues signaling solidarity between Nanako and her readers. Nanako follows the greeting with an interpersonal request that readers "Please excuse [her] grammar and spelling mistakes." In this way, she is able to strategically position readers both as fellow Anime fans and as a certain kind of audience—the kind that attends to content and rhetorical structure rather than grammatical correctness and spelling alone.

Nanako's statement that she is an English learner who is "trying to improve her writing skills" can be viewed as having a particular socially situated meaning in the context of fanfiction.net that differs significantly from the meaning the statement might have in another context. One of the major defining elements of fanfiction.net is the built-in review function where readers can click on a link in a story to post a review. Most authors end their fictions with a request that the audience R&R (read and review), and some authors will even refuse to write the next chapter in a sequel until they have received a certain number of reviews—the point being that reviews are at a high premium in this space. Nanako's self-identification as an ELL who is trying to improve her writing in this context can be seen as a strategic action that, as mentioned before, not only positions the audience as certain kinds of readers, but also serves in this Discourse as a strategic *activity exchange* that focuses on "getting others to do things" (Fairclough, 2003). In the context of a review-oriented writing space, Nanako's statement can be viewed as a request for readers to review her fiction in order to help her improve her writing.

Nanako goes on to explain that because she needs to improve her writing, "this story might be really sucks." Interpersonally, this statement shapes how the audience can negotiate or respond to the meaning of the statement (Gee, 1999; Halliday and Matthiessen, 2004). In choosing the modal verb *might*, Nanako opens up a space where, through reviews, the audience is able to interact with her about whether or not her story really "sucks." However, the humble nature of her self-introduction as an ELL who wishes to improve her writing and her admission that the story might contain grammatical and spelling errors strategically work toward enlisting supportive and helpful feedback from the audience. Thus, she places herself in a position where she most likely will be able to practice writing and learn from her participation and interaction in this space. And, as evidenced by the 1,700 reviews she received on this fiction, Nanako did manage to elicit responses from readers, most of whom assured her that her writing does not "suck."

Clearly, Author's Notes are a point where online fanfiction writing diverges from the writing classroom, in the sense that fan authors assume an interactive, dialogic learning space where they are able to communicate with and receive almost immediate response from readers via the Internet. Moreover, she is able to leverage her knowledge of the fanfiction site and her facility with the social register or Discourse of fanfiction.net to play a formative role in shaping the activity and to at least influence how the audience will provide feedback to her text. This is in contrast to classrooms where the curriculum and the teacher largely determine the sort of activity and instruction taking place, and where student participation and feedback is generally guided by the rules of Writing Workshop.

HYBRID LEARNING SPACES

As Giroux (1996) points out, with the proliferation of networked ICTs and media, "youth increasingly inhabit shifting cultural and social spheres marked by a plurality of languages and cultures" (p. 68) and negotiate hybrid spaces that allow for interaction across accustomed geographic and temporal borders. The notion of hybridity is useful for understanding the negotiation of meaning taking place as fans design texts in the fanfiction community (Black, 2005a; Chandler-Olcott and Mahar, 2003a), as well as for understanding what counts as expertise in Anime fandom. Linguistic and cultural hybridity are salient elements in many

Anime-based fanfictions. Because Anime and its print-based counterpart Manga are Japanese cultural productions, many of the series are set in Japan and China and are steeped in Japanese and/or Chinese language and culture. Thus, first-language (L1) English speakers are not automatically at an advantage in creating popular texts, as Japanese and Chinese linguistic and cultural elements are at a high premium in Anime-based fanfiction.

In contrast, ELLs with Asian backgrounds, such as Nanako, often have insider or expert status in this regard and will integrate such cultural and linguistic knowledge into their fictions. In the following example, Nanako draws on her L1 to convey the emotionally charged mood of a conversation between the two Chinese characters in the Japanese-based *CCS*.

> "Dui bu qi Xiaolang…zhen de he dui bu qi…(I'm sorry Xiaolang, I'm really sorry) I know you must hate me right now…I never knew I would hurt you and Sakura that much…" She sobbed (Tanaka Nanako, 2002).

In this post, a reviewer responds to Nanako's use of Hànyǔ Pīnyīn, which is a system of romanization of standard Mandarin Chinese (Wikipedia, 2005).

> Congratulations! I deem you another Han Yu Ping Ying champion! :D It's rare to find many people who understand how to use this phonetic spelling of the Chinese language correctly, but you have proven that you can through the Mei-Lin/Syaoran conversation! Great job on that aspect of your fic! Overall, of course, your fanfic is wonderful! I've been meaning to review but keep forgetting ^^; Please update soon! :D (Hope, 2003).

In this way, the reviewer recognizes Nanako's identity as an expert and insider in Anime-based fanfiction due to her facility with the Chinese language. The post also acknowledges Nanako's ability to draw on her L1 in creating a fiction that is accessible and appealing to the broader fanfiction community.

The preceding example is also an illustration of how Nanako is able to leverage the genre of *CCS* fanfiction to negotiate the tensions of composing in an L2. Within the *CCS* site, an ELL's writing may be valued for its creativity and introduction of interesting information about Anime or elements of Japanese and/or Chinese culture above features such as grammatical correctness and conventional forms. This is a point of divergence from classroom spaces where, in spite of intended foci on writing processes and building on students' experiences and abilities, there remains a marked underlying emphasis on grammatical and orthographic conventions that is evident during class lessons, guided peer-review sessions, teacher conferences, teacher modeling, assessment, and through the examples of print present in the classroom literacy environment (Atwell, 1998;

Moje et al., 2001). Moreover, with the emphasis on conventions and writing within specific academic genres, classroom-based composition does not allow much room for the sort of cultural, linguistic, and genre hybridity that can be found in fanfiction. ELLs are rarely given the opportunity to compose in their L1s in school, much less to integrate knowledge of an L1 with their developing textual and social practices in English.

COMMUNITY PARTICIPATION

Process-based approaches in formal writing instruction are intended to illustrate the recursive, social, and communicative nature of composing by having students exchange drafts, share them in small peer groups/dyads for feedback, and meet with the teacher for writing conferences, so they can receive feedback and then return to various stages in the writing process to work on areas that need attention (Atwell, 1998). Thus, student writing is mediated through the knowledge of peers and teachers. In some respects, this is a point of convergence with the fanfiction community, as fan authors' writing is also mediated through interactions with other fans and their feedback. For example, many submit their chapters to an official proofreader/editor/reviewer, known within the fanfiction community as a "beta reader," for feedback on their work. After revising and editing the text according to the beta's suggestions, they may resubmit it to the same beta, may choose another reader for additional review, or may post the revised version online as is.

Although beta readers and teachers might be fulfilling a similar function in the writing process, the evaluative aspect of the teacher's role creates a fundamental difference between the two that Nanako expresses when she explains that she does not like to write in school "cuz its gonna get graded n i dun wanna get a bad mark" (Tanaka Nanako, 2005). Another essential difference between this official review role in the affinity space of fanfiction.net and in the school space of a classroom is that in school the teacher is usually the only person who can be the beta reader and can have the final say in when it is appropriate to publish a piece of writing. On the contrary, with fanfiction, the role of beta reader can be filled by multiple peers according to various criteria, such as familiarity with genre, friendship, command of English language, knowledge of characters, and/or knowledge of Japanese language and culture, that provide all members of the affinity space with the opportunity to act as beta readers and to display valued forms of knowledge in this space. In addition, only the fan author has the final say in when a fiction is ready to be published on the Web, which ultimately upholds the author's agency and control over her or his writing.

Peer review is another point where the literacy practices of the fanfiction community diverge significantly from those of schools. First, these spaces differ greatly in terms of what constitutes a peer. In posting their fictions online, ELLs have access to a broad community of peer reviewers that is not bounded in the same ways that a space such as a classroom is. Classroom peers are generally determined by age and location, whereas online peer groups are voluntary and can encompass a range of ages, locations, socioeconomic groups, education levels, and linguistic backgrounds. In addition, because peers in the fanfiction site share an affinity for Anime, they come to the activity of reviewing with a shared point of reference. Because of this, fan writers can be confident that there will be some common underlying knowledge about their topic and that their topic is of interest to the audience. This is a point of divergence from classrooms in two respects. First, in classrooms students often are writing in response to prompts on topics that they have little interest in and/or knowledge about. And second, even if students compose on topics that are personally meaningful, this does not mean that their readers, teachers, and classmates will share their knowledge of or interest in a topic.

Peer feedback also contributes to Nanako's construction of her identity as a successful fanfiction author. Reviewers offer minor but specific comments on elements of the composition through various posts. A significant commonality is that readers end each review with a request for more "chappies" or chapters or ask the author to "update soon." In the first post, a reviewer includes comments on areas of the text that need development, that is, the relationship between Sakura and Syaoran, "Awwwww … that was kawaii. You've developed your character's beautifully and plot has begun to rise, now we need some S+S action!!Lol, so update it already, ok?*wink*" (anon, 2002). In another post, a reviewer offers specific suggestions for making the fiction more comprehensible by pointing out potential trouble sources (Nystrand, 1986) in the text, but follows with a request for more chapters.

> AW! That is just so CUTE! Great story!! I'd just like to mention that sometimes I'm a tiny bit mixed up becoz the pronouns or the names of the people who are doing the actions are not mentioned in the beginning of the phrase. So plz, can you put them. Even though it kills your fingers. Heehee. OOPS, sowwy, I didn't mean to be evil. I'm just like that. Btw. MORE CHAPPIES! (anon, 2003).

In another example, a reviewer writes "This is so cute! You keep bouncing between past tense and present tense, but otherwise, I've got nothing to complain about" (anon, 2002). Another reviewer responds to Nanako's use of alternative symbols to indicate dialogue between characters by modeling the use of quotation marks in her post. The reviewer writes, "like when they are saying something…you use this symbol 'Hi, how are you?'" (anon, 2003). This type of feedback provides

ELLs with "just-in-time" information (Gee, 2004) or on-the-spot minilessons on specific elements of their composition that impede comprehension or need development. Such focused and dialogic forms of feedback have been shown to be effective in scaffolding L2 (Guerrero and Villamil, 2000) and L1 (Nystrand, 1986) writing. Moreover, the way that critique in reviews generally is tempered by positive input still enables the author to maintain confidence and motivation to write and helps to create a strong sense of an eager audience waiting for the story to continue, all of which helps ELLs to construct and maintain an identity as an accomplished writer or designer of fanfiction.

DISCUSSION

Research on writing and language acquisition foregrounds the importance of encouraging students to become active learners who integrate their experiences of both the word and the world (Freire and Macedo, 1987) as a means of achieving power and control over their own thinking and learning (Alvermann and Phelps, 2002; Atwell, 1998). Much of popular writing pedagogy is intended to be responsive to the needs and life experiences of a diverse student population. Nonetheless, due to institutional and curricular constraints, difficulty often arises in the implementation of such pedagogies in formal instructional settings such as classrooms, resulting in a situation that offers students little opportunity to actively make meaning and to shape their own learning. In a discussion contrasting the traditional possibilities for learning offered in schools with those of online sites, Lankshear, Peters, and Knobel (1996) point out,

> The book, the classroom, and the curriculum can be viewed as intermeshed fixed enclosures which operate in concert to separate educational engagement from wider spheres of social practice: substituting reliance on texts for an integrated experience of word in relation to world, and in the process conferring heavy responsibility on the teacher to organize curricular activities and materials, and interpret meaning and experience. (p. 154)

Thus, classrooms are all too often constructed as "spaces of enclosure" where curricular objectives and officially sanctioned forms of knowledge often supplant student experience and take precedence over broader interactions with the world and forms of knowledge outside the classroom. In contrast, networked online environments, such as fanfiction.net, in many ways present an optimal site for the enactment of writing activities such as those promoted through pedagogies such as Writer's Workshop. It seems that one of the most salient elements that adolescents find motivating about the fanfiction space is the potential for change and transformation that this space offers—in essence, it offers them power and control over their own thinking and learning.

Although fanfictions are derived from preexisting pop cultural texts and artifacts, there is no authoritative genre, meaning, or interpretation to take precedence over the writers' own reworking and/or understanding of the texts. Authors in fanfiction sites seem to relish the opportunity to experiment with writing by extending preexisting genres and media forms and by challenging a variety of text and language conventions. Such practices indicate that students, especially ELLs and struggling writers and readers, may benefit from ample opportunities to experiment with and test out hypotheses about language and composition. By experimenting with different genres, conventions, and modes of expression, students may be able to gain meta-awareness and insight into why these genres and conventions exist and how they are useful, thus making them more inclined and better able to use them when necessary. Moreover, they need opportunities to display and build on their personal strengths through literacy and textual practices. The freedom afforded in fanfiction sites enables ELLs to write about topics of their own choosing and, through sophisticated writing and reading practices, engage with texts that stem from and are relevant to their lives. Furthermore, through their local interactions and engagement with texts that are not "enclosed," they are able to engage in powerful meaning-making activities and actively shape the norms, artifacts, and tools of the fanfiction space on a global scale by introducing linguistically and culturally hybrid texts that are taken up, distributed, and reproduced within the fan community at large.

As computers and the Web continue to grow as vital means of communication, information exchange, and as means of traversing traditional borders (Giroux, 1996; Lankshear and Knobel, 2003), the literacies of navigating and accessing online spaces will be increasingly relevant to academic and economic success, as well as to civic participation at both the local and global level (Warschauer, 2002). As Burbules (2004) argues, in much of the talk that goes on around students' engagement with on-and offline spaces, the real is generally associated with physical space and the virtual with digital space. Thus, it is seldom acknowledged that classrooms in and of themselves are *virtual* spaces (Burbules, 2004), where educators construct activities and experiences for learning. From this perspective, educators have the potential to design meaningful activities that incorporate many of the same aspects of online communities that youth find so engaging—what Burbules calls the "transaction elements of interest, involvement, interaction, and imagination" that promote a sense of meaningful immersion in a learning experience (p. 174). It follows then that educators and researchers alike might be able to learn a great deal from looking at grassroots spaces such as online fanfiction sites, where all participants have the opportunity to play a part in shaping the learning space and determining the sort of knowledge that is valued—and where participants clearly demonstrate the elements of interest, involvement, interaction, and imagination.

Moreover, as Freire and Giroux (1989) point out, "Learning is not merely about the acquisition of knowledge but also about the production of social practices which provide students with a sense of place, identity, worth, and value" (p. xi). This chapter provides a glimpse into a space where ELL youth are engaging in sophisticated literacy and learning activities and are successfully using English, as well as their personal, cultural, and linguistic backgrounds, in ways that contribute positively to their identities as competent writers, interactants, and legitimate members of global communities. The chapter also foregrounds the difficulties many teachers face in implementing engaging, interactive, and student-centered pedagogical approaches in bounded classroom spaces. As such, it generates ideas about how classroom activities could be expanded into networked spaces (e.g., school intranets, classroom Web sites, Web quests, Web-based writing activities) as complements to the professional guidance and support that language educators provide for students in print-based and computer-assisted activities. Therefore, this chapter may afford some insight into how popular culture and networked computer environments might be integrated with what we already know about effective writing pedagogy and SLA to develop learning activities that students will find meaningful, motivating, and empowering across their social, literate, and learning activities both in and out of schools.

NOTE

1. All names and titles are pseudonyms.

REFERENCES

Aljaafreh, A., and Lantolf, J. (1994). Negative feedback as regulation and second language learning in the zone of proximal development, *Modern Language Journal, 78*,4.

Alvermann, D., and Hagood, M. (2000). Fandom and critical media literacy, *Journal of Adolescent and Adult Literacy, 43*(5), 436–446.

Alvermann, D., and Phelps, S. (2002). *Content reading and literacy: Succeeding in today's diverse classrooms*. Boston: Allyn & Bacon.

Atwell, N. (1998). *In the middle: New understandings about writing, reading, and learning*. Portsmouth, NH: Boynton/Cook.

Barab, S., Barnett, M., Yamagata-Lynch, L., Squire, K., and Keating, T. (2002). Using activity theory to understand the contradictions characterizing a technology-rich introductory astronomy course, *Mind, Culture, and Activity, 9*(2), 76–107.

Bekerman, Z., and Silberman-Keller, D. (2004). Non-formal pedagogy, epistemology, rhetoric, and practice, *Curriculum and Teaching, 22*(1), 45–63.

Black, R.W. (2005A). Access and affiliation: The literacy and composition practices of English Language learners in an online fanfiction community, *Journal of Adolescent and Adult Literacy, 49*(2), 118–228.

Black, R.W. (2005b). Online fanfiction: What technology and popular culture can teach us about writing and literacy instruction, *New Horizons for Learning Online Journal, XI*(2), Retrieved December 15, 2006 from http://www.newhorizons.org/strategies/literacy/black.htm.

Burbules, N. (2004). Rethinking the virtual, *E-learning, 1*(2), 162–183.

Calkins, L.M. (1994). *The art of teaching writing.* Portsmouth, NH: Heinemann.

Chandler-Olcott, K., and Mahar, D. (2003a). Adolescents' anime-inspired "fanfictions": An exploration of multiliteracies, *Journal of Adolescent and Adult Literacy, 46*(7), 556–566.

Chandler-Olcott, K., and Mahar, D. (2003b). Tech-savviness meets multiliteracies: Exploring adolescent girls' technology-mediated literacy practices, *Reading Research Quarterly, 38*(3), 356–385.

Dyson, A. (1997). *Writing superheroes: Contemporary childhood, popular culture, and classroom literacy.* New York: Teachers College Press.

Engeström, Y., and Miettinen, R. (1999). Introduction, In Y. Engeström, R. Miettinen, and R. Punamaki (eds.), *Perspectives on activity theory* (pp. 1–18). New York: Cambridge University Press.

Fairclough, N. (2003). *Analyzing discourse: Textual analysis for social research.* New York: Routledge.

Fanfiction glossary, retrieved on March 22, 2005 from http://www.subreality.com/ glossary.htm

Fiske, J. (1992). The cultural economy of fandom, In L. Lewis (ed.), *The adoring audience: Fan culture and popular media* (pp. 37–42). New York: Routledge.

Freeman, D., and Freeman, Y. (2001). *Between worlds: Access to second language acquisition, 2nd ed.* Portsmouth, NH: Heinemann.

Freire, P., and Giroux, H. (1989). Foreword, In H. Giroux and R. Simon (eds.), *Popular culture, schooling, and everyday life.* Westport, CT: Bergin & Garvey.

Freire, P., and Macedo, D. (1987). *Literacy: Reading the word and the world.* Westport, CT: Bergin & Garvey.

Gee, J. (1999). *An introduction to discourse analysis.* London: Routledge.

Gee, J. (2002). Literacies, identities, and discourses, In M. Schleppegrell and M. Colombi (eds.), *Developing advanced literacy in first and second languages: Meaning with power* (pp. 159–175). Mahwah, NJ: Lawrence Erlbaum Associates.

Gee, J.P. (2004). *Situated language and learning: A critique of traditional schooling.* New York: Routledge.

Giroux, H.A. (1996). Slacking off: Border youth and postmodern education, In H. Giroux, C. Lankshear, P. McLaren, and M. Peters (eds.), *Counternarratives: Cultural studies and critical pedagogies in postmodern spaces* (pp. 59–80). New York: Routledge.

Giroux, H.A., and Simon, R.I. (1989). A pedagogy of pleasure and meaning, In H. Giroux and R. Simon (eds.), *Popular culture, schooling, and everyday life.* Westport, CT: Bergin & Garvey.

Guerrero, M., and Villamil, O. (2000). Activating the ZPD: Mutual scaffolding in L2 peer revision, *Modern Language Journal, 84*(1), 51–68.

Halliday, M., and Matthiessen, C. (2004). *An introduction to functional grammar, 3rd ed.* New York: Oxford University Press.

Heath, S. (1983). *Ways with words: Language, life and work in community and classrooms.* Cambridge: Cambridge University Press.

Hine, C. (2000). *Virtual ethnography.* Thousand Oaks, CA: Sage.

Jenkins, H. (1992). *Textual poachers: Television, fans, and participatory culture.* New York: Routledge.

Lam, E. (2000). Literacy and the design of the self: A case study of a teenager writing on the Internet, *TESOL Quarterly, 34*(3), 457–82.

Lankshear, C., and Knobel, M. (2003). *New literacies: Changing knowledge and classroom learning.* Philadelphia: Open University Press.

Lankshear, C., Peters, M., and Knobel, M. (1996). Critical pedagogy and Cyberspace. In H. Giroux, C. Lankshear, P. McLaren, and M. Peters (eds.), *Counternarratives: Cultural studies and critical pedagogies in postmodern spaces* (pp. 149–188). New York: Routledge.

Moje, E., Willes, D., and Fassio, K. (2001). Constructing and negotiating literacy in a Writer's Workshop: Literacy teaching and learning in the seventh grade, In E. Moje and D. O'Brien (eds.), *Constructions of literacy: Studies of teaching and learning in and out of schools* (pp. 193–212). Mahwah, NJ: Lawrence Erlbaum Associates.

Nardi, B. (ed.). (1996). *Context and consciousness: Activity theory and human-computer interaction.* Cambridge, MIT Press.

New London Group. (1996). A pedagogy of multiliteracies, designing social futures, *Harvard Educational Review, 66*(1), 60–92.

Nystrand, M. (1986). *The structure of written communication: Studies in reciprocity between writers and readers.* Orlando, FL: Academic Press.

Ohta, A. (2000). Re-thinking interaction in SLA: Developmentally appropriate assistance in the zone of proximal development and the acquisition of L2 grammar, In J. Lantolf (ed.), *Sociocultural theory and second language learning* (pp. 51–78). Oxford: Oxford University Press.

Purves, Alan. (1998). Flies in the web of hypertext, In D. Reinking, M. McKenna, L. Labbo, and R. Kieffer (eds.), *Handbook of literacy and technology: Transformations in a post-typographic world* (pp. 235–51). Mahwah, NJ: Lawrence Erlbaum Associates.

Scribner, S. and M. Cole. (1981). *The psychology of literacy.* Cambridge: Harvard University Press.

Spradley, J. (1980). *Participant observation.* New York: Holt, Rinehart and Winston.

Squire K.D., and Jenkins, H. (2003). Harnessing the power of games in education, *Insight, 3*(1), 5–33.

Steinkuehler, C.A. (2006). Massively multiplayer online videogaming as participation in a discourse, *Mind, Culture, and Activity, 13*(1), 38–52.

Stone, J.C. (2005). Lessons on teaching writing from website design, *New Horizons for Learning, 11*(2). Retrieved December 15, 2007, from http://www.newhorizons.org/strategies/literacy/stone.htm.

Street, B. (1984). *Literacy in theory and practice.* Cambridge: Cambridge University Press.

Super Cat. (1999). A (very) brief history of fanfic, *The fanfic symposium*, retrieved May 1, 2005 from http://www.trickster.org/symposium/colyear.html#2003.

Vygotsky, L.S. (1978). *Mind in society* (M. Cole, V. John-Steiner, S. Scribner, and U.E. Souberman, trans. and eds.). Cambridge: Harvard University Press.

Warschauer, M. (2002). A developmental perspective on technology in language education, *TESOL Quarterly*, 36, 3.

Wikipedia. (2005). retrieved March 22, 2005 from http://en.wikipedia.org/wiki/Pinyin.

CHAPTER NINE

Close TO THE Edge: The Poetry OF Hip-Hop

MARY STONE HANLEY

Young poets in the United States perform across the landscape of hip-hop, North and South, and from left to right coasts, "spittin'" lyrics and poetry. Gano and Ascalon declare rhythmically with musicians in a poetry slam performance (August, 2005): "It's the spit shot from lungs that breaks open the beat of meaning!" The poets meet at street corners, clubs, malls, schoolyards, pool halls, gyms, and vacant lots, wherever anyone will listen and respond. They play with metaphor, simile, alliteration, and other such literary gymnastics while navigating rhythms in a stream of meaning. Crowds of young people applaud their verbal agility and smirk or boo at any lack of imagination. The wordsmiths spit fires of passion that only the young can claim, pushing against the borders of language and consciousness set by the previous generation. They speak to their truths, amazed at the ability of the word to shake the world, to change, to move themselves, each other, and perfect strangers, which ultimately makes no one a stranger.

At the same time, older adults listen to the edges of popular culture and bemoan the heat of youth in the same way that their parents did, "I just don't know what's wrong with these kids today"—the refrain of parents, and their parents, and their parents. Unfortunately, what they miss when they stand outside are the cultures of youth, is the fascination of witnessing the rising tides of generations, and the reflections of centuries of memory in the ebb and flow of life. They also miss the important opportunity to ask provocative questions when the world of ideas and pleasures can be a confusing place for those entering adolescence and adulthood. As educators we might miss the voice, motivation, and genius of the sometimes blank staring, hooded, and disengaged youth who tap their pencils or bob their heads to beats that teachers cannot hear while they drone on about gerunds and participles.

What has often concerned and frightened parents and others throughout the past centuries has not been popular culture so much, but the Blackness in popular culture. Black music and its rhythms and language, Black sensuality, Black dance and physicality, and Black style are unwelcome in many White homes—and in some Black homes as well. Like a dominant social gene, however, young people continue to find their own marginalized status expressed in the rhythms of a subordinated Black culture. Herein is a revolutionary aspect of hip-hop; it has democratized public spaces for the voices of youth, providing them with a late-twentieth-century soapbox from which to speak when so many people in power would like to silence them. Mihn-Ha (1991) explains the possibilities of artists to transform society,

> The ability to confer aesthetic status on objects and representations that are excluded from the dominant aesthetic of the time is a way of asserting one's position in social space. It is a way of defying the ethical censorship of the ruling classes whose aesthetic intolerance and aversion to different lifestyles defines them as possessors of legitimate culture. (p. 230)

How the story gets told, and by whom, are crucial keys to its significance. Thus, creating the poetry of hip-hop is a political act. The fact that the forms are Africentric and the language is based in working class and underclass values is significant because it represents a rupture from within the dominant culture that represses and marginalizes the voices of Blacks and youth.

However, when examining discourse, Foucault (1972) asks who is speaking and who is silenced. Who has the authority, who has given the authority for the speaker, and who listens and believes? In the case of hip-hop there are some rap artists who internalize concepts that include commodification and misogyny, using those ideologies to interpret and express their reality. Others consciously choose to use rap music as a public space from which to excite resistance to a subordinate status. From either perspective, these artists mirror the economic, political, and cultural structures of society. Their stories, emerging from a culture of projected Anglocentric and patriarchal superiority, drag internalized oppression and/or a critical consciousness with them. The artist may create, but what she or he knows and creates may, or may not, be liberating.

POPULAR CULTURE

The dialectics of the culture of youth in the United States is a conundrum of tensions. In a society in which consumption and profit are central factors of the national economic and social culture, those who are not considered to be involved in the process of creating economic capital are marginalized. Social class stratifications among and between people of color, women, youth, and gays and lesbians create even more complex challenges. Giroux (1996) points out how the intersection between education and economic conditions are troublesome for youth. He asserts that in addition to deplorable economic conditions youth are confronted by irrelevant social institutions that unfortunately hold central positions in their lives. The schools exemplify these institutions with Eurocentric curricula that are "often resistant to analyzing how racial, class, and gender differences intersect in shaping that curriculum, [thus] schooling appears to many youth to be irrelevant as it is boring" (p. 13).

Herein lays the significance of a study of popular culture to education. In view of the pervasive nature of the popular culture media in the lives of youth, and the need for skills and knowledge to interrogate their meanings, an education that is neither reflective, engaging, nor relevant would seem to create a calamitous future for individuals, leaving them powerless before an onslaught of hegemonic messages and self-interests that may be detrimental to their lives. A fundamental difference between power and powerlessness is agentive social consciousness. Freire (1970) speaks about the transformative nature of resistance consciousness as he maintains that "To no longer be prey to its [oppression] force one must emerge from it and turn upon it. This can be done only by means of the praxis: reflection and action upon the world in order to transform it" (p. 36). Mind-numbing education eliminates praxis and reinforces powerlessness.

A study of popular culture, and in this case hip-hop, can also help educators to understand the extent of its effect on the consciousness of students who are hip-hop artists, those who listen to the music and words, and the subsequent effects on society and schooling. Equally important, an investigation of hip-hop, an expression of marginalized youth, and its rich African and socioeconomic and political roots, may crack open the supremacist world view of educators enough for them to perceive the many nuances and voices at play in youth culture. To that end, this article examines the cultural roots, aesthetics, poetry, and educational possibilities of hip-hop.

THE AFRICAN ROOTS OF HIP-HOP

Rap music, the first hip-hop poetry form, as it emerges in the context of African diasporic cultures, is best understood when framed by its three main sources: music, poetry, and orality, or performance. African and African American music emphasizes improvisation and interaction. The call-and-response pattern, an activity in which everyone participates, is a manifestation of the communal nature of Black music. Improvisation is also a way of being in the African tradition and may be a factor in the resiliency of the people of the African diaspora. Malone (1996) ties "the ability to disregard outer form yet retain inner values" (p. 26) in African diasporic cultures to the same improvisational quality of the music.

In traditional West African cultures, music and dance were inseparable. Malone (1996) cites Thompson, who explains the five traits of western African music that are also present in dance: "dominance of a percussive concept of performance, multiple meter, apart playing and dancing, call and response, and songs of allusion/dances of derision" (p. 15). Malone explains:

> "Multiple meters" refers to the use of cross rhythms. Musicians create tension in the music by playing several different rhythms at the same time. ..."playing-apart" for musicians refers to the practice of drumming different overlapping rhythms at the same time, with each rhythm contributing to the polymetric whole ... Call and response is a special form of antiphony, wherein a caller alternates his lines with the regularly timed responses of a chorus. (pp. 16–17)

Adding the words of the singer, poet, or *griot* (storyteller and oral historian) to the music carries the knowledge, wisdom, and meaning of generations meshed with circular and repetitive beats of polyrhythmic patterns.

Malone (1996) describes the last trait of African music and dance, songs of allusion/dances of derision:

> Songs of insult, topical songs, and songs of incitement are present in many traditional cultures. The ability of skilled singers to make spontaneous additions to songs and recreated lines is valued. Songs of allusion serve as vehicles of social control. Satire is used to preserve indigenous values and wisdom. People who have stepped outside the bounds of approved social behavior face the risk of being reprimanded publicly through song. (p. 17)

Southern (1983) observes that in eighteenth-century Africa, "poet and musician typically were one and the same person" (p. 18). Rap utilizes all of these African-based techniques: improvisation, call and response, polyrhythmic and polyphonic music, and the traditions of the poet-musician.

THE WORD—POETRY AND ORALITY

The other current that flows into the reservoir of rap is the Afri-cultural gift with words, both written and spoken. The relationship of music and poetry can be seen in the Black oral traditions in children's games and rhymes, the sermons of

Black ministers, and even shouts and cheers (Gates and McKay, 1997). The verbal traditions parallel music and dance forms with the techniques of call and response and repetition of phrases and rhythms to poetically express their ideas and feelings. As in music, the inventiveness of the individual through verbal expression is highly prized. A memory of teaching through allusion and satire that I have from my own childhood is a riddle that my mother and I ritually recited whenever my mother felt I needed to be reminded of the importance of humility. My mother would say to me, "You know what the fly said to the lightening bug?" My response was always, "No. What?" She'd reply, "You think you're bright, but it's just your ass." Social control was a process of bonding accomplished through the playful use of language and humor.

Signifying is another example of metaphoric, figurative, and ironic language in Black speech that parallels the songs of insult and the dances of derision described above. "Sounding" or "ranking," a form of signifying, is a verbal duel of friendly insults and one-upmanship, as in "I went to your house and wanted to sit down. A roach jumped up and said, 'Hey this seat is taken!'" The response is: "So, I went to yo' house and stepped on a match, and yo' mama said 'Who turned off the heat?'" (Lee, 1991). The ability to "give and take a lick," to take an insult and quickly reply with a wittier response is a part of the improvisational *be* mentality in African American folklore—*be* there when oppression comes, and *be* there when it's gone. All these aspects of orality can be found in hip-hop word play.

THE POLITICAL ECONOMY OF RAP'S BEGINNINGS

Rap music began in the South Bronx of New York City in the mid-1970s. This was the period of US history that Rose (1994) calls postindustrial America. Across the country, and especially in the northeast, it was a time of economic transition. The declining industrial base and the loss of accompanying relatively well-paid and stable union jobs were replaced by unstable service jobs established to fulfill the needs of the telecommunications, finance, and information industries. The economic and cultural foundation of the country was in flux. Rose describes the transition:

> The growth of multinational telecommunications networks, global economic competition, a major technological revolution, the formation of new international divisions of labor, and the increasing power of finance relative to production, and new migration patterns from Third World industrializing nations have all contributed to the economic and social restructuring of urban America (p. 27)

In 1975, New York City was in default on its loans, denied a federal bailout, and had to develop an austerity program. At the same time, construction of the

Cross-Bronx Expressway, destroyed tens of thousands of homes, leaving the South Bronx a wasteland of demolished and abandoned buildings, poverty, and with a limited economic base. From these bleak conditions emerged an expressive form of music and dance, and a culture of resistance known as hip-hop in which youth groups—"crews or posses"—made music, danced, and created graffiti art. The urban context that necessitated making a way out of no way, and the "be" mentality that for centuries had sustained the African diasporic people, supported them as they continued to adapt and transform—to improvise. Spirituals, gospel, blues, jazz, rhythm and blues are each branches of music that have carried all or some African cultural forms throughout diverse eras and technological developments, and each has contributed to rap music. Each branch was shaped by and reflected the contradictions of its era. Spirituals were often used as signals to escape slavery. The blues evolved during a period of Jim Crow and virulent White supremacy. Rose's (1994) description of rap music as the expression of the contradictions in an urban environment afflicted by a declining economy, the marginalization of youth, the exploitation of the poor in the inner cities, and the development of technology for recording and listening to music are the external factors that helped to create a music grounded in the experience of its creators. Understanding the economic conditions that spawned rap music is crucial because the songs they create present the artists' experiences and desires.

Rap historians (George, 1998; Ogg and Upshal, 2001, Rose, 1994) agree that Clive Campbell, aka Kool Herc, a Jamaican immigrant, was the first to lay the basis of what would be called rap. As a disc jockey (DJ) in the Bronx in the 1960s and 1970s, Herc created a back track of musical rhythms and extended dance music at community dances by switching back and forth between songs. Dances lasted longer, and his choice of highly percussive breaks provided exciting opportunities for dance, some of which evolved into break dancing.

DJ's would hook their equipment to any electrical source, sometimes a hot-wired light fixture in an empty lot, and begin to play. Young people would gather, and the party started, a Phoenix among the ruins of the South Bronx. DJs teamed with masters of ceremony (MCs) who rapped between or during the songs or back beats, "creating spoken rhymes, catch phrases and a commentary about the DJ, the clientele, and themselves over the beats" (Toop, 1984). Using rhythm, story, and rhyme, MCs thrilled audiences until they became the main performers.

Competition among MCs in New York was intense. The contests took the form of boasting or competitive bragging in songs of derision and signifying, as MCs demanded respect for the excellence of their word skills. George (1998) describes this form of communication as a unity of pride and arrogance among Black males, who dominate the field of rap music. He states that the use of bragging in hip-hop is a form of resistance and claims that "Black male pride is a weapon and an attitude. It is an attack on the negative and it is a way to spin the negative on its head" (p. 51).

The polyphonic and polyrhythmic music, orality, improvisation, call and response, the connections between music and dance, and the ways in which all are used to express individual excellence and style are ancient African roots that flower into contemporary musical expression. Expressive individualism, a development of distinctive personality and spontaneous behaviors (Allen and Boykin, 1992) in rap music merges with signifying in the oral tradition and becomes ritualized as a boast. Rappers boast about their ability to rap, to "flow," to fight, to challenge, to be "players" and lovers, drive fancy cars, and drink expensive liquors. Boasting can also be tied to the African songs of derision because boasts are not only meant to acknowledge the skills of the rapper but to diminish the reputation and standing of the opponent as well.

COMMERCIAL RAP

From the analysis of rap music played on commercial radio stations it would appear that rap artists, most of whom are young Black men, are at war. They describe grim and dangerous communities, where a man must maintain a warrior's posture and presentation. The lyrics in these songs reveal men who refuse to be diminished, who are prepared to fight for the position of king of the hip-hop hill. The war appears as a rivalry in boasting about rapping, as when 2 Live Crew (1986) rapped, "I've been rhymin' and designin', and always tryin'/Our beats are always strong, and never dyin'/The lyrics I recite, I say with power/So step aside or get devoured." Or they brag about prowess in street violence, as when Mobb Deep (1995) raps, "From these streets that we done took/You walkin' with a head down, scared to look/You shook, cause ain't no such things as halfway crooks." Rap music provides a public space for the establishment of power and voice. Unfortunately, the main enemies in this war appear to be each other.

Thus, commercial hip-hop is full of contradictions. On the one hand, it releases power; on the other hand, capitalist record producers suck it away. The history of capitalism and neocolonialism is replete with examples of how the privileged classes establish a buffer social class that serves as a valve for frustration and anger, providing the masses with a model of possibility and success to emulate which is acceptable to the ruling class, thereby controlling the insurgent responses of the oppressed. Rappers, young men from impoverished or working-class backgrounds, who defend their manhood by turning their musical wrath on each other, rather than direct it at the source of oppression, serve to reproduce the very conditions that they lament.

TECHNIQUE

Two artistic techniques that reflect the genius of rap artists, and also obfuscate the meaning of their narratives, are the uses of the first person and metaphor. Rappers are storytellers, and like all storytellers they use their imaginations to create characters and situations. Most of the threats of violence are metaphors about skills in MCing, as in the example of "RE:DEFinition" when Mos Def (Black Star, 1998, track 4) says, "Son, I'm way past the minimum, it's a verb millennium. My rap's hold a gat [gun] to your back, like Palestinians." The metaphorical violence of the MC boast also is easily confused with the gangsta rap that describes gang violence, with no allusion to boasting about verbal agility.

The other convention in rap lyrics that may be misleading is the use of the first person in almost all of the songs. Rappers portray themselves as if they have done all they describe, when in actuality, like any creative artist, rap artists create meaning through the vehicle of story, in this case musical stories. Some rappers, like Tupac Shakur and Biggie Smalls, were indeed involved in dangerous activities, as their deaths attest. However, as the young woman with whom I had lunch said, "All of 'em ain't talking about what they know, they just saying that so they can make some money." Ogg and Upshal (2001) state, "They separate John Wayne from the character he's playing, they separate Robert DeNiro from the character he's playing. They never separate rappers from the lyrics they're performing" (p. 142).

ALTERNATIVE PERSPECTIVES IN RAP

Hip-hop culture has many variations and threads of meaning that parallel and intersect. Debate about the directions of hip-hop are as diverse as its people, including an opportunity for the poor to "make it" in an uncaring world. Others see hip-hop as a means to foment social change and social justice. Nic, a fourteen-year-old Latino MC expressed his idea about the importance of hip-hop when he told me, "I see it as a unifying force, I mean it has the potential to lead a revolution, It [hip-hop] has the power to unify globally you know what I mean, *globally* you got hip-hop and graffiti you got it in Brazil in Japan, everywhere. ..."

The element of social consciousness evident even from the earliest rap music is still created by the current field of artists in the category of what students told me was *Conscious Rap*, music written to express critical consciousness about society. A rap group representing this category of music is Dead Prez. The song *Police State* (Dead Prez, 2000, track 5) presents an alternative perspective as they declare,

> Bring the power back to the street, where the people live
> We sick of workin' for crumbs and fillin' up the prisons
> Dyin' over money and relyin' on religion for help
> Organize the wealth into a socialist economy
> A way of life based off the common need
> And all my comrades is ready, we just spreadin' the seed

However, these songs that carry messages that critically examine social conditions and suggest alternatives are not the songs that are repeatedly played on the radio. I interviewed a twenty-eight–year–old African American man who had been rapping for fourteen years. I asked him why he thought *Conscious Rap* was not what is heard on the radio. He replied, "You got middle class White kids [MCs] talking about guns and killing, imagine the power of talking about political change."

INFINITE TOMATOES

Underground hip-hop is the space that is in the hands of the youth themselves, outside of the glare of commercial constraints. Here they return to the roots of hip-hop as a culture of the streets and communities of young people. Here artists write poetry, lyrics, create beats, and perform in any space that is conducive to expression. Nic and Damian, ages fourteen and twenty-five, respectively, two MCs that I interviewed speak of possibilities for creativity in hip-hop to explain its importance in their lives. Damian said, "Creation is poetic, so that there is some order to it. But, in order there is always an infinite possibility, and I think that's what's a part of it [his interest]—that's there's always a possibility to create something that is infinite." Nic added, "Like an infinite point of view from the person, like poetry, I read a whole bunch about Talib Kweli can do that. He could make a whole bunch of poems and metaphors about a tomato; so it's just infinite about tomatoes; it's incredible, it just caught my attention right there." Hip-hop writers are empowered to speak through poetry in a firestorm of stoop-and-street-corner literacy. In underground hip-hop culture, artists produce their own work in cottage industries, much of which critiques social contradictions.

VARIATIONS IN HIP-HOP POETRY

With the aesthetics, history, and politics of hip-hop in mind I now examine the forms of poetry. Hip-hop poetry is foremost a performance art. Words, rhythms, beats, techniques such as call and response, and repetition ignite emotion and pleasure to build community through a common experience. Collins (2003) asserts that "to hear a poem is to experience its momentary escape from the prison cell of the page, where silence is enforced, to a freedom dependent only on the ability to open the mouth-that most democratic of instruments-and speak" (p. 3). Indeed, the most extraordinary thing about the explosion of poetry and the people who create it is the democratic nature of the movement. I have observed poetry slams, performances, and open mic events that embraced young and old, male, female, people of all races and ethnicities, poor and well off, sharing the same space, embracing each other's creativity and respecting each other's voice.

The literary forms of hip-hop includes rap lyrics; words in rhythm and rhyme added to musical beats; and spoken word, performance poetry that may not have rhyme or rhythm and that very often includes critical thought. Rap performance forms include *rapping*, the recitation of the words to beats and music, *battling*, a rivalry between MCs to determine who is verbally more creative with words and ideas, and *freestyle*, individual improvisational poetry with rhythm and rhyme that is based on words that the MC takes from the audience.

Spoken word is connected to the Beat poets of the 1960s and poets such as the Lost Poets and Gil Scott Heron of the 1970s. Rap music's emphasis on the performance of words recharged poetry as a means of meaning making through popular culture so that spoken word poets have become poet-actors. They may use musicians or even props, but the salient aspect of the performance is the expression of ideas and emotion through poetry. Spoken word artist Kelly Zen-Yie Tsai (Bond, 2005) explained the relationship of the poetry forms and said, "It's really all one family. Spoken word and hip-hop are like cousins in the family, just like page poetry is a cousin in the family. Everyone is going to have their different influences and variations, but basically it's all one."

Erudite critics may show disdain toward the poetics of spoken word and rap. Their notion of poetry is word forms on a page, whereas hip-hop poets make poetry an embodied experience. The democratic impulse in hip-hop is to speak to power; the aesthetic is to say it well. The performance of the work is about sharing and through sharing to move people with one's skills in the art form.

LITERACY OF HIP-HOP

Although educators lament the literacy of students, a culture of wordsmiths swirls all around us. I have met middle-school students who cut classes to go to the mall, not to shop or ride the escalators, but to meet friends to stand in groups and play with words. Never in my life's experience have so many young people been excited by words and their ability to use them. Some of these students are the same young people whom educators assume have no interest and lack the discipline for learning. One African American high school student told me he studies to be a good MC.

He said, "You got to know something to be able to say something. You just can't get up there and say stupid stuff. So, when I run out of ideas I read anything and everything. I read and read until I start to get ideas." It would benefit teachers and their students to pay attention to the interests and efforts that abound in the hip-hop culture.

HIP-HOP IN SCHOOLS AND COMMUNITIES

An example of the use of hip-hop in the school curriculum is a poetry workshop sponsored by a university and two school districts for high school students, particularly those who were not known for their academic achievement, to work with local adult poets in developing their poems. Students were bused from their schools to the university where they spent the whole day thinking, discussing, writing, and performing poetry. There was a hip-hop workshop attended by many of the participants, a combination of some of the White students from Advanced Placement courses and Black and Latino students from the last-chance schools for the willful and resistant. The workshop leader, an African American man who is an MC, instructed the students on the conventions of poetry. He wrote a list on the board that included simile, metaphor, imagery, alliteration, assonance, consonance, onomatopoeia, meter, rhythm, and rhyme scheme. He asked for definitions and a young man, his skin almost the color of the black do-rag he wore, with sagging oversized pants and a toothpick that he chewed constantly while he rocked back and forth on two legs of his chair, knew the meaning of all the words. When it was his time to share his poetry he did so with the attitude of assurance, and with a crooked grin, he took the toothpick out of his mouth. He asked for words from the audience, and used their words to freestyle, improvising poetry in rhythms and rhymes that spoke of the trials of being young and Black in a White world. He decried boring education, wars, and corrupt politicians. When he finished, the applause was explosive. He had fractured the notion for many in that room that Black males are nonachieving illiterates. This was an example of equity pedagogy described by Banks and Banks (1995), which is "an environment in which students can acquire, interrogate, and produce knowledge and envision new possibilities of that knowledge for societal change" (p. 153).

I am forever amazed by the amount of concentration and knowledge that the poet and other freestylers engage. They speak of the flow, a metaphor for being completely immersed in the process of creating. Csikszentmihalyi and Schiefele (1992) assert that intrinsic rewards of creating art are so enjoyable that … the reward is innate. As such, the … experience is called the "flow experience." When people are in the flow no extrinsic rewards are necessary, and participating in the activity is preferable to doing anything else. Thus, the young man with the toothpick proved that all people are learners when they have a purpose. Internal motivation comes from relevancy.

IN COMMUNITIES

I experienced the power in the verbal culture of hip-hop to meld traditions and communities, when I attended what was publicized as a Spoken Word Open Mic in a city on the West Coast. I was early. The site was a high-end curiosity shop, long and narrow, with the ubiquitous coffee stand in the corner. Large and small masks from traditions as diverse as Europe, China, and sub-Saharan Africa hung like gargoyles alongside fragile statuettes, gems, rocks, and butterflies pinned in glass display cases. The next to enter were the organizers of the event, and the mistress and master of ceremony, a mother-and-son duo, poets and short story writers, an intergenerational dedication to language. Other participants strolled in, in large and small groups, finding their seats, trying to get close to the stage. Those who came late stood in the back and along the sides. There was an eight-year-old African American girl and her mother and father. A gray haired white man in a suit and tie sat with his equally conservative—and rather nervous—lady friend. They sat beside a group of young black men, some with do-rags and some with locked hair, who greeted a mixed group of Filipino and Latino youth. A few young white males entered, more black youths in sagging pants—one with gold teeth. African American teenaged young women, Native American youths, male and female, Latino teens who brought a five-year-old, a group of vocal Asian American young women, a forty-something black man, and me, a middle-aged African American woman made a standing-room-only crowd of about 100 people, who came to do one thing—play with words. And we did.

The first twenty minutes were a free-write. The audience suggested three words, and everyone wrote poetry for twenty minutes using those three words. Then each person was encouraged by hand clapping and foot stomping, and vocal support, like "show them some love" and "I know you have something wonderful to share with us. Don't be shy." The eight-year-old African American girl read her poem and encouraged her mother and father to read. The Suit read his poem, although no amount of encouragement could get his companion to read hers. Even the five-year-old Latino boy drew a picture about the words. His sister translated its meaning to the gathering. Poets from diverse backgrounds made themselves vulnerable and presented long and short poems, some funny, some sad, some with rhyme and rhythm, some in free verse, some rather trite, others challenging form or raising critical questions about society and social justice. Whatever was offered was welcomed and applauded. It was a feast of meaning and community that the second part of the evening continued with the performance of poetry that had been written beforehand.

I have used this open mic technique with high school students and under-graduate college students. What is most wonderful is how much I learn about each student as they perform their work. I write and share as well. We build community through our vulnerability.

CONCLUSION

Rap music is thoroughly rooted in ancient African traditions that wind their ways of orality and rhythm through stories, songs, and places across centuries and emerged in the streets of the South Bronx in New York City where imaginative and articulate, but marginalized, youth seized the figurative weapons of language to express their rage. The spoken word movement blossomed in the soil of hip-hop. Literacy is a central component of the culture of hip-hop, in which rap music emphasizes mental and verbal dexterity. Mos Def (Talib Kweli, 2000, track 5) demonstrates his agility as he raps, "Yo, I am the world renowned, verb, adjective, adverb/Pronoun, preposition, suffix, prefix/Original or remix, sunburst and eclipse/Me and Kwe' combine like strands on a double-helix/My speech seasoned, with dialect of my region/Booga-nam Brooklyn Bed-Stuy Eastern/Where youth and policemen, they nah reach agreement." Here is imagery, metaphor, even grammar performed in an art form that may connect youth and teachers to creative expression and critical consciousness.

REFERENCES

2 Live Crew. (1986). Check it out y'all. On *2 Live is what we are* [CD]. Riverside, CA: Lil' Joe Records

Allen, B.A., and Boykin, A.W. (1992). African American children and the educational process: Alleviating cultural discontinuity through prescriptive pedagogy. *School Psychology Review, 21*(4), 586–596.

Banks, C.A.M. and Banks, J.A. (1995). Equity pedagogy: An essential component of multicultural education. *Theory Into Practice, 34*(3), 152–158.

Black Star. (1998). RE:DEFinition. *Mos Def and Talib Kweli are Black Star* [CD]. Los Angeles: Rawkus Entertainment.

Bond, M. (2005). Kelly Zen-Yie Tsai, DEF poet and spoken word artist. Gothamist [on-line], Available at http://www.gothamist.com/archives/2005/08/30/kelly_zen-yie_tsai_def_poet_spoken_word_artist.php

Collins, B. (2003). Poems in the air. *The spoken word revolution: Slam, Hip-hop and the poetry of a new generation* (pp. 3–5). Naperville, IL: Sourcebooks.

Csikszentmihalyi, M., and Schiefele, U. (1992). Arts education, human development, and the quality of experience. In B. Reimer and R. Smith (eds.), *The arts, education, and aesthetic knowing: Ninety-first yearbook of the National Society for the Study of Education* (pp. 169–191). Chicago: University of Chicago Press.

Dead Prez, (2000) Published by the War of Art Music (BMI)/Walk Like Warrior Music (BMI)/Hi Yo Silver Music (ASCAP)/Gold Touch Music (ASCAP) All Administrated by the Royalty Network, Inc.

Foucault, M. (1972*). The archeology of knowledge and the discourse on language.* New York: Pantheon.

Freire, P. (1970). *Pedagogy of the oppressed.* New York: Seabury Press.

Gano, J. (poet, emcee) and Ascalon, M. (poet, emcee). (August, 2005). *2005 Northwest Poetry Slam Competition.* [spoken word poetry performance]. Seattle, WA, The Mirabeau Lounge.

Gates, H.L., and McKay, N. (eds.). (1997). *The Norton anthology of African American literature.* New York: W. W. Norton and Company.

George, N. (1998). *Hip-hop America.* New York: Viking.

Giroux, H.A. (1996). *Fugitive cultures: Race, violence, and youth.* New York: Routledge.

Lee, C. (1991). Big picture talkers/words walking without masters: The instructional implications of ethnic voices for an expanded literacy. *The Journal of Negro Education, 60,* 291–303.

Malone, J. (1996*). Steppin' on the blues: The visible rhythms of African American dance.* Urbana: University of Illinois Press.

Mihn-Ha, T. (1991). *When the moon waxes red: Representation, gender, and cultural politics.* New York: Routledge.

Mobb Deep. (1995). Survival of the fittest. *The infamous* [CD]. New York: Loud Records, LLC.

Ogg, A., and Upshal, D. (2001). *The hip-hop years: A history of rap.* New York: Fromm International.

Rose, T. (1994). *Black noise: Rap music and Black culture in contemporary America.* Hanover, NH: Wesleyan University Press.

Southern, E. (1983). *The music of Black Americans: A history.* New York: W.W. Norton and Company (p. 7).

Talib Kweli and Hi Tek featuring Mos Def. (2000). This means you. *Train of thought* [CD]. Los Angeles: Rawkus Records.

Toop, D. (1984). *Rap attack 2: African rap to global hip-hop.* London: Pluto Press.

CHAPTER TEN

Advertising AND Consumerism: A Space FOR Pedagogical Practice

VIRGINIA S. FUNES

Advertising is, overwhelmingly, an enemy of the classroom. This project proposes, nevertheless, the transformation of advertising into an educational opportunity, an opportunity to spark a flame of inquiry and to awaken a critical consciousness of advertising.

In addition to being viewed as an enemy of the classroom, advertising inspires confusion and disjuncture in the teaching environment. This stems from an apparent contradiction between the ethics of teaching versus the ethics of advertising—the former centers on "duty" and "being" whereas the latter centers on "want" and "appearing." Teachers are uncomfortable when faced with advertising: their proposal is to explain things "as they are" to learners who "must" learn. This proposal is contradictory with respect to advertising, and the resulting clash can lead to a double revelation, without doubt paradoxical and disturbing for both sides: advertising as imperative and normative, and teaching as activator and manipulator of wants and pleasures.

Television commercials are cultural texts in which dominant ideology is codified in order to influence the audience's social representations of reality and their problems. The mechanisms used by the media to influence the audience's representations are difficult to detect and often go unnoticed. It is considered that practices focused on analyzing media cultural texts will enable a distancing from which learners may go beyond being mere spectators and, through a progressive decentralization of their perceptive experiences, will be able to contextualize and, as a consequence, "defamiliarize" that which is generally accepted as obvious and normal. This process will also enable learners to analyze their behavior as audience members, and it is an indispensable requisite to understanding the media strategies used to teach certain contents and values.

Finally, this project considers the didactic application of advertising in formal education. Instead of transmitting content, the goal is that the student learns to learn. The methodology proposes a phased deconstruction of the traditional transmitter-message-receiver scheme in order to place the experience of the learner first. Then responsibility indeed falls to the teacher-facilitator who must conduct the learning process taking place in the triple condition of the learner—as consumer, as citizen, and as an increasingly competent spectator of the advertising show. This process will enable the learning of a language used to express knowledge that escapes traditional textbooks and that is deeply anchored in the cultural consumption of young people.

THE ADVERTISING IMAGE AS A TOOL OF SOCIAL CONTROL

Advertising images are powerful tools of social control. Born of, and focused on, the emotional aspect of the audience, they present value frameworks and models of homogeneous behavior with the singular aim of driving willpower toward the market.

The advertising image preserves an implicit and legitimate social model that openly presents standardized representations of reality. Advertising messages not only describe the products they aim to sell, but they also put forth other issues. Through advertising, lifestyles are discouraged or promoted, and ideologies are praised or condemned. People are convinced of the social utility of certain behavior and habits, while dreams, feelings of euphoria, and perfection are sold.

Television advertising creates a mythology of the object in which private wishes become public; it invades people's lives on a daily basis with a parade of suggestions, instructions, and images that are spectacular, speculative, and fascinating.

In today's mass communications hypermarket, audiences are sold and the spectator's attention is bought. Audiences are a central part of the commercial transactions between the communication industry and advertisers. Nowadays, the most valuable product is the public's loyal and devoted visual attention. The content of programs is no longer as important as the incessant and spectacular flow of advertising images, and the provocation of their message. Thus, television programming serves only as a background for the greatest show on earth—commercials.

It is evident that the visible discourse of advertising can change the meaning of objects to the extent of converting them into authentic fetishes and that the psychological pressure that audiences bear is precisely what drives their consumption of said objects.

In the contemporary world, advertising as a hegemonic discourse replaces traditional myths and results in a contemporary mythology in which the cult of objects transforms itself into a sense: of wanting to be, of wanting to be able, and of wanting to do. The prevailing discourse surrounding advertising is centered on desire and the principle of pleasure (González Requena and Ortíz de Zárate, 1995). However, this strategy of persuasion based on the stimulation and management of desire nearly always appears together with a normative discourse based, in the final instance, on the duty to consume as the means to experience belonging, or social integration.

Audiences' consumption and consumerism are controlled and manipulated by goods manufacturers. This is because the survival of our economic system is based on the fact that what is produced must also necessarily be consumed. It is precisely here where advertising's authoritarian character lies—as the most effective means producers have of assuring an addicted consumer market, managing mass demand, and creating false needs.

The capitalist system imperative of creating needs and linking them to aspirations and deep desires defines the framework in which consumption and product advertising act. Yet the demand for creating such a link originates in the system of production. According to the latter, advertising would be a phenomenon particular to capitalism. In today's globalized society, economic benefit has become the goal of any human activity, and all information technologies are basic institutions of the consumer society. These technologies homogenize behavior, transmit the latest, act as systems of social checks and balances, and are the principal stage for many social conflicts.

As globalization's neoliberal conception gains ground (a concept according to which all rights are not equal), modern developments and innovation appear to the majority as objects for consumption and to many people as no more than a show.

Consumer goods provide us with quality of life, security, personality, and independence. Advertised objects are flaunted for their added value, giving them a certain supersaturated significance. Objects are not consumed for what they are but as something that distinguishes a person. Objects are acquired not only to be used but to be exhibited as a symbol of belonging to a reference group or lifestyle. As a result, every object not only alludes to its usefulness or practical purpose but also to a certain imitation of lifestyles and cultural habits held by hegemonic groups. As Baudrillard states (1974, p. 5), "Objects' possibilities extend well beyond their functional utility and it is in this excess of presence that they acquire a prestige meaning, where they designate identity and the social status of their owner/user."*

In other words, the receiver not only consumes a certain product in the economic market but also acts as receiver of a given cultural text in the communication market (Lomas, 1996a). Meanwhile, advertising experts know that rational arguments may be refuted and, therefore, employ other resources: feeling, aesthetic beauty, humor, congeniality, erotic promise, and emotions. Little reference is made to the actual product. Instead, a consumer prototype is presented on which we (consumers) can model ourselves and in so doing socially integrate into that position. The object is a guarantee of social identity by means of the viewers' identification with a brand.

The television viewer/consumer does not master the differentiation of readings (product denotative and value/symbols connotative) proposed by advertising texts, and views the texts with certain skepticism while criticizing them within parameters such as truth, lies, and reality—categories in which advertising discourse does not reside, based instead on illusion, symbol, pleasure, and desire.

WAYS OF SAYING AND WAYS OF DOING

Within such a sociological context, it must be understood that advertising discourse is loyal to its assigned intent within the economic system for which advertising acts as a messenger and support. For that purpose, modern advertising does not aim its efforts at merely providing information regarding the qualities of the products existing on the market. Instead, it intends to be as effectively persuasive as possible in legitimizing a certain conception of life and of the world.

In accordance with this pragmatic intent, as Lomas (1996a, 1996b) states and develops, advertising communication absorbs most of the formal resources of the current means of expression and, in a studied practice of textual polyphony, uses them to achieve the presentation of its commercial promises as believable (obviating categories of truth/falseness).

It may be wondered whether a real advertising discourse exists, that is, whether it possesses specific and distinctive signals of textual identity that differentiate it from the rest of discourse practices deployed in people's communication exchanges or whether the show that is persuasive advertising must be considered as a meeting point among diverse forms of discourse. If the latter is true, the advertising discourse would be a text pastiche in which other texts are imitated and parodied, and other textual voices are echoed. Plagiarisms, allusions, quotes, and paraphrases would confirm the presence of texts of diverse origin in the advertising discourse, thus rendering it a perfect example of textual polyphony (Bakhtin, 1975).

If an analysis of the uses and forms of advertising communication is to be defended from a pragmatically inspired semiological perspective (Lomas, 1996b), then the language of advertising is but a specific discourse type that complies with certain conditions of enunciation and reception, that has a concrete intent, appears in precise cultural contexts, and is explicitly marked so that it is habitually recognized by its listeners without difficulty. Consequently, advertising discourse appears as a scenario of certain forms and messages in which sense is created from enunciated stereotypes deployed in cultural and communicative contexts in accordance with pragmatic criteria of coherence, appropriateness, and efficiency. It is not possible to understand an analysis of the uses and forms of the persuasive power of advertising via the study of the significance of a given commercial but only within the universe of content and significance that advertising campaigns represent.

ADVERTISING AS PEDAGOGICAL DISCOURSE

Among all media languages, the existence of advertising discourse presents a paradox: despite its omnipresence, it is totally invisible. The compulsive ubiquity of advertising text in the different mass media and all the manifestations shaping and giving sense to advertising language provoke a hypnotic effect on the decoding capacity of the audiences.

The social representation of advertising produces an informational dynamic that allows one to see certain aspects of reality while at the same time blocking other aspects from view. Its visible side is a discourse about objects, but its hidden face legitimizes an entire social system.

We can succeed in consciously perceiving the interaction of codes present in the advertising message, such as photographic technique or any rhetorical figure employed. However, there are many aspects in the advertising discourse that constitute its invisible side.

When we reflect on the advertising text and we ask ourselves who is communicating and what for, how reality is reconstructed in the representations advertising makes of it, which axiological scale is taken as a reference, or how audiences identify with the advertising message, we are approaching advertising's invisible side without a doubt.

Advertising also acts as an authoritarian discourse that is primarily unidirectional information from the sender to the receivers. According to Prieto Castillo (1987, p. 30), the commercial and propaganda intentions of advertising make up its informative essence. We can label advertising as an antidialogue action having its own particular traits (conquest, division, manipulation, and cultural invasion), as Paulo Freire (1980) describes it, and as the radical opposite of dialogue and authentic communication among people.

The semiotic codes selected and combined in a given advertising message lead audiences to a single interpretation, which is the one that really matters to the sender. Bearing this in mind, the advertising message may be considered to be a pedagogical discourse, as it is capable of generating sentimentally indolent and noncritical masses, redirecting them toward the practice of consumption within the limits of a symbolic universe that advertising itself can create.

Advertising as a pedagogical discourse includes three types of practices: semiotic, ideological, and economic. (see Figure 1)

Semiotic practice supposes the most superficial stage in the critical analysis of an advertising text. The selective use of certain elements (framing, lighting, color range, the location of elements within the frame, camera movements, etc.) provokes selective learning in both male and female consumers. Through this practice, objects are imbued with meaning, thus becoming easily recognizable to the public. From this perspective, advertising also constitutes a system to build and rebuild the meanings that provide value to products. All television commercials organize those meanings into signs that are then transferred to products (Goldman, 1992).

Like all ideological discourses, advertising as an ideological practice addresses audiences with the aim of imposing a certain system of representing the world and, above all, of assigning specialized behavioral rules to people, rules that are conditioned by the underlying social structure of that system of representation itself.

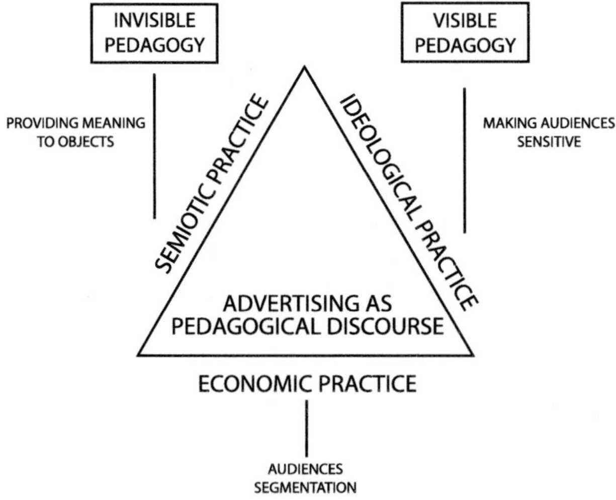

Figure 1.

From this perspective, advertising's principal objective is that of sensitizing audiences, orienting them toward the market. In a figurative sense, the ideological practice constitutes the invisible pedagogy of advertising discourse—its hidden curriculum.

Finally, considering advertising as an economic practice supposes acknowledging that not only does it provide the financial support for the media informative structure but also that those media are advertisements themselves that convey information and entertainment capable of capturing audiences for advertisers.

Therefore, the media's main product is not programs but audiences because what advertisers try to achieve is access to those audiences (hypothetical male and female consumers) by purchasing media broadcast time. In turn, the media sell segments of audiences in certain time ranges to advertisers. Hence, it seems clear that the real product bought and sold is the audience; they are the media's only true product.

POPULAR CULTURE, MEDIA CULTURE, SCHOOL CULTURE: INTERSECTIONS

The notion of culture refers to a battlefield for meaning in which multiple values, voices, and intentions are reflected. This implies considering the intensity of social contradictions within linguistic and symbolic systems. A culture comprises social practices and representations that assert or deny certain values, interests, and commitments that are part of a symbolic capital in a hegemonic or determined position. We are faced with two interwoven cultures that are simultaneously in conflict in everyday life and in educational spaces.

On the one hand, school culture is made up of a set of practices, knowledge, and representations produced and reproduced by schools. Yet this culture also includes means of communicating and transmitting knowledge that enable people to act socially (beyond the school context) according to the logic of the school. In that sense, school culture is a way of producing, transmitting, and reproducing that tends toward the rational organization of daily social life.

On the other hand, media culture is part of the popular culture in which students interact. Quite frequently, there is a serious gap between the pedagogical experiences provided by formal education and the audiovisual world we live in (truly a parallel and nonsystematic school). In the classroom, teachers officiate a liturgy of the past, exhaustively analyzing lessons locked in books, whereas students belong to a generation that cannot find its place at school. It is a generation of video games, multimedia, DVDs, and a participative digital society interconnected through the Internet.

One of the most serious problems educators should be reflecting upon today is the contradiction that exists between the educational system and the sociocultural environment into which new generations of students are born into and in which they grow up.

Marshall McLuhan expressed this contradiction in a very pertinent way:

> There is a world of difference between the classroom and the integrated electric information context in modern homes. Today's television-watching child is instantly attuned to the codes of adult news: inflation, disturbances, war, taxes, crime, beautiful people in their bathing suits. That child is perplexed when s/he enters the nineteenth-century environment still characterizing the educational system, with little bits of information neatly ordered and structured in patterns and topics, fragmented and classified. It is, naturally, an atmosphere very similar to that of any factory, with its inventories and assembly lines (…). Today's child is growing up in an absurd way since s/he lives in two worlds and neither of them fosters growth. Growth: that is our new task and it is total. Mere instruction is not enough. (1987, p. 14)

Judith Lazar also refers to the contradiction between the two worlds but from the standpoint of mutual reproaches:

> The child is trapped between two radically different cultures. One is book-based, officially recognized, cited as reference. The other, that of television, is fought against and yet, universal. On the one hand, school speaks to students about classical culture defined as noble. On the other hand, before the small screen, the child is immersed in a mosaic culture that appears as a sub-culture to most teachers' eyes. (1985, pp. 19–20)

Never before, perhaps, has such a profound gap existed between what happens in the classroom setting and in people's vital contexts. Most likely, it will require more than audiovisual equipment to bridge this gap.

The educational institution of is out of phase, revealed in the fact that some decades ago, when written culture was dominant, the illiteracy rate was high. Nowadays, that rate has been notably reduced, but the socially hegemonic culture is the audiovisual one, and there is currently a large mass of audiovisually illiterate people.

We are, then, faced with an emerging cultural shift that radically questions the monolithically transmissible character of knowledge, a shift that reassesses people's practices and experiences and throws light on mosaic knowledge made up of mobile objects, diffuse borders, and intertextualities.

This polyphonic effect of the discourse is strengthened by the phenomenon of remediation (Bolter and Grusin, 1999) whereby old media are appropriated by new media[1] without critical commentary. This oscillation is central to understanding how a medium can both reinvent its predecessors and transform its contemporaries. Therefore, if it is true that today people do not read or write as in the past, it is because they neither do nor do they make representations as in the past.

Consequently, new generations know how to read, but their reading is imbued with the plurality of texts and writing styles available today. The cultural subjects of this new generation are drawn from the connection and disconnection of technological devices rather than from the figures, styles and practices of old traditions that define "culture."

Most adults and people in the educational universe face this new culture with a distant and preventive attitude, resenting and resisting that which renders much of their knowledge obsolete. They blame this culture for the crisis in intellectual and even ethical values. On the contrary, young people experience a kind of empathy that goes beyond their ease in relating to and using the language of audiovisual devices to include an expressive complicity with those devices' stories, images, sounds, fragments, and velocities.

The current situation is our starting point to reconsider the issue of teachers' communicative effectiveness in the social framework of an omnipresent audiovisual culture. We need, then, a conception of education and school that feeds off and into the communicative ecosystems present in society and provides enough autonomy to allow us to be discerning while enveloped in symbolic mechanism.

It is in this way that this document considers the use of advertising images in an educational context in order to promote a differentiation of those readings suggested by advertising texts. That is, a denotative reading of the product, and a connotative reading of the values and symbols. This would enable us to grasp a language in which knowledge circulates—knowledge that escapes the textbook and that is deeply anchored in the cultural consumption of young people.

TWO CONTRASTING WORLDS

Neil Postman describes the paradoxical situation of the child confronted for the first time by traditional education saying that schools nowadays face a different kind of student, one molded by the electronic mass media, which favors images, immediacy, nonlinearity, and fragmentation. Postman asserts that today's student does not feel at home at a traditional school that emphasizes "sequential presence, social order, hierarchy, continuity and rejection of instant gratification" (cited in D.P. Ely, 1984, pp. 97–98).

One of the most serious problems that education should be considering today is precisely that divergence (or even contradiction), from the standpoint of communicative parameters, between the school and the society for which pedagogy theoretically educates, between the school context and the sociocultural environment in which the student grows. Whereas at school the means of hegemonic expression is verbal, in society it is iconic and audiovisual. Whereas school teaches mainly *in* the spoken and written word and *with* the spoken and written word, in society the student fundamentally receives audiovisual messages. This leads to a student who is facing a dichotomy. First, there is an avalanche of images and mosaic culture, characterized by immediacy, nonlinearity, ubiquity, dispersion, random chaos, seduction, and fascination without critical reflection. Then there is analysis, structure, rigor and systematization, verbalism, and logic—but all with detachment and the incapacity to seduce.

Some of the traits defining these contrasting worlds can be summarized as follows:

SCHOOL	MASS MEDIA
Humanistic culture	Mosaic culture
Verbal hegemony	Audiovisual hegemony
Abstraction	Concrete ideas
Analysis	Immediacy
Logic	Sensations
Systematization, structure	Dispersion, random chaos
Linearity	Ubiquity
Personalizing will without seductive capacity	Fascination capacity, with depersonalizing risk

What is most worrying about the contradiction between these two universes is perhaps the last element in the comparison. That is, the comparison between seduction with depersonalizing risk and the attempt at personalization without capacity to fascinate. Students are fascinated or seduced by mass media, toward which they do not easily form reflective and critical attitudes. On the contrary, at school they often develop fairly reflective and critical attitudes, but they are rarely fascinated, even when audiovisual techniques or resources are incorporated into teaching.

This divergence or contradiction is particularly serious because the iconic culture in which the student interacts—a kind of iconosphere in which the student is immersed—ends up transforming his or her taste, perceptive habits, or even mental processes, rendering many of the means of communication traditionally used in school old-fashioned and ineffective.

ADVERTISING AS NONFORMAL EDUCATION

In an educational system that still preserves many rigid components from the past, advertising as an object of study engenders uncertainty. To some people, justifying its inclusion in academic curricula seems a difficult task, and in any case, it is not seen with certainty that it would be pedagogically useful. In the little educational space given to advertising, it causes a somewhat of a scandal, which hits at what might be called the "ethics" of the institution.

The ethics of teaching and the ethics of advertising seem to derive from contradictory sources. Teaching is based on concepts of "duty" and "being." While, advertising would derive from "want" and "appearing." Hence, the teaching discourse aims at explaining things "as they are" for a receiver that "must" learn them, whereas the advertising discourse addresses a receiver who "wants" and "desires" in order to show him things "as they appear."

This collision of ethics leads to situations that are a symptom of teachers' uneasiness when approaching advertising, and of the particular scandal advertising discourse arouses in teachers, or in their educational role and the near impossibility of matching school and consumption in an operative way.

In fact, this collision can bring about a mutually uncomfortable revelation on both sides: on the one hand, advertising, seen from a teaching perspective, shows the imperative and normative character it always tries to hide. On the other hand, teaching, when confronted with advertising, is revealed as an activator and manipulator of desires and pleasures.

We are not alone when faced with a militant rejection by teachers of the materialistic ethics that advertising imposes. School's discursive strategy reveals, at a closer look, that the programs of "duty" try to incorporate pleasure- and desire-associated values (motivational theory applied to pedagogy, mainly in the guidelines for modern teaching and active pedagogy).

Whereas, including advertising in the classroom will reveal its strategies of desire management and, more importantly, duty management. It is easy to be certain that the known persuasive strategy centered on desire stimulation is nearly always accompanied by a normative discourse, ultimately based on the duty of social integration.

DIDACTIC APPLICATION OF ADVERTISING
IN FORMAL EDUCATION

According to Joan Ferrés (1994b), there are three ways in which video material may be incorporated into the school context: as video lesson, as video support, and as motivating program.

In the case of video lessons, curricula contents are developed through a program in a systematic way, with a structured and gradual development that has precise educational objectives.

When using video as support, images accompany the teacher's presentation, that is, images are implemented as illustration, reinforcement, or as complementary to the spoken word.

Finally, the motivating program is the one that has neither an explicit educational intent nor a content-systematic presentation. However, because of its style, format, or content, it can exercise an educational influence.

Using this kind of material aims fundamentally at providing postvideo follow-up tasks with the teacher taking the essential role of mediator. He or she is responsible for integrating those images into a didactic unit, as most television images may serve as a motivating program.

The educational use of advertising messages is suggested on the basis of this latter methodology.

A critical and reflective use of advertising from an endogenous educational model (Kaplún, 1998) is suggested. Such an approach centers around students who learn and emphasizes the process. It is not about education that informs but education that forms, that seeks to form learner-spectators.

The aim is to achieve an action-reflection-action process in which the student starts from his or her own experience and social practice. The teacher's role is to stimulate the analysis and reflection process, to facilitate it, to foment investigation, to create controversy, to question, to listen, to help the group express itself, and to provide the information necessary to move forward in the process. The process does not revolve around the teacher but around the group of students. "In the communicative interactions among the three elements- teacher, student, context -it is the teacher's participation as mediator that most contributes to significant learning, to creating a fundamental link between new ideas and concepts and the students' cognitive background" (Gutiérrez Martín, 2002, p. 6).

More than teaching something or transmitting contents, what matters here is that the subject learns to learn, that he or she is able to reason alone, that he or she can go beyond merely empirical and immediate facts and verifications that surround him/her (naïve consciousness activated by perception), that he or she develops his/her own skills of deduction, to make connections, and to find synthesis (critical consciousness activated by reflection and analysis).

The project developed here is based on the subject's active participation in the process by getting involved, investigating, questioning, and looking for answers. In short, it is an education that constantly raises questions in its pursuit of demythologizing the social reality of the subject who learns.

In order to support this critical reading of advertising, it will be necessary to rely on students' self-identification as spectators and their intent (or lack of) while contemplating or receiving advertising (prefeeding stage). In stage 1, it is advisable to start developing spontaneous comments on the selected advertising spots, having students in different groups then compare their readings and conclusions.

This procedural methodology differs from the classical "transmitter-message-receiver" scheme in which the speaker/teacher starts the communicative process, and states the contents and ideas he or she wants to communicate while the student-spectator addressee acts as a mere receiver of the message. Therefore, the teacher's main role is not to transmit ideas but to gather experiences from students, select from them, order them, and organize them. After structuring these ideas, the teacher will provide feedback so that students can internalize their ideas, analyze them, and reflect on them.

After students view the ads, the goal of this stage of the process is not to ask students: "Which are the value-conveying images that add value to the advertised products?" This is not an activity of audience indoctrination, as with such a formula the sensitive, affective, and emotional dimension provoked by any image is censored, thus prioritizing the logical and rational dimension. In an adequate use of audiovisual document, the rational, analytical, and reflective aspects have to be the aim of the process. This method intends to achieve critical reflection through emotion.

It is essential, therefore, for students to comment on the images through spontaneous verbalizations about the reactions the images have provoked in them. These reactions may range from attraction to disgust, shock, or indifference. The intention is to motivate students to see advertising in a whole new light, making the aspects that constitute advertising and its own particular underlying ideas easier and more evident to them. In turn, this motivation implies students may "talk" about advertising, comment on it, rethink it, and speak about themselves as subjects-audience and about their interaction with advertising references.

In stage 2, progressive distancing from the first reactions will take place. The teacher's role is very important here, as the teacher will act as a learning facilitator and mediator. The teacher will be in charge of introducing rational questions to let students account for their emotional reactions. It is a dialogue and discussion phase.

While working on this stage, students should assume a triple standpoint: as consumers, as citizens in dialogue with the symbols and values of their time, and as increasingly critical spectators of the advertising show.

The global aim of a critical reading of advertising must be to contrast the reality of the product being sold with the values and images used to sell it, and so this method explicitly insists on a reading that is not independent from the commercial itself, but one that participates in a controversial dialogue with the reality of the object advertised.

With that purpose in mind (see Figure 2), it is important to start characterizing the advertised product both functionally and socially through a debate on whether it is really needed, a debate about its functional features, and its social

Chart . A global frame for the analysis of commercials

1. Which product do commercials sell?

- Product identification, uses description and purchase objective traits (function competence, consumer information, manufacturing details, packaging)
- Product social meaning
- Current brand positioning

2. Who is the product sold to?

- Time, day and television station; how the product is inserted in the program
- Average viewer of the television station/ timetable

3. What do commercials say about the product features?

- Commercial type
- Technical resources to present product features:
  - Icon-visual parameters (narrative pace, shots detailed study, objects, characters)
  - Sound code: verbal messages, music, noises
  - Relationship among sounds, verbal messages and icons

4. What other social values do commercials use to make the product/brand more attractive?

- Commercial real content:
  - Plot and theme
  - Suggested lifestyle
  - Universe of promoted values

- Technical resources to present the values suggested by the product or brand: Icon-visual parameters, sound codes, relationship sounds, verbal messages and icons

5. Conclusions

- Type of information that is relevant to influence purchase acts of given product
- Opinion about suggested lifestyle
- Commercial quality as a persuasive message:
  - Message adequacy degree to target
  - How noticeable the commercial is compared with others in the same period
  - How noticeable the commercial is compared with others in its sector

Figure 2.

connotations through the use and possession of such a product or brand. From there, it is necessary to find out to whom the commercial is addressed, contextualizing it within different population segments at which mass media are targeted and analyzing what is being suggested about the lifestyle of the consumer prototype presented in the commercial. The process concludes with spot analyses and critical reflection.

It is essential to teach students about linguistic, rhetorical, and audiovisual resources that are found in advertising messages. The aim is not merely to identify them in the commercials later but to analyze the ultimate sense of their contribution to the construction of the intent of the message.

In order to make progress in demythologizing spots, a deeper study of what is said about the products should be made. Such an analysis will consider the way the message is expressed and what is not said about the product. It will be useful to see the type of commercial used[2] as each of them involves certain spectator-consumer implicit resources as well as textual codification and organizational strategies that will determine different critical reading strategies.

Such an approach would mean reflection on the images through students' own experiences. The ultimate aim of this methodology is to take advantage of the emotions, feelings, and the pleasure evoked by all television images.

This method also achieves another goal: the teaching-learning process becomes more motivating and coherent, whereas emotion can become an opportunity for reflection. It should be applied to both when working to "educate in the media" as well as when working on "educating with the media."[3]

The methodology implemented here is conceived as a framework adaptable to the particular characteristics of each commercial while a more exhaustive treatment of some parts may be developed. What is important is to make explicit some conclusions in which the focus on the contrast between the reality of what is being sold and the tools used for that aim is respected.

The objectives of this teaching-learning process as a whole could be expressed as follows:

- To analyze the ends and the social function of advertising
- To understand the relationship between commercials and the type of receiver/consumer they are aimed at
- To develop a critical attitude regarding television commercials, which aim to persuade and transfer ideology
- To understand the pragmatic resources of advertising discourse, its intent, and its capacity to persuade
- To compare linguistic, rhetorical, and icon-verbal resources integrated in different advertising messages

The contents that we propose in order to achieve the abovementioned objectives could be selected from the following:

Concepts

- The origin and function of advertising
- Advertising classification and typology
- Narrative structure, characters, and physical surroundings

- The rhetoric of the advertising image
- Advertising, fashion, and consumption
- Stereotypes
- Sale of values

PROCEDURES

- Comprehension of the general sense and ends of the advertising discourse
- Analysis of linguistic, rhetorical, icon-verbal resources present in different commercials
- Interpretation of pragmatic resources according to their intent and capacity to persuade
- Cooperative work, discussions, and debates on different advertising messages
- Written work on the conclusions related to the different task sets proposed
- Production of commercials that critically reproduce the discursive resources typical to advertising

ATTITUDES

- Critical assessment of television advertising as an expression of the aims and social function of advertising messages
- Active and critical reception of different advertising messages
- Reflection and assessment of the possibilities of manipulation and persuasion that advertising discourse offers
- Critical attitude toward the diffusion of models or stereotypes that imply discrimination or undervaluing (due to cultural, social, political or sexual reasons) in advertising discourses

CONCLUSION

We have analyzed how advertising as social discourse results from two levels of convention: communicative and cultural. What are at stake, therefore, are the codified or ritualized foundations of the very society from whence advertising emerges. Hence the ease with which advertising can provoke skepticism, uncertainty, and uneasiness. Yet, advertising can also be—and this is what the chapter is about—the opportunity to create a constructive initiative and to raise critical awareness about such a construction, that is, a space for the practice of a style of pedagogy that is exploratory and that foments discussion.

In this respect, knowledge about advertising may present an extraordinary opportunity. To explore advertising is to place oneself in front of an ever valid "document": the discourse spreading across all areas of social communication; an exponent of the connection between the symbolic world and the economic world (i.e., between the universe of material production and that of intellectual production)—a discourse that organizes customs and consumption as well as desire and everyday dreams.

Let us consider that the influence of advertising on teenagers has not only a quantitative impact (because of its permanent redundancy in their lives) but also a qualitative one: advertising defines a real informal education as it pursues generational homogeneity. Advertising shows teenagers only one model of social insertion: they are mere objects of consumption, and consumption is the means to happiness. We can also see that most advertising is either addressed to teenagers or mimics the discourse of youth as part of the permanent quest for new consumers for the future.

From a teaching perspective, advertising communication should be understood as a mosaic of textual procedures, whether linguistic or not, in which a symbolic universe of meaning becomes manifest. Education should contribute to unmasking the tricks of seduction and persuasion use din commercials to stimulate stereotypes of pleasure, evasion, submission, or power which, in turn, are ideological referents.

The pedagogical purpose of the educational appropriation of advertising is associated with a comprehensive and meta-communicative understanding of advertising tools and of their use in cultural contexts of reception and production. The idea is to encourage scholarly knowledge of advertising texts that will prompt spectator competence aimed at a critical understanding of the messages conveyed by advertising. Educational knowledge in this respect implies knowing how advertising messages are created, and for what purpose they are created.

It should be remembered that the school environment is the only setting in which knowledge of the expressive codes of advertising may be assembled while at the same time fomenting a critical attitude toward the ideological sense of advertising messages. It is up to education, then, to view advertising in a whole new light, to be able to pose the question whether it is worth seeing life in a different way from that suggested by advertising.

NOTES

* Translated from the Spanish.
  1. On the first page of *Understanding Media*, Marshall McLuhan insisted that the content of a medium is always another medium: the content of writing is speech; the written word is the content of printing, and printing is the content of the telegraph. Cf. M. McLuhan (1964). *Understanding Media: The Extensions of Man*. New York: McGraw-Hill.
  2. For this point, it is recommendable to analyze spots bearing in mind the guidelines of critical analysis developed by Péninou (1972), Saborit (1994), and Ferrés (1994b). Similarly, Jakobson's functions of the message (1963) will be taken into account for verbal intervention.
  3. Joan Ferrés (1994). He proposes two ways of integrating television into education: (a) educating in television, which assumes turning television into an object of study (educating in audiovisual language and critical media analysis, bearing in mind its technical, economic, ethical, cultural, and ideological dimensions) and (b) educating with television, which implies incorporating it into all curriculum areas and in different teaching levels.

REFERENCES

Bakhtin, M. (1975). *Teoría y estética de la novela*. Madrid: Taurus.

Baudrillard, J. (1974). *Crítica de la economía política del signo*. México: Siglo XXI.

Berman, R. (1981). *Advertising and social change*. Beverly Hills, CA: Sage.

Bolter, J.D., and Grusin, R. (1999). *Remediation: Understanding new media*. Cambridge, MA: The MIT Press.

Ely, D.P. (1984). Les deux mondes de l'élève, In Zaghloul, M., *L'education aux medias* (pp.93–106). París: UNESCO.

Featherstone, M. (2000). *Consumer culture and postmodernism*. London: Sage.

Ferrés, J. (1994a). *La publicidad, modelo para la enseñanza*. Madrid: Akal.

Ferrés, J. (1994b). *Televisión y educación*. Barcelona: Paidós.

Ferrés, J. (2000). *Educar en una cultura del espectáculo*. Barcelona: Paidós.

Ferrés, J. (2002). Televisión y comunicación inadvertidas, in *Educación para la comunicación. Televisión y multimedia* (interactive book). Madrid: Máster de Televisión Educativa y Corporación Multimedia.

Freire, P. (1980). *Pedagogía del oprimido*. Madrid: Siglo XXI.

Funes, V. (2005). Espectadores, los alumnos del siglo XXI. *Comunicar, 24*, 105–112.

García Matilla, A. (2002). Una televisión para la educación en el siglo XXI. Mucho más que un servicio público esencial, in *Educación para la comunicación. Televisión y multimedia* (interactive book). Madrid: Master de Televisión Educativa y corporación Multimedia.

Goldman, R. (1992). *Reading ads socially*. New York: Routledge.

González Requena, J. (1995). *El discurso televisivo: espectáculo de la posmodernidad*. Madrid: Cátedra.

González Requena, J., and Ortiz de Zárate, A. (1995). *El espot publicitario. La metamorfosis del deseo*. Madrid: Cátedra.

Gutiérrez Martín, A. (2002). Nuevos medios y productos para la educación: ¿un nuevo modelo de comunicación educativa?. In *Educación para comunicación. Televisión y multimedia* (interactive book). Madrid: Máster de Televisión Educativa y corporación Multimedia.

Jakobson, R. (1963). *Essais de linguistique générale. Trad. franc. et introduction de N. Ruwt*. Paris: Editions de Minuit.

Kaplún, M. (1998). *Una pedagogía de la comunicación.* Madrid: Akal.

Kilbourne, J. (2000). *Can't buy my love. How advertising changes the way we think and feel.* New York: Touchstone.

Lazar, J. (1985). *École, communication, télévision.* París: PUF.

Lomas, C. (1996a). *El espectáculo del deseo (usos y formas de la persuasión publicitaria).* Barcelona: Octaedro.

Lomas, C. (1996b). A este lado del Edén (Ética, estética y retórica de la publicidad). *Textos, 7*, 53–68.

Luke, C. (coord.) (1999). *Feminismos y pedagogías de la vida cotidiana.* Madrid: Alianza.

Mattelart, A. (1991). *La publicité.* Paris: Editions La Découverte.

McLuhan, M. (1987). *El medio es el masaje.* Barcelona: Paidós.

Péninou, G. (1972). *Intelligence de la Publicite. Étude sémiotique.* Paris: Robert Laffont.

Pérez Tornero, J. (1994). *El desafío educativo de la televisión.* Barcelona: Paidós.

Pérez Tornero, J.M., Tropea, F., Sanagustín P., and Costa, P.O. (1992). *La seducción de la opulencia. Publicidad, moda y consumo.* Barcelona: Paidós.

Prieto Castillo, D. (1987). *Discurso autoritario y comunicación alternativa.* México: Premia Editora.

Ramonet, I. (1981). *Le Chewing-gum des yeux.* Paris: Alain Moreau.

Saborit, J. (1994). *La imagen publicitaria en televisión.* Madrid: Cátedra.

CHAPTER ELEVEN

If Ideas WERE Fashion

DAVID WONG AND DANAH HENRIKSEN

INTRODUCTION

Standing in a Paris Metro subway, somewhere between Les Champs d'Elysees and L'Arc de Triomphe, I gaze at the glossy placards above the seated passengers. Givenchy, Piaget, Lancome … a variety of alluring, attractive images. I think about the thousands of Metro riders who also gaze at these evocative images and, perhaps, are inspired to imagine a different world, a different way of living. As I scan the stretch of images along the line of the windows, my gaze suddenly stops. It's a simple, but engaging graphic of the earth and a single star. To one side, it says (in French), "When you look at Alpha Centauri—the closest star to Earth—you are watching something that happened over four years ago." Like the images for perfume and furs on either side, here is an advertisement, except it's for a science idea. Here in Paris, where the distinction between style and living is beautifully blurred, I am inspired to wonder, "What if ideas were fashion?"

WHY CONSIDER IDEAS AS FASHION?

We are fascinated with fashion. In its presence we look or turn away, imitate or reject, admire or dismiss. We spend an extraordinary amount of time, energy, and money to fashion ourselves and the world around us. Middle and high school students are especially fashion conscious. Most students would agree that their lives are made more interesting, meaningful, and beautiful by fashion.

We as educators should be envious of the intensity of observation and imagination associated with students' fascination with fashion. If only our own teaching could be as engaging. We may also wish that our teaching transformed the students' world as much as the experience of fashion seems to. Thus, we propose that provocative implications emerge from the question, "What if ideas—substance of school—were fashion?" We discuss how the phenomenon of fashion can be a framework for thinking about teaching and learning.

To propose that subject-matter ideas could be fashion is to imply similarities between the *New York Times* Style section and the *Educational Researcher* Featured Article section, between FCUK and F=MA, between students in school halls and students in shopping malls. Within the circles of "serious-minded" scholarship, our proposal runs the risk of crossing the fine line between the cutting edge and over the edge of scholarship. Here are a few reasons why we think it is a risk worth taking.

Fashion is a deeply engaging experience. Fashion fascinates middle and high school students. One only needs to note the amount of time, energy, and resources they expend on fashion to be convinced. Furthermore, fashion engages not just young people but adults as well, not just in this culture but across cultures, and not just today but throughout the ages. We call fashion a "deep inclination" because the attraction to fashion has been evident in a wide variety of people over long periods of time. Because fashion is a deep inclination, we propose that it has the potential to be the basis for creating powerful educational experiences.

We note here that the primary goal of our work is to identify new ways in which school can become more compelling to students. We begin by first looking at the kinds of situations in which students seem to be naturally deeply engaged. The casual observer may note that this is already the cornerstone for pedagogical strategies such as student-centered instruction. In these approaches, the basic task is to describe how the subject matter of school can be connected to topics that interest students. In our approach, we are less concerned with topical similarities between the students' lives in and out of the classroom and more concerned with finding similar experiential qualities between life in and out of school. For example, in fashion experiences students are compelled by the imaginative consideration of possibilities and by visual or tactile forms of expression. They may be fleetingly transformed or revived in the experience of fashion. If this is so, we recommend that educators strive to create instructional experiences that similarly enliven students.

Thus, our intention is not simply to suggest that teaching should be more engaging by making connections to things that are currently hip or "in fashion" among students (although this is not a bad idea and is the main thrust of most approaches that take students' interests seriously). Instead, we recommend that educators become more attuned to the psychological qualities that make the experience of fashion so absorbing. With this knowledge teachers may begin to create experiences with similar qualities in the classroom.

How can the substance of school be similar to objects of fashion? To equate ideas with iPods may seem a contrived metaphor with little redeeming value.

Yet we would ask scholars to hold off this reflexive reaction, and engage in some "methodological belief" and willingly "try on" an unconventional perspective (Elbow, 1986). In moments of playful open-mindedness, we might consider how the underlying psychological, social, and cultural dynamics in the rise of a new fashion item—say an iPod—are similar to the dynamics of being absorbed by a new idea in class. Both involve the awakening of perception, the engagement of thinking and feeling, and the interchange of viewpoints and experiences with others. Without making any claims about the relative worth of iPod and school ideas, we can agree that the experiences share educationally relevant qualities.

We push the comparison further and point to one notable difference: students rarely find the experience of school as engaging as fashion. By "engaging," we refer to more than the engagement of the emotion, but also to the intellect— the very part of the student that schools seek to stimulate and develop. Anyone who doubts that fashion engages the intellect need only look at teenagers playing popular video games. Notice the detail in their observations, the depth of their knowledge, and the richness of their discussion and analysis. Similarly, in the realm of fashion experience we can find the same sharpness of perception and the same sensitivity to detail and nuance. If only students could distinguish the differences between plant and animal cells as easily and eagerly as some can distinguish real from knockoff Louis Vuitton handbags!

To fashion is to imagine, create, and express. It should be clear by this point that we are primarily concerned with the experience of fashion and not with the objects of fashion. Of particular importance in the experience of fashion are the involvement of the imagination and the consideration of the possible. Whether trying on a new outfit or designing a science project, the fashion experience evokes anticipating, hoping, dreaming, wishing, desiring, and becoming. The energy, drama, and meaning of the experience are in exploring the imaginative bridge between the actual and an allusive possibility. At its best, education can and should do the same. Within the framework of Dewey's aesthetics, the meaning of intense, transformative experiences emerges from exploring the imaginative bridge between the actual and the possible (Dewey, 1934; Jackson, 1998).

Although we have pointed out the ways that fashion fascinates people and is an integral part of what it means to be human, we also recognize that there may be a strong negative reaction to our suggestion that ideas could be fashion. There is no shortage of aphorisms expressing this sentiment:

"Fashion is something that goes in one year and out the other."
Denise Klahn, writer.

"Fashion, n. A despot whom the wise ridicule and obey." *The Devil's Dictionary*, 1911.
Ambrose Bierce, writer.

"We forfeit three-fourths of ourselves to be like other people."
Arthur Schopenhauer, philosopher.

"I cannot and will not cut my conscience to fit this year's fashions." In a letter to Committee on Un-American Activities of the House of Representatives, 1952. Lillian Hellman, playwright.

We acknowledge that the lens of fashion has pitfalls as well as potential. Ironically, many authors and readers of this volume may be among the most severe critics of the fashion idea. Those who are familiar with societal inequities and cultural means by which these inequities are sustained are likely to be especially wary of the realm of fashion. Furthermore, although the fashion metaphor emphasizes inspired imagination and original expression, it can also connote frivolous action and slavish conformity.

But, what provocative metaphor of learning has ever been immune to unflattering interpretation? Associationist models of learning were seen as simplistic and mechanical, the computer metaphor was devoid of emotion, the expert/novice paradigm smacked of authoritarianism, and the various forms of postmodern perspectives have been dismissed as hopelessly relativistic. We think of it this way: A metaphor or perspective is a suggestion to be explored rather than an assertion to be proven as true or false, or good or bad. The role of the metaphor is to express a new idea in a comprehensible way or an existing idea with renewed clarity and power. In their role as professionals, teachers explore these possibilities and determine for themselves the meaning and value of any new idea. We hope the fashion metaphor is unusual and provocative and, thus, has potential to lead the open-minded educator to explore new possibilities for engaging their students.

To ensure that the metaphor is understood, we define key terms clearly and specify what is and is not part of association between fashion and learning. First, we define the educative fashion experience as one that is mindful, rather than mindless. Sure there are both kinds … the key is to understand the difference. By "mindful" we are not suggesting that the experience should be a dry intellectual activity but rather one of vital and lively perception.

Second, we see value in emphasizing the creative aspect of fashion. Life is made more interesting, meaningful, artful and beautiful in fashion. In fact, when "fashion" is considered as an active verb-meaning "to form"—an undeniably creative and existential flavor emerges. In an existentialist's worldview the meaning of life is created primarily through individual choices and actions. Thus, the relationship between fashion and life takes on even greater significance. We might see that all our conscious acts, even the act of not acting, are existential choices, or "fashion statements." To fashion something, be it an idea or an artifact, is to give meaning to one's existence (Dewey, 1958; Nietzsche, 1978; Sartre, 1943). In this light, the intense curiosity that students have for fashion is more than interest in mere accoutrements but in a deeper, more significant desire to become a certain kind of person (Back, 1985; Brubach, 1999; Davis, 1992; Steele, 1985).

Further consideration of the meaning of fashion as an act of creating highlights its close relationship with "style." Interestingly, common perceptions seem to be much more positive about style than fashion. Perhaps the term "style" better conveys individuality and expression of self, whereas "fashion" connotes conformity and suppression of self.

"The style is the man himself."
Greek proverb

"Proper words in proper places make the true definition of style."
Jonathan Swift, writer.

"The most original thing a writer can do is to write like himself. It is also his most difficult task."

Robertson Davies, writer.

Thus, if we consider that fashion can mean to style or to create, then the purpose of education is to help students "to fashion" a worthwhile existence, rather than "to be in fashion." Indeed, the elements of style—originality, flair, and confidence—seem to describe equally well the goals of both fashion and education.

How to find a good idea: Taking a fresh perspective on enduring educational issues. Although scholarship in education values originality, it is, in fact, an inherently conservative endeavor. The value of any new piece of work is largely associated with the degree to which it is grounded in and gives credit to the work that preceded it. The explicit and implicit conventions of scholarship demand that new ideas be firmly grounded in an existing conceptual framework or legitimately born from one of the "parent" disciplines such as psychology, philosophy, anthropology, and sociology (Shulman, 1986).

In this spirit, we wish to acknowledge the "family resemblance" of our work to other scholarship in education. The metaphor of learning as the fashion of ideas actually shares much in common with mainstream metaphors such as learning as identity formation, learning as participation in meaningful shared activity, and learning as language appropriation (e.g., Gergen, 1994; Lave and Wenger, 1990; Vygotsky, 1978). Connections to other scholarship facilitate the comprehension and assimilation of new ideas and lessen the possibility that new ideas might be summarily rejected because they seem too incomprehensible or unconventional.

Sometimes, new ideas emerge from within an existing paradigm—a conceptual system that provides a perspective for seeing, describing, and understanding educational phenomena such as highly motivated behavior. At other times, as with our work, new ideas are conceived outside the parent disciplines. Instead of returning to academic disciplines for inspiration, we looked at culture, broadly speaking, for ideas about highly motivated behavior. We looked at both pop culture and art culture; we looked at contemporary culture as well as culture through history. We asked, "What kinds of phenomena do people seem to be deeply engaged by across time and across age groups?" One enduring phenomena of fascination was fashion: people of all ages, across time, are drawn to fashion. (Examples of other "deep inclinations" include an almost innate fascination with sublime experiences, the idea of redemption, sex and violence, heroes, and tales of love overcoming great odds.)

(Note: Our break from the parent disciplines may remind some readers of action research (e.g., Carr and Kemmis, 1986) and grounded theory (e.g., Glaser, 1992). However, there are significant differences in how we identify phenomena of interest and develop central constructs.)

One final thought on this matter: given the relatively minimal impact of educational scholarship on educational practice in the past century, we feel safe in pointing to a need—perhaps a dire need—for educational scholarship that reaches beyond our "parent disciplines" in search of new ideas. There is no shortage of intelligent people in the areas of fashion, advertising, and marketing. Professionals in these domains regularly affect the lives of many people. We have much to learn from them.

THROUGH THE LENS OF FASHION: WHAT WE MIGHT SEE IF WE CONSIDERED IDEAS AS FASHION

Once we identified fashion as a "deep inclination," we took a closer look at its expression in classic and contemporary art, literature, and scholarship. In this process, we gained a deeper appreciation for the phenomenon and a firmer basis for generating implications for education. We searched for fashion phenomena in which people—especially young people—were deeply engaged. In this section, we discuss two examples—the Apple iPod and the television show *What Not to Wear (WNTW)*. These examples are contemporary and popular—hardly the kind of citations one finds in the literature reviews of most serious scholarship. However, there is no denying the audience's intensity of attention, imagination, and eagerness associated with these particular phenomena. Because this kind of intense engagement is a central aim of educators, we believe there are lessons to be learned from a closer examination of these fashion phenomena.

THE APPLE IPOD: FASHION, ADVERTISING, IDEAS, TEACHING

The Apple iPod is a portable digital music player that comes in a variety of colors, sizes, and storage capacities. First introduced in 2002, the iPod has since become a massive commercial success. Although many other portable digital music players are available, the iPod has become the must-have item and in 2005 dominated the competition with an astounding 87 percent share of the market (actually down from a high of 92 percent). What accounts for the iPod's success? Granted, iPods are a well-designed piece of technology, but we might also say this of a kitchen spatula. With apologies to architect Michael Graves and his line of high-fashion kitchen utensils available at your local Target store, the iPod is more likely to be at the top of many gift wish lists. Among the many brands of portable, digital music players on the market, the iPod is the most coveted. Something has elevated the iPod beyond pleasant functionalism into the realm of fashion. Ask for an explanation from young iPod owners and you are likely to hear that iPods are, in a word, cool. Why is the iPod such a fashion phenomenon and what can we educators learn from it?

Silhouettes: Ads and the Inspiration of Imagination

It may be important to observe that not only is the iPod itself considered cool, but the advertisements for the iPod are also the objects of intense observation and discussion. The "Silhouettes" ads are probably the best known in the iPod advertising campaign. These ads have appeared in print, television, and Internet media and consist of dancing silhouettes against a solid neon background. The Silhouette ad campaign was created by the TBWA\Chiat\Day advertising firm and won the Grand EFFIE Award (the preeminent award in the world of advertising/marketing that recognizes "creative achievement in meeting and exceeding advertising objectives"). The awards are based two-thirds on results achieved and one-third on creativity. Seth Stevenson (2004), a reporter for Slate and National Public Radio, described the iPod ads in this way:

> let's talk about what the ads get right. For one, the songs (from groups like Jet and Black Eyed Peas) are extremely well-chosen. Just indie enough so that not everybody knows them; just mainstream enough so that almost everybody likes them. But as good as the music is, the visual concept is even better. It's incredibly simple: never more than three distinct colors on the screen at any one time, and black and white are two of them. What makes it so bold are those vast swaths of neon monochrome. This simplicity highlights the dance moves, but also—and more importantly—it high-lights the iPod. The key to it all is the silhouettes. What a brilliant way to showcase

a product. Almost everything that might distract us—not just background scenery, but even the actors' faces and clothes—has been eliminated. All we're left to focus on is that iconic gizmo. What's more, the dark black silhouettes of the dancers perfectly offset the iPod's gleaming white cord, earbuds, and body.

"Silhouettes" is, indeed, a powerful ad. The music and images converge to create a compelling sense of style and cool. The ad seizes the viewer's attention and attunes them to the concept of the iPod.

Of course, not every ad is as compelling as "Silhouettes," nor is every viewer moved by these ads, nor is every person crazy about iPods. Thus, in order to understand how the ad works its magic we start with the assumption that there is nothing inherently compelling about the ad itself, nor about the iPod. The experience of any ad, product, or idea becomes compelling when there is a certain quality to the interaction between it and the audience. What are these qualities? In our opinion, the magic of fashion is that it inspires the imagination. iPods and Silhouettes are cool for this very reason. Specifically, there is a consideration of possibilities, of a world that could be. The realm of imaginative possibility can include personal and interpersonal qualities, physical, intellectual, and emotional capacities, or the nature of the world around us. In the experience of fashion, as we move back and forth between what is and what could be, we feel movement, growth, and a greater sense of vitality.

How do the iPod Silhouettes ads inspire the imagination? Here are a few possibilities:

- The dancers are vibrant and expressive: those who respond to "Silhouettes" are likely to also wish they could be so able to be so beautifully moved by music.
- The music, image of the person, and the movement are ultrahip. The more you aspire to be part of the culture suggested in the ad, the more compelling it will be.
- The design of the ad focuses our attention on certain things and not on others. Like good teaching, the art of the ad is to draw attention to what is important. In the case of Silhouettes, it is music, movement, freedom, fun, and, of course, the iPod itself.
- Silhouettes both seizes and holds our attention. The sound, contrast, movement, colors are "catchy" and grab our attention right away. However, like all good advertising, art, and, teaching, the beholder is rewarded for spending time and looking closer (see Dewey's 1913, *Interest and Effort in Education* for a discussion of catching and holding attention.) For example, the silhouettes turn out not to be quite completely monochromatic black. In the nuances of shading, the careful observer begins to see

facial features, clothing, and accessories (other than the iPod). Also, after repeated viewing, one cannot help wonder "how did they do that?" The amount of discussion on the Internet on this topic attests to Silhouettes power to catch and hold viewers' interest.

To wish, to aspire, to hope, and to wonder involve the imaginative consideration of possibilities. The possibility of being alive with greater skill or intensity is compelling.

The experience continues beyond the advertisement to the product itself. The power of the ads is related to the degree that the imaginative bridge spans reality and a conceivable possibility. It is difficult to feel compelled by that which is completely beyond the realm of the possible. "Silhouettes" and other effective fashion experiences create fantasies that lie beyond what exists but not so far beyond that they seem impossible or unattainable. To the degree that "to exist" means to live, the stretching of existence from what is to what could be is, literally, to expand what it is to be alive.

Beyond the Ad: From Imagined Possibility to Fashioned Reality

So far in this discussion of iPod ads, the focus has been on the experience of the advertisement. Granted the experience of the ad may be compelling, but what else is? What happens when the commercial is over? When the page is turned? Is the experience of fashion only in the moment? First, the value of experiences that are "only in the moment" should not be diminished for one simple reason: life is "only" a series of moments. Furthermore, a deeply felt moment leaves an impression that, in turn, shapes future moments. As Einstein famously noted, "A mind that has been stretched will never return to its original dimension."

Thus, the real issue of concern to educators is how the "momentary" experience of the advertisement influences subsequent moments of experience. The belief that present experiences either enhance or diminish possibilities for subsequent experiences was fundamental to Dewey's (1938) philosophy and views of education (he called it the "principle of continuity of experience"). Furthermore, the imaginative consideration of possibilities was an integral element of learning. In educative experiences, possibilities are not only conceived but explored. From this exploration come new perceptions, relations with the world, and understanding and sensitivity.

The goal of all advertising and marketing is to get people to invest in a product. What happens to the experience over once a person has purchased an iPod? For some, nothing: the ad is observed, perhaps with "interest," but nothing subsequent is affected. Others may be compelled by the ad to purchase an iPod. As a fashion phenomenon, individuals may "try on" some of the imagined possibilities to see how they "fit" with who they are or would like to become. Perhaps, in their lives with an iPod, they will listen more intently to music or dance with new enthusiasm. Perhaps, they will see themselves or others will see them as more sophisticated or cool. Perhaps, the iPod will open up new opportunities for interacting with others by sharing music or the details of each other's iPod experiences. In these ways, fashion and ideas live on beyond the immediate experience of advertisements.

Silhouette's Implications for Education: Image and Imagination

The power of images. In the iPod's Silhouette ads, the look, the sound, and the movements all cohere to give the ad a distinct feel of style and fun. For other ads, the feel can be completely different. For example, Nike's famous "Freestyle" shoe commercials exude grace, athleticism and confidence. Old Kodak film commercials were well known for their dripping sentimentalism. The *feel* or *sense* is the heart of the aesthetic experience—it is what strikes us first, moves us through the experience, and lingers with us afterward. To create images that evoke a distinctive and powerful feel is central to the art of fashion and advertising. It is also central to the art of teaching.

Images and descriptions abound in school textbooks, posters, and lectures. Why is it that these images usually fail to seize the students' imagination? Perhaps, these images are typically not artistic—that is, they were not created to evoke an aesthetic experience. Instead, many images are intended to be descriptive or illustrative and represent ideas in a straightforward manner. However, in artistic images, ideas are evoked rather than represented. The images are more implicit than explicit, more connotative than denotative. Imaginative thought and feeling are stirred in situations that are suggestive, alluring, and intriguing.

Let us reconsider the images we might use in schools. What if teachers and students in art, creative writing, or multimedia courses were given the charge to create images that stirred the hearts and minds of students? The intent of these "image makeovers" would be for these visual, aural, and textual pieces to become more artistic in their design and more aesthetic in their experience.

The all important "buzz" When it comes to subject matter ideas, how often do students excitedly ask their friends "have you heard...?" or "did you see...?" Any marketer will tell you that the buzz—the spontaneous sharing of information—is a crucial to the success of any product. The buzz can emerge in a variety of ways. For example, what exactly made Juicy Couture the uniform of choice for the high school crowd? Perhaps, in a saturated market, the faint buzz that resonates below the radar might have had a larger impact than the ubiquitous campaigns.

The fact that Juicy's fame developed through word of mouth steeped the company in cultish cool from the onset. Also, the genius of Juicy's often explicitly monikered clothing is the inherent self-promotional factor. Whether adorning the likes of a Hollywood hipster or teenage trendsetter, there is never a question as to who created the ounce of cotton proudly proclaiming "Juicy Debutante" or "Old School Juicy." Much of Juicy Couture's perceived legitimacy among teenagers is rooted in the joint adoration of peers and idols, rather than in a manufactured image hyped by a corporate entity. Students have literally given the company its advertising legs, strutting their logo-emblazoned drawstring pants throughout the corridors of high schools across America.

Although the way that the buzz comes about may vary from one fashion phenomenon to another, the bottom line is that people are spontaneously talking about IT. The energy of the buzz is evident in the telltale phrases "Have you seen ..." or "Have you heard ..." If subject-matter ideas are to be fashion, then educators need to become more savvy about the nature of "the buzz" and how to create it.

The model image. When we consider the images of fashion, we may be inclined to think of the celebrities. We may be tempted to think that star power is a driving force in any fashion happening. For example, Nike ads are famous for featuring well-known athletes at the height of their careers. Nike maintains an absurdly deep stable of superstar athletes—Tiger Woods, Michael Jordan, Mia Hamm, and Lance Armstrong—to name only a few. However, it would be shortsighted to conclude that we are compelled by fashion only because of the celebrity image. Successful advertising campaigns have been created both with and without recognizable celebrities (T-Mobile's Catherine Zeta-Jones and Verizon's "Can you hear me now?" guy or U2 singing and anonymous silhouettes dancing on iPod commercials).

If successful ads do not necessarily involve celebrities, we might think that these ads are successful because the people are attractive. The people in the iPod ads may not be celebrities, but their silhouettes make it clear that they are attractive and talented. Or, make a quick flip through any magazine and you are likely to encounter images of people who may not be celebrities but are still more attractive, much more attractive, than ordinary folks. The world of fashion and advertising seems to be the exclusive the domain of attractive people. Is this true, and is it a problem?

Certainly, celebrity and attractive people help to draw attention to a product. There's no point in trying to debate or over-theorize this simple observation. It is not our task in this chapter to conjecture about whether this inclination is cultural, biological, learned or otherwise. It is also not our intent to go on at length about the social and moral implications of this inclination. Suffice to say, our fascination with certain kinds of people is a powerful inclination. This inclination has the potential for both positive and negative consequences. Our primary task in this chapter is to appreciate the positive potential and to consider ways this potential can be developed for educational purposes. We take our inclination to notice attractive people as a matter of fact and a starting point for other considerations. Questions such as "What makes someone attractive in addition to celebrity status and physical beauty?" emerge as more interesting to us than whether this inclination is good or bad.

We suspect that the people in successful ads, whether they are well-known or not, represent ideas in ways that evoke feelings of connection and possibility. Thus, a picture of Einstein standing at a chalkboard may not actually be the best advertising image for the laws of gravitation. Do kids really relate to him as a person, or is it just that crazy hair? Also, the iconic image of Einstein with his tongue out does not really give the feel of what it would be like to really be moved by a physics idea. The iPod Silhouette ad, by contrast, directly expresses the experience of being with the iPod. You want to get an iPod because you want to be part of that experience. Thus, if the science teacher's goal is to sell a science idea, perhaps a more compelling image would show an anonymous high school student in the grip of a powerful idea. For example, the ad might express her dawning realization that both she and the moon in the night sky are held captive by the gravitational attraction with the Earth.

WHAT NOT TO WEAR: FASHION, TEACHING, AND LEARNING

In this section, we focus more directly on the issue of practice and address the question, "If ideas were fashion, how might we teach?" To begin, we emphasize that there is no one right way to teach ideas as fashion. We endorse any instructional approach that inspires students to imagine possibilities, helps them create an existence that is more worthwhile and beautiful, and, in general, provides opportunities for them to experience how "cool" ideas can be.

It may be coincidence, but there has been a recent convergence of fashion and instruction in popular culture. The "expert re-fashioning" genre seems to be more popular than ever on television. In one week of cable television program viewing, one can observe experts helping novices refashion their clothes, hair, face, and body. And, the inclination to make over does not stop at personal appearance. Other targets of expert-assisted renovation include one's house, car, family, and lifestyle.

We emphasize again that we make no claims about the value of any of these programs or any fashion phenomenon in general. Our point is that the popularity of these programs is evidence for a strong interest in being helped at fashioning. These shows tap into something and we aim to understand this source of potential energy.

There are many examples in this expert re-fashioning genre. We focus on one of the most popular, longest running shows. *What Not to Wear (WNTW)* is a hugely popular show on Discovery's The Learning Channel with a relatively simple premise: two style experts, Stacey London and Clinton Kelly, help re-create the fashion sensibilities of a person who has been deemed to need a "fashion intervention." Within the larger framework of the ideas-as-fashion metaphor, the format of this show may be woven into an educational representation, considering subject-matter ideas and learning in the same light as new clothes and fashion sensibility.

Each episode begins with a different candidate, nominated by friends and family members to receive style expertise and advice, as well as a budget for a new wardrobe. The process begins by breaking down the participant's fashion missteps and misguided ideas with a brutally honest evaluation from resident experts Stacey and Clinton. Acceptance of the benefits of a fashion budget, advice and stylized look is contingent upon the participant's willingness to try new things, be open to a new personal fashion sensibility and recognize its effect upon both their intrinsic life and their experience of the world. They must allow the experts to honestly critique and in many cases throw away (or donate) their existing wardrobe in favor of a fresh set of ideas.

These new fashion ideas are important in that they are tailored to the personality and individualism of each participant. There is no "one-size-fits-all" approach to putting everyone in a universal trendy look, but fashion is viewed as a means to visually express something about oneself and to experiment with a personal aesthetic. The primary rule for learning about fashion here is that *"you've got to try it on"* in order to fully experience the possibilities of a concept. Though participants may initially doubt the hosts' advice, they must try their suggestions and consider them fully before deciding to accept or reject them. The result is that individuals often come to appreciate items that they never would have considered and develop a more educated sense of what works and does not work.

Since its inception several years ago, the show has styled many participants, each with a distinctive flavor and unique vibe to their new look. There are of course, some general rules for good all around fashion sense (i.e., kick those socks and sandals to the curb), but for the most part each person is treated as a distinct individual in the experience.

The final stage is the reveal when the individual presents their new look and discusses the ways in which their outlook on fashion and on themselves has evolved. Final comments and reactions have been marked almost overwhelmingly by a positive shift in self-image and associations with fashion, which begs the question of why does fashion and style create such a distinct and positive feeling of excitement for the participants and the audience?

We hang art on our walls and decorate our homes to complement and express ourselves in our surroundings. Why do we find fashion, and the feeling that it creates, so compelling? Ultimately there are two questions that can be anticipated within the fashion/learning associations that we draw. Although we find *WNTW* to be a persuasive format, the first question to ask is, "What difference does it make, what you wear?" This question begs the same answer as its education-centered counterpart, "Why should it intrinsically matter to the student what they think or what they learn?" The answer to both questions may be that these things, ideas, and fashions create a reflection from within. We take cues and images of the self through the ways in which the world sees us. Identity is, to some degree, always a reflection of the world around us. In the *WNTW* ideal, this is referred to as "style from the inside out." Fashion and appearances are explicit ways to affect these cues—but what students may come to realize is that ideas and knowledge have value for this same reason.

WNTW and Implications for Learning

The expert/novice paradigm revised. With its clear emphasis on the right and wrong way to do things and the passing on of wisdom from teacher to student, the model of instruction in *WNTW* may seem glaringly old "fashioned" and outdated. Progressive educators would question how learners could possibly voice their own ideas or take charge of their own learning given Stacy and Clinton's teacher-centered didactics. Similarly, scholars of the postmodernist cloth would surely object to the experts' privileged access to the truth about what not to wear. Oh, the hegemony!

It may seem strange to note that Stacy and Clinton are hardly alone in being out of step with the current educational mindset. Numerous other television programs follow a similar expert-centered approach to dispensing advice. One need only glance at the program schedule for The Learning Channel or Home and Garden Television to witness our collective eagerness to sit at the feet of experts.

Similarly, one would be hard pressed to find shows that feature the egalitarian learning community favored by many progressive and postmodern educators. Why can't Stacy and Clinton be "guides on the side" rather than "sages on the stage" and encourage their students to explore their own fashion ideas? Even the Socratic Method—a perfect blend of progressive student centeredness and *WNTW*'s confrontational dramatics (at least, when Socrates was the teacher)— has not been picked up by any of the popular instructional television shows. Why is this so?

The easy explanation would be that the instructional methods of *WNTW* serve the primary goal of catching and holding the interest of the television audience.

This is popular television after all and, therefore, strives to entertain rather than educate. However, only the most puritanically serious-minded critic would insist on such a stern separation between entertainment and education. To think that a good educational experience does not entertain and that good entertainment does not educate is just plain wrong. In fact, we suggest that *WNTW*'s appeal has a lot to do with its educative qualities. Stacy and Clinton are engaging not only as actors but also as educators. We enjoy watching their dramatic methods precisely because they are so self-assured, strong, and direct. Furthermore, their teaching engages not only because of its dramatic methods, but because of its dramatic effects. Most of the "learners" on the show begin with skepticism or flat-out resistance but end up expressing sincere gratitude for the way the experience changed them. Thus, it would be simplistic and arrogant to dismiss the pedagogy of *WNTW* as having "only" entertainment value.

If we took the popularity of *WNTW* and its relatives seriously, here's what we might see. First, we would quickly realize that professionals working in the fields of art, fashion, entertainment, and education share the same goal of creating compelling experiences for their audiences. In considering ideas as fashion, we might see learning new ideas as an aesthetic phenomenon and that educators have much to learn from those who have a highly sophisticated appreciation for the aesthetic qualities of powerful experiences.

Second, *WNTW* illustrates how professionals in arts and entertainment are adept at finding and evoking dramatic tension. The creators of *WNTW* understand how to artfully work the tension between good and poor ideas, teacher and student, and what is and what could be.

Third, even though *WNTW* resembles the traditional expert-novice paradigm of teaching, its basic epistemology has been significantly "updated" (to use a term borrowed from home design shows). In the typical expert-novice study, the expert and novice define the beginning and end of a continuum of learning. Instruction relies on the force of logical reasoning to move novices closer to the experts' way of seeing. *WNTW*, along with the metaphor of ideas-as-fashion, highlights how learning is motivated not just by the power of abstract reason but also by the real, practical consequences of the idea. In this updated version of the expert-novice approach, "teachers propose and learners dispose." That is, the expert gives reasons why the suggestion is a good one and really "works" for the person. In the end, however, it always comes down to the individual's own lived experience with the idea/fashion. Thus, unlike the classic expert/novice model, it is not a foregone conclusion that learners will move closer to the expert's point of view. However, because ideas are fashion, they will have tried on the idea, experienced its effect, and, as a result, have a greater appreciation for it.

Educational scholars will remind us that Dewey offered this same perspective on learning long ago. In fact, basing meaning in the practical consequences of an idea is a central feature of pragmatism as expressed by philosophers such as Charles Peirce, William James, and Richard Rorty, as well as John Dewey. We are not so ahistorical and besotted by *WNTW* as to proclaim Stacy and Clinton as visionaries of a new philosophy of meaning. Instead, we suggest that *WNTW* provides a compelling, contemporary illustration of pragmatism's central argument. *WNTW* reminds us that ideas, like fashion, must be lived in and experienced in order to understand, appreciate, and judge their meaning and significance.

IF IDEAS WERE FASHION: A FEW OTHER PROVOCATIVE IMPLICATIONS

Our goal here is to enliven the perception of our readers. In case the metaphor of ideas as fashion and the examples from popular culture have failed to be sufficiently provocative, we offer two final implications.

Style is substance. For many, this idea strikes a jarring and dissonant note. The distinction between the realm of style and the more substantial matters seems natural and intuitive. Indeed, it is a contrast that runs deep in our society. In schools, we want our students to learn substance: that which is deep, meaningful, and enduring. In contrast, we are inclined to think of style as that which is superficial and ephemeral. In art, style may be the form or technique of a painting but not its meaning. In language, style is the manner of expression but not the content. Yet so much of the weight of an artist's message is inextricable to its form. Similarly, the meaning of language is not just in the words, but how the words are expressed. (See Postrel's *Substance of Style* [2003] and Sontag's "On Style," in her book *Against Interpretation* [1966] for two different takes on why the separation of style from substance is not particularly worthwhile.) Finally, consider the classic "big question": where is the meaning and significance of one's life? Is it somewhere within us—bestowed upon us by another or inherited from others? Or, perhaps, it exists in living—created and re-created in our interactions and experiences. Life's meaning and value—its most important quality—is on the surface and ever changing. Thus, life's meaning, its very substance, is fashioned.

Teaching as advertising, learning as shopping. When exploring the realm of ideas as fashion, one soon encounters the association between fashion and consumer culture. This is a complicated issue, and once again, charges of superficiality and insubstantiality must be addressed. Granted, the consumer culture of fashion is a veritable breeding ground for vanity, greed, thoughtlessness, and other moral infirmities. "To consume" can mean to eat or drink in large amounts or to destroy something completely by fire or disease. A "consumable" is something that is impermanent, used up, or discarded after use. However, "to consume" also means to fill somebody's mind or attention fully (e.g., to be consumed in compelling or passionate experiences). All educators surely aspire to this intensity of engagement for their students. To be consumed in the experience of fashion can no doubt be perilous. This is true of all intense experiences. The lesson here is not to avoid intensity but to be aware of it, to modulate it, and, in the case of the novice, to trust in the wisdom and care of others.

If we can hold in abeyance the reflexive disdain we may have for consumer culture, other interesting implications may emerge. If ideas are fashion, then learning is the art of shopping. As good shoppers, students know how to be open to inspiration, "try on" many different things, and enjoy the experience. Ideas are to be tested in the same way as hats, scents, shoes, or music. We imagine, experience, and evaluate how a particular idea enriches our world. In this view, the task of the teacher is to educate the students' "shopper" sensibility and to help them have more intense and fulfilling shopping and fashion experiences. Experts in advertising and marketing make it their business to be attuned to the experience of the shopper and may be a source of helpful insights for educators (e.g., Rogers, 1983; Solomon, 1985; Underhill, 2000).

Similarly, if learning is shopping, then teaching is advertising. Teachers offer a well-chosen line of products—subject-matter ideas—and are skillful at promoting them. They realize that a fine balance exists between classic and trendy style. They are exquisitely sensitive to what moves their customers and skillful at creating needs where no need existed before. They are versed in the aesthetic and appreciate that new ideas must be felt—not just comprehended—before students can be moved. Finally, as merchandisers, teachers fully realize that the customer has every right to not like or "buy" what they are selling. Teachers cannot force their students to make their "product" part of their lives. The best educators can only hope—and this is no small hope—that students will fully experience and appreciate worthwhile subject-matter ideas. In both education and fashion, whether or not an idea finds a place in a student's way of life is a matter of "informed taste." In our opinion, this is a worthwhile goal of education.

No doubt, many people will find it crass to think of education in these terms. Unfortunately, this reaction does a double disservice. First, it turns a blind eye to the fact that schools have always been connected to the marketplace idea (Powell, Farrar, and Cohen, 1985), and considering questions of value and utility is essential to any thoughtful plan of education. Second, a quick dismissal idea of learner as shopper undervalues the experience of the shopper. The appeal of shopping spans all ages, all cultures, and all periods of history. Like fashion, the allure of shopping seems to be an example of what we have called a "deep inclination." Perhaps we overlook the value of the shopping experience because of the association between women and shopping. We should be especially cautious of this prejudice. This warning applies to men for obvious reasons, as well as women, for less obvious reasons. In an article appearing in *Vogue*, feminist scholar, Elaine Showalter (1997) boldly asserted, "But for those of us sisters hiding 'Welcome to Your Facelift' inside 'The Second Sex,' a passion for fashion can sometimes seem a shameful secret life. ... I think it's time I came out of the closet." Later, she added wryly, "For years ... I've been trying to make the life of the mind coexist with the day at the mall."

At times, the experience of shopping can be characterized by excessiveness that can easily spill over to gluttony. And, yes, shopping can be mind numbingly dull and can resemble a trancelike state of mind. However, in the moments when shopping becomes an act of fashioning it is an intensely human and vital experience filled with imagination, anticipation, inquiry, and reflection. As educators, we aspire to give our students this kind of experience.

CONCLUSION

The main task of our work is to find ways to make school experiences more engaging and meaningful to middle and high school students. To find provocative and worthwhile ways of conceptualizing this task, we looked not only to the field of education and its parent disciplines but also to the popular culture of the students' world and the kinds of experiences they find compelling. In this way, the "ideas-as-fashion" metaphor emerged.

Where do we go from here? Our plan is to seek the assistance of both educators and professionals from the world of marketing and advertising. As a team, we would develop an "ad campaign" to inspire students to find a few well-chosen school subject-matter ideas fashionable to think and talk about. Isn't it cool to consider that popular movies and classic literature draw on a small handful of powerful themes? Or doesn't it inspire the imagination to realize that plants are the only living things on Earth capable of converting the sun's energy into a form that can be used by animals? Granted these ideas have been around for a while and have yet to catch on. Despite this fact, we are not yet ready to give up. We should resist the urge to "blame" students for their lack of interest in these ideas. Perhaps, educators themselves must first believe that these ideas are genuinely cool. Perhaps we need to recruit the help of professionals who make it their business to make things fashionable. Some skeptics may still have difficulty imagining how these ideas could be fashionable in any way. However, this vision becomes more viable when one considers how "incredulous" it is that oversized jeans, the Backstreet Boys, or the mullet hairstyle could have ever become wildly popular. Our "advertising campaign" for creating a fashion of ideas will have three elements: evocative print ads for the ideas, a strategy for creating a "buzz" among students about the ideas, and suggestions for developing a classroom culture that supports the fashion of ideas.

Some "serious-minded" educators may quickly judge our fascination with style and fashion as superficial and frivolous. They will question the appropriateness of finding scholarly inspiration in popular culture phenomena. We quietly suspect, though, that a significant portion of the educational community will be open to the suggestion that important contributions can come from places and people outside traditional academic circles. Yes, this work is "popular" in that ideas and examples are drawn from a pop-culture that is contemporary, public, and easily accessed, rather than an academic culture that is abstract, difficult to access, and arcane. However, because fashion is a deep human inclination, it is the kind of experience that can be found and appreciated across time periods, age groups, and culture. We believe the "ideas as fashion" metaphor may resonate deeply with three important audiences: scholars, practitioners, and students. If this were true, then these ideas are "popular" in every positive sense of the word.

REFERENCES

Back, K.W. (1985). Modernism and fashion: A social psychological interpretation. In M.R. Solomon (ed.), *The psychology of fashion* (pp. 3–14). Lexington, MA: D. C. Heath/Lexington Books.

Brubach, H. (1999). *A dedicated follower of fashion*. London: Phaidon Press.

Carr, W., and Kemmis, S. (1986). *Becoming critical: Education knowledge and action research*. London: Falmer Press.

Davis, F. (1992). *Fashion, culture, and identity*. Chicago: University of Chicago Press.

Dewey, J. (1913). *Interest and effort in education*. Boston: Houghton Mifflin.

Dewey, J. (1934). *Art as experience*. New York: Perigee Books.

Dewey, J. (1938). *Experience and education*. New York: Collier Books.

Dewey, J. (1958). *Experience and nature*. New York: Dover Publications.

Elbow, P. (1986). *Embracing contraries: Explorations in learning and teaching*. Oxford: Oxford University Press.

Gergen, K. (1994). *Realities and relationships: Soundings in social construction*. Cambridge, MA: Harvard University Press.

Glaser, B.G. (1992). *Basics of grounded theory analysis: Emergence vs. forcing*. Mill Valley, CA: Sociology Press.

Jackson, P. (1998). *John Dewey and the lessons of art*. New Haven, CT: Yale University Press.

Lave, J., and Wenger, E. (1990). *Situated learning: Legitimate peripheral participation*. Cambridge, UK: Cambridge University Press.

Nietzsche, F. (1978). *Thus spoke Zarathustra: A book for none and all* (W. Kaufmann, trans.). New York: Penguin.

Postrel, V. (2003). *The substance of style: How the rise of aesthetic value is remaking commerce, culture, and consciousness*. New York: Perennial.

Powell, A.G., Farrar, E., and Cohen, D.K. (1985). *The shopping mall high school: Winners and losers in the educational marketplace*. Boston: Houghton Mifflin.

Rogers, E.M. (1983). *Diffusion of innovations* (3rd ed., pp. 19–40, 175–196). New York: Free Press.

Sartre, J.-P. (1943). *Being and nothingness: An essay on phenomenological ontology* (H. Barnes, trans.). New York: Washington Square Press.

Showalter, E. (1997). The Professor Wore Prada. *Vogue*, December, pp. 80, 86, 92.

Shulman, L. (1986). Those who understand: Knowledge growth in teaching. *Educational Researcher*, *15*(2), 4–14.

Solomon, M.R. (ed.). (1985). *The psychology of fashion*. Lexington, MA: D. C. Heath/Lexington Books.

Sontag, S. (1966). On style. *Against interpretation and other essays* (pp. 15–36). New York: Farrar, Straus & Giroux.

Steele, V. (1985). *Fashion and eroticism*. New York: Oxford University Press.

Stevenson, S. (2004). You and your shadow. Posted on *Slate*, Tuesday, March 2, at 10:05 AM PT. Available online at http://www.slate.com/id/2096459/

Underhill, P. (2000). *Why we buy: The science of shopping*. New York: Simon and Schuster.

Vygotsky, L.S. (1978). *Mind in society: The development of higher psychological processes*. Cambridge, MA: Harvard University Press.

CHAPTER TWELVE

Popular Culture AND THE Teaching OF History: A Critical Reflection

CARLOS ANTONIO AGUIRRE ROJAS

Almost four decades from the salutary and important irruption of the worldwide Cultural Revolution in 1968, which unfolded and spread throughout the length and breadth of the entire world between 1966 and 1969, it is quite clear that this event has transformed the world in a profoundly radical and complete manner as well as the modern structure of the generation of knowledge, and the transmission of such knowledge, that is the contemporary school institution. Reference is made to a total transformation of the school apparatus, which not only explains the unusual popularity enjoyed by pedagogical science during the past three decades, but also the deep changes in relations between teachers and students, along with changes in teaching methods and the mutation of the social role itself of these academic spaces within global societies throughout the world.

Among so many other beneficial changes that this Revolution of 1968 (Aguirre-Rojas, 1993; Braudel, 1993; Wallerstein, 1991) brought with it, we can also count the definitive breaking off with the old hierarchical structure based on the *Magister Dixit* principle, which assumed that all of the knowledge within the classroom was concentrated in the professor, and it assigned to the students the role of passive parties receiving such knowledge. But when Chinese students legitimately questioned the disconnection of this knowledge learned in the classroom from the experiences of the real and everyday world, or when the French students cried out their slogan of "Professors, you are old! And your knowledge is also old!" what enters into a crisis is precisely the relationship of hierarchy between teachers and students, as well as that false assumption of the omniscient knowledge of professors in the face of total ignorance on the part of the students.

Then, there comes a reevaluation of the role of that collective student body in the process of generating knowledge, accepting their active and fundamental role within this academic space and redefining from this vantage point and in a global context the respective roles of the professors and of the students involved within these processes of teaching and learning. Thus, it is no coincidence that after 1968 one of the fundamental problems of modern pedagogy was precisely to establish how it might be possible to rescue the knowledge dispersed to students and to make it bloom within the classroom, and which knowledge, when recovered, can undoubtedly also generate newer and richer knowledge in regard to different studies and researched themes.

One of the essential lessons of the multiple 1968 cultural revolutions was to reintroduce *the active, creating, and generating roles of the great social groups* within the different social processes in which they participate daily, which not only became evident within the heart of educational institutions but also reproduced itself over the length and breadth of the social body, expressing itself in the cultural plane as well as in the historical plane, and that of economics, social relations, or the most diverse human spheres in all possible orders. These active and creative roles of these popular classes and masses, which up until recent times prior to the end of the 1960s, had been generally ignored, excluded, or even denied by the immense majority of social scientists in general.

Therefore, it is not a question of sheer chance that ever since seven lustrums ago, the technique of *oral* history has grown and expanded and become popular, subject to the idea that those who really *make* history should also be the ones to help in *constructing* and *writing* such history. Then again, it has only been a few decades since the beginning of *social* history, that of those great collective actors of history, ended up by giving itself complete legitimacy in practically all of the historiographies of the world, causing the flourishing of studies related to popular beliefs or regarding the daily lives of the working classes or in connection with the peasant economy of vast rural groups subject to the societies before the French Revolution, among others.

It is also within this general framework, created by the worldwide Cultural Revolution of 1968, when a systematic renovation begins in all areas of study, analysis, and characterization in the vast dominium of what is commonly known as "popular culture," which in the 35 years hence has been the object of more studies and debates than during the 100 years preceding 1968 (Aguirre-Rojas, 2004b).

This systematic and rigorous study of popular culture that shall not only break with false and limited aristocratic visions that completely denied the very existence of such popular culture, but also criticize the still condescending and paternalistic visions regarding that subordinate culture, which they consider a simple result, derived, dependent, and secondary to their own culture of the elite or of the supremacy of their class over all others.

With the goal of trying to search deeper and more carefully into this complex theme of the recent characterization of popular culture, we believe that it is worthwhile to recover the perspective that has been developed by Carlo Ginzburg, the Italian historian, who constructed the most complex and subtle model for the study and analysis of this same culture of subaltern classes in history up to this point—a perspective that not only offers a complete critical model for the analysis of the history of subaltern cultures but also several important clues to decipher in a novel manner this rich and highly diversified link between the culture of the dominant classes and the culture of the socially subordinated classes.

Therefore, by reconstructing the referred critical model for the cultural history, it shall be possible for us to get some important elements to understand how we need to teach history now in the beginning of the third millennium in which we are living today.

DECIPHERING THE CULTURE OF THE SUBORALTERN CLASSES

What are the main features that characterize this new model of critical analysis subaltern cultures proposed by Carlo Ginzburg? Within this model, how are the complex relations conceived between hegemonic and subaltern cultures, which are relations that include certain "dialogues" or specific exchanges to closed and irreducible confrontations? The first important idea that underlies this model of cultural history is the thesis that the history of culture is an absolutely recent field, very young and incipient within historic studies in general, and is, therefore, a *field still under construction*, referring to the definition of the diverse problem issues and of the different items it covers but also regarding the finer and more adequate elaboration of its main concepts, its methodological paradigms, its explanatory models, and its main articulating hypothesis (Ginzburg, 1980).

The culture of the subaltern classes, as Ginzburg pointed out could *not* become an object of study before the historic discipline opened up to the vast field of its dimension as *social* history, as history of the classes, of the masses. The great collective groups of society, known to all, would not occur until the second half of the nineteenth century, until the revolution that Marxism implied for the evolution of the science of history (Aguirre-Rojas, 2000b).

Even the birth of social history, the affirmation of the mentioned history of popular culture, developed very slowly and progressively, thanks to twentieth-century anthropology and historiography. The concomitant abandonment of the aristocratic, traditional, and anachronistic position continued on still for decades even after the rise of Marxism to relegate popular culture to the plain and simple status of "folklore" or "popular arts and traditions."

Side by side with this feature of cultural history, still very young, is the clear thesis that culture is not something that is unitarian nor homogeneous but a field of divided and contradictory forces that is always formed by two different universes—that of *hegemonic* culture (and not only dominant) and that of multiple *sub*altern cultures (and not only popular culture). Following the important and decisive lessons of Antonio Gramsci, Ginzburg conceived the culture of the dominant classes as being hegemonic, that is, as a culture that not only exercised domination by means of imposition or total subjugation but also by creating a certain cultural "consensus," which at the same time that it "takes possession" of certain themes, motifs, and elements of the subaltern cultures, to deform them and use them as weapons for their own legitimization, and also urges it forward to permanently promote different efforts to diffuse its own culture within these subordinate classes, obviously directed toward firmly establishing and making the mentioned hegemonic culture acceptable on the part of those submitted classes themselves.

Likewise, and trying to overcome both the "transclassist" vision of culture (implicit in the concept of "mentality") as well as a "generic classist" vision of culture (underlying to the term "popular" culture, that is the culture of the amorphous and undefined, but also nonexistent "people"), Carlo Ginzburg is going to set forth more the notion of "subaltern cultures," that is, of multiple cultures corresponding to the different subaltern classes and to the different subaltern social groups, that even though they find themselves in the referred situation of "subaltern" and of submission, this does not mean that they do not affirm their *own culture*, which is *different* from the hegemonic culture, even if they are submitted by the latter, but that they maintain their own *specific logic* and their *own singular expressions* that are only typical of itself, nourishing the cultural resistance of the oppressed and the necessary permanent renovation of the hegemonic cultural efforts of the already referred dominant classes at the same time.

This conception clearly characterizes the referred hegemonic culture and the subaltern cultures, leading Carlo Ginzburg to assert a double thesis—which is paradoxical only in appearance—for the author of *The Cheese and the Worms*, the space of culture is at the same time a *permanent battlefield* where hegemonic and subordinate cultures incessantly face each other. Simultaneously, it is a terrain identically marked by a movement of *constant circularity* where both cultural versions constantly exchange cultural elements, cosmovisions, motifs, and configurations as part of the same cultural battle that interconnects and overdetermines them in general.

Once having radically overcome the idyllic but false vision of a "mentality" that would be common to Julius Cesar and the humblest of his soldiers, or to Christopher Columbus and the last of his sailors, Ginzburg instead emphasized the fact that the global social conflict that characterizes and has characterized the immense majority of human societies throughout history is also reproduced within the cultural sphere, systematically opposing the culture of the dominant classes with the culture of the popular classes within an asymmetrical framework that favors the dominators and the elites in power.

At the same time, to make this construction of a cultural hegemony on the part of the privileged classes of a society possible is when this permanent *cultural circularity* develops, which determines that only those messages, codes, and visions of the dominant class are able to socially take roots and affirm themselves, because it is this class that manages to legitimately *connect and refunctionalize* this domination one way or another to the themes, problems, conceptions of the world, or *previously* existent cultural elements that have also been previously disseminated and have taken roots in the same cultures of the subaltern classes.

In the other extreme, it is also clear that the subordinate classes never accept this hegemonic cultural imposition of the dominant classes passively and calmly but are persistently submitted to a recodification that, beyond its vocation of legitimizing the status quo, again filters attitudes of resistance and even open cultural rebellion, taking possession of certain elements of such hegemonic culture to use them in their own daily struggles, as well as to constantly recreate and generate new figures and elements of culture that has not yet filtered through the hegemonic code, that remain as genuine expressions of that inexhaustible and constantly renewed subaltern culture of multiple faces and dimensions for some time (Ginzburg, 1991).

To continue with the above examples, this also explains the fact that even after more than one millennium of continued and renewed, although never totally achieved, "Christianization" (Ginzburg, 1989), the European peasant culture continues to survive and reinterpret Christian cosmogonies from the naturalist, radical, utopian, and materialistic perspective that is characteristic of those subaltern classes. This is reflected so clearly in the case of the audacious and courageous peasant, Menocchio, the same way as we see the indigenous people of New Spain pay homage to images of the Virgin Mary, that only covers an interior space where the little figures of the diverse autochthonous indigenous variations of the previously mentioned goddesses of the earth and fertility lie hidden.

This should not lead us to the false and naïve idea that, stemming from this confrontation, the hegemonic culture, or each subaltern culture, is in turn homogenous entities or that they function with a logic that is sole, univocal, and not subject to modification. Quite the contrary.

In view of this circularity or "dialogue," and of this permanent confrontation between both cultural fields, each one consists of a complex display of positions and elements that encompass positions that from the side of the dominant classes, that only clearly and directly strengthens social domination, or, on the side of the subordinate classes, only vindicates—without any ambiguity—radical resistance leading to totally subverted domination to many diverse positions that include a range of possible *intermediate positions* at both extremes of the corresponding cultural spectrum. Therefore, the culture of the popular classes shall contain the same elements of a triumphant hegemonic culturing process that plainly and simply legitimizes economic exploitation, political despotism, and social domination and discrimination, or the subaltern culture can include other figures that are *non*functional to such domination but are equally tolerated and subsistent within this vast cultural universe, together with cultural figures that embody very different degrees of reinterpretation and refunctionalization of the main messages of the hegemonic culture from the perspectives of the subaltern classes and cultures (Ginzburg, 1979).

The same is true for hegemonic culture, which, far from being monolithic, is also a varied display of positions, which is undoubtedly dominated by one that legitimizes and justifies the existing social order, but within which can appear positions *of criticism* of such official culture, which from the inside, contradicted and questioned that same cultural hegemony.

Thus, breaking with a conception still very widely disseminated up to the 1970s, which considered hegemonic culture as well as the subaltern cultures as *homogenous* and boringly *univocal* and *coherent* constructions, Carlo Ginzburg critically defined his limits from positions that sometimes idolized a supposedly popular culture without criticism, conceiving it as always "benign," positive, and revolutionary exempt of any sin whatsoever, as well as from the notion of a dominant culture without faults, one that is purely repressive, subduing, omnipresent and that absolutely denies the existence of subaltern cultures. In the same way, Ginzburg defined his limits from inverse positions that also view cultures as blocks built from one material. They considered popular culture as a mere set of superstitions and purely irrational beliefs, totally subject to affectivity and of magical and symbolic visions that today are already "primitive," anachronistic, and backward, at the same time calling the dominant culture as the only true "scientific" culture, rational, progressive, creative, innovative and "worthy" of being systematically studied and examined.

This intrinsic diversity and heterogeneity in each cultural space and its mutual relations, that in any case does *not eliminate* the fact that it is an *asymmetrical, hierarchical, and permanently unequal* relationship, a relationship in which "the dice are loaded" so that victory is ensured for the dominant and hegemonic classes in power most of the time. If the culture is hegemonic, it is so in the way it expresses the ideas and the *Weltanschauung* of the dominant class, which by means of imposition and consensus ends up possessing hegemonic visions within a given society. For this, they also have available multiple means and points of support that range from the monopoly of reading and writing—and also preparing written testimonies and of documents of all kinds (Ginzburg, 2003) —to the very construction of language and elements of discourse, which by being "theorized" and "defined" by such hegemonic classes, also become domesticated and adapted to express in the best possible way that same unequal and asymmetric world that has created them and that permanently refunctionalizes them but also stems from the fact that such hegemonic classes always possess the material means both for the most extensive dissemination and projection of their own ideas and cosmovisions, as well as for the repression and the blocking of the different forms and figures of the subaltern cultures.

For centuries and millennia, the culture of the popular classes has been an exclusively *oral* culture, and even today it continues to be *predominantly* so. This implies that in passing from this dominant condition of this culture, toward the field of the written terrain, it shall always suffer violence and deformation. In the first place, with its reinsertion within the terms and concepts of a language already resignified by the hegemonic culture, and in the second place, its inevitable "translation" on the part of whoever is writing, who—in the great majority of cases—also belongs to such dominant or hegemonic classes (Aguirre-Rojas, 2001).

However, and once more in a manner that only appears to be paradoxical, if it is true that this hegemonic culture has at its disposal all of these means to impose itself and take possession over the subaltern cultures, this imposition or strategy is permanently carried out and updated precisely because—in spite of its condition of subordinateity and subordination—the culture of the popular classes continues to be a strong culture in itself with an enormous underlying historic density, with a certain degree of irreducible autonomy and with an inexhaustible source of regeneration and renovation that is its own, which is impossible to expropriate in the final analysis.

However, it is only possible to adequately perceive all of these specific traits and features of the subaltern cultures when one places oneself, as Carlo Ginzburg also proposed, from the "point of view of the victims," from the perspective and the singular manner of cultural perception of the same submissive, exploited, and discriminated classes.

From this new conception of the "popular" or subaltern cultures, it could be interesting to see the point of the new teaching of the history, new ways of generating and transmitting historical knowledge, which developed all over the world after the worldwide cultural revolution of 1968 once again.

A NEW TEACHING OF HISTORY

After reconstructing the complex model that Carlo Ginzburg proposed for studying subaltern cultures, it is worthwhile to question ourselves if this same proposal could be projected beyond the specific ambit of the analysis of culture and if it is true that this proposal contains lessons of a more general nature—for example, the problem of teaching current history to clarify for us what type of history we should be teaching in our schools today.

This is a question that, in our opinion, we should answer affirmatively. When Carlo Ginzburg proposed this new explanation of such cultural phenomena, he proposed a way to see it from a profoundly *critical* vision, which is also a *dialectic* vision. This critical and dialectic vision that makes absolute oppositions less rigid, causing them to be more fluid and relative, at the same time showing the specific interrelations that are established among the elements of a particular relation researched in each case. This can therefore also be applied to other false oppositions or alternatives that for decades have been the core of several main debates among historians over the past 150 years. We refer to false alternatives that the historians of today still have to face and, from the lessons we might infer from the works of Carlo Ginzburg and his very specific theorization of popular culture, can in fact be fully surpassed and overcome and to be able to construct the profiles and general elements of a new type of history, one that is more scientific and more complex and is a history that we should be teaching now.

The series of false alternatives that were set forth in the past, and even in the present, as part of the "great debates" among historians, have constantly exerted pressure on the latter so that they choose or decide among different objects of study, but also among different orders of the phenomenon of reality, as well as among diverse techniques or methods, or paradigms, or forms of approximation toward their different research themes.

There has been an unending debate as to whether history should be occupied, most of all, by general, reiterative, and universal elements within history or whether its attention should concentrate more on the unique, unrepeatable, and singular nature of historic developments. The eternal controversy has continued to this day between those who defend the empirical and scholarly work of the historian and those who instead defend the philosophy of history and the metafactual and essentially discursive construction of the historian. The same thing happens when we try to oppose microhistory to macrohistory, a purely descriptive history to interpretative history, the individual to the masses or any other form of "collective," economic, or social history to the history of mentalities or to cultural history, the history of structures and of strong inertias of the history of the active agents and of the actions, the same as "objective" history to "subjective" history, and quantitative, serial, and anonymous history to individual, live and lived history, or the history of long duration to the history of events, the "truly scientific" history to "ideological" or "politically committed" history, or eclectic or "without orthodoxies" history to that history that is rigidly limited to the application and repetition of one sole historic model.

However, as it is absurd to rigidly oppose popular culture to hegemonic culture, viewing them as two universes that exclude each other—with no link among them—it is just as senseless to postulate these false alternatives among the different forms, levels, or elements of history, setting them forth as choices or positions to be taken that mutually exclude each other and one that would be in radical opposition with regard to their possible main historiographic results. Because it is quite clear that in all of the foregoing cases, we refer only to *false oppositions* and *false elections or alternatives* that are dissolved and eliminated immediately as we carefully read the works that have been bequeathed to us by the most important authors and defenders of the *genuinely critical* history of the past century and a half—from Karl Marx himself and even the most recent and current critical historiography for example, that of Carlo Ginzburg, and all the group of Italian microhistory (Aguirre-Rojas, 2003a, 2003b). Because, as stated by the French historian, Fernand Braudel, the science of history is the sum of *all* of the possible histories, past, present, and future (Braudel, 1980), the same way that truly critical history implies the consideration of *all* of those elements, perspectives, dimensions, orders, methods, techniques, and paradigms that some historians pretend to falsely oppose, arguing this supposed and nonexistent element, excluding nature, and at times, even antithetical among them.

Because it is clear that history is, in its profoundest essence, a complex and permanent dialectic between a series of universal, repeated, common, and general elements, with other singular, unique, exceptional, and particular elements, a dialectic that in this *double* course explains to us why certain regularities and clear tendencies exist within history, but at the same time asks why this history *never* repeats itself. That is, why is history *not* a simple eternally variable accumulation of permanently different facts, characters, events, and processes that would prevent all and any rational and scientific analysis? Neither is it a mere change of form or "outfit" for a history that would then be cyclical and eternally repeated, in addition to being tediously foreseeable.

To the contrary, and far from the *historicist* position that has yielded to its love affair regarding this unique and singular nature of what is historic—the vulgar Stalinist position—that asserted that the laws of history led all nations of the world toward "socialism," critical history recovers the *permanent* need at all times, and in each specific historic analysis, to recover the general elements as well as the particular ones, restoring in each case, finely and subtly, its complex overlapping and specific dialectics.

It is possible to set forth the same considerations regarding the discussion, and the retaking by those who defend the postmodern point of view in history, between history as a simple task of erudition or scholarship and the handling of hard and verifiable "facts" that are subject to rigorous verification and on the other hand, history as a pure "free construction" by the historian, as an almost metaphysical exercise of the invention of objects, problems, techniques, and results that culminate in the invention of discourses and pseudotruths that are in agreement with a certain "regime of truth" (de Certau, 1978; Veyne, 1979; White, 1973).

If we are to assume that history is both a work of erudition and scholarship as well as of interpretation, the false opposition equally dissolves, once more interconnected within a specific dialectic where the erudite laboring and strict establishment of the facts only marks the starting point and the limits of the interpretation. This provides the latter task with its raw material and its support platform and where interpretation restores the true sense and significance of those facts by getting to the bottom of its profound essence and coherently rebuilding its intrinsic rationality and logic.

Equally sterile is the false alternative between being dedicated to the study of the great global processes and historic problems over long periods of time and taking spatial units of analysis of great dimensions or concentrating on small and delimited themes of history, tackling particularly limited problems over short periods of time and within limits that are more local, regional, or of reduced dimensions. That is, there is a false opposition between making macrohistory or general history, or on the other extreme, microhistory of small and particular things.

However, philosophy taught us quite a long time ago that what is general only *exists and becomes evident* by means of that which is particular. At the same time it lectures us that what is particular is essentially a mode or a specific figure of deployment of generality or universality. Once again this means that what is general and what is particular are always overlapping and intertwined, and that it is *not* possible either to separate the macrohistory dimension from the microhistory one, without being at risk of falling, be it in the pure and simple metaphysical speculation of the fragile and even brilliant generalizations—however always erroneous—of the diverse philosophies of history, or in the pure anecdotic and picturesque description of microhistories of a small town, a small city, a locality, or any small region whose descriptions lack any lesson or teaching of a *general* order for all historians.

Returning to the teachings of French historian, Marc Bloch, now extended by means of Italian microhistory, recall that the first condition for any local or regional or particular history "to be useful to the *entire* corporation of historians" requires us to address "problems of a general order," explicitly and consciously, which in this case, must be resolved "from and with the elements it is provided with" by that particular locality or region or example of situation that is studied or researched (Bloch, 1983). The only way to avoid constructioning unreal and fantastic models of the supposed human historic evolution is to again confront concrete, minute, singular histories, including the diverse individual cases in that microhistoric dimension, thus restoring the permanent interrelation and compelled feedback of macrohistory with microhistory and vice versa.

Another false alternative, which frequently appears in discussions of those who study history, is that which opposes the history of individuals or of the false or true "great men" and even those of the elites—be they political, military, economic, or intellectual—to the collective and social history of the social classes of the popular groups, the masses, and the great majorities that are almost always ignored or given less consideration by traditional, positivistic historians. However, if one main progress is accomplished by the current critical contemporary historiography from its beginnings that coincides with the development of Marx's project and up until today, it is precisely an organically incorporating these diverse collective and majority actors and players of society. This does *not* mean that we must completely *abandon* and ignore the history of all kinds of individuals, great personalities, and elite groups. On the contrary, it is precisely this organic incorporation within history of the classes and of the popular sectors, which allows us to recover in a *new form*, but more richly and with more pertinence, those same individual and small group histories, redimensioning such histories to provide fair and just proportions that correspond to them in reality.

History is undoubtedly made by the masses, and leaders in a complex mesh that synthesizes and at the same time combines the participation of the social classes with the individuals itineraries, which also interweaves and overlaps the activity and actions of these multiple and plurifaceted majority groups of the population with decisions and the acts of the so-called great men. If the popular classes as well as the individuals are important for this critical history, it is evident that it is impossible to advance the research of history without considering *both* elements in their reciprocal interrelations. The Belgian historian, Henri Pirenne, proposed to resolve the dilemma that history was faced with in his time—between psychology that studied the individual and its diverse manifestations and sociology that studied the social groups and societies (Pirenne, 1937)—in the just and fair sense of studying the individual as an acting member of such social groups and the groups and social classes as conglomerates and articulate syntheses of those same concrete, distinct, and acting individuals.

It is a false opposition between individual and collectivity, which in another aspect, transforms into the antinomy of the individual against the social context and that does become particularly evident in the classic problem of the *historical biography*. The reason is that once this field of historical analysis is addressed as a central theme, that is, of the critical reconstruction of the complete long journey and of the diverse curves of the life of a certain individual, again with the reappearance of the false alternative of characterizing this individual, either as a clear product and its concrete expression in its specific context—reducing its individual singularity to the conditions of what its circumstances have been, that is, to its "milieu" and to its "time"—or in the other case, of exaggerating the active role and the transforming and producing potential of such an individual thus reducing that context of its action and its different historical works and achievements to the role of a mere "backdrop," which is actually unessential and secondary to such works and actions.

Up to now traditional and positivistic historians have reproduced this false antinomy between social context and historic individuality, considering the individual as a type of simple "marionette or puppet" of the circumstances, a product of its environment and of its time, and which fatally had to be generated into a given trend or situation, in order to fulfill its predetermined historical role, or at the other extreme, conceiving the circumstances as a set of almost random conditions that do not explain much of the *singular* life of this individual—and more so in relation to the individual that it may have been able to be—to accomplish what it did due to its exceptional genius and singular and unrepeatable extraordinary character.

However, from reading such works as Karl Marx's *El 18 Brumario de Luis Napoleon Bonaparte* or Norbert Elias's *Mozart, Sociology of a Genius*—as well as Lucien Febvre's *Martin Luther: A Destiny*, not to mention Jean-Paul Sartre's brilliant *Critique of Dialectic Reason*—the critical historian knows very well that separating the individual in this brutal and dialectic manner from this context makes *no* sense. The historian knows also that it is equally absurd to place both terms against each other, forcing to choose between them. On the contrary, it is necessary to always begin to research *the individual in the context, immersed in such context*, explaining concretely how that context molds the individual and forms it to express itself *through itself and in itself*, at the same time reconstructing how that individual is inserted into that context in order to project its action and to affirm and deploy its diverse initiatives, *transforming* this context with the multiple impacts of its actions, shaping the concrete figures in the same contextual space using a complex network of increasing concentric circles that form its entire world of diverse relationships.

By reconstructing mobile and changing contexts, that instead of being rigid and predetermined beforehand, by conceiving individuals that evolve, grow up, mature, choose, and remake their life strategies in regard to such changes and reconfigurations of their multiple contexts, the critical historian also overcomes the false dilemma or alternative between individual and context, reconsidering under new terms the old and very debated theme of the historic biography (Levi, 1989).

This is a new way of approaching historic biography, which also dissolves the false opposition between structural histories, or the heavy and limiting structures or inertias of history, and the history of the active agents and of the subjects who are the creators of their own history and active transformers of the world by revolutions and social movements. This false opposition that is not identical to that of individuals and contexts—but does connect with it in a very close way when it projects these contexts as the heavy "structures" of history, slow in forming, slow in lasting and staying, and slow in destroying themselves and being transformed, at the same time that it occurs from the individual toward the "subjects" of history in general, be they social classes or revolutionary movements, the same as small or large active social groups.

However, as explained by Marc Bloch and Fernand Braudel, history is simultaneously change and permanence. Therefore, it is a complex and interactive synthesis of such structures that, indeed, remain in effect during long periods of history, together with processes and realities that change and are substantially modified. All of the prior, as a frame and at the same time as the result of a whole diverse and complex range of individual and collective actions, that may well have a fundamental bearing in changing such processes and structures or, at times, may be lost in minor or insignificant effects, when they encounter the major or minor resistance that these structures and processes may have toward their own transformation and historical changes.

Because history includes revolutions that succeed and fail, movements that are visible and socially assert their demands, together with others that perish under repression without having achieved social dissemination or becoming solidly established in society, the same is true for individuals who reach their goals of possibly changing their world alongside others who succumb to social pressures or circumstances. All of this is within the different historic scenarios where structures tumble before our eyes, and others who resist change and tenaciously remain, in multiple ranges of social realities, sometimes more and sometimes less sensitive to change and to the impact of the actions taken by these individuals. Since there are no revolutions capable of making an absolute *tabula rasa* of the past, there are no structures or societies that are completely immune to the passing of time and the actions of individuals. It is then clear that for critical history, there does not exist the false dilemma between structure permanence and change produced by agents, but there exist complex dynamics of social actors who partially reinvent the world every day, within a universe of processes and structures that die or are slowly dying, until they finally disappear.

The historian *does not* have to choose between providing a history of long permanencies and heavy inertias, those structures of long historic duration defended so many times by Fernand Braudel, or, on the other extreme, a history of the agitated and changing daily events, of times of revolution or of social conflicts renewed each day but instead a true synthesis that will reconstruct the history of events and trends and cycles and the structures overlapping into one entity—the whole complex set of facts, phenomena, and processes of different historic times, unfolded in the many temporary registers, of global actions that contains the history of societies and of men.

History is neither purely objective nor purely subjective. Instead it is precisely a complex dialectics of the relationship between object and subject in which educators undoubtedly form the students. It is also true that "the educators need in turn to be educated," and this "education" is provided many times by students themselves. If individuals are the result of circumstances, circumstances are also created by individuals, repeatedly and interminably—a movement that is of historic dynamics itself.

This demonstrates why there is no sense in constructing a history stemming "from the subject"—supposedly opposed and different from "objective" or "structural" history. It makes no sense to also try, by exaggerating its importance, to overestimate the history of mentalities or cultural history as being more relevant, more "universal," or more all embracing than economic history, political history, or social history. As if it were not evident that all history is at the same time "subjective" and "objective," made by man, classes, and social actors, history is also conditioned by structures, objective conditions, and material circumstances. In addition, history is *total*. It is as relevant and as much a priority to study the cultural as well as the social, the economic as well as the political, and the psychological or the geographical. Instead of falling into the recurrent "fetishism" of the specialist in a specific field or problem space, where it might be conceived as "the most decisive" and "crucial," that which is "the key to the comprehension of the totality," where we must assume the importance of the always-essential link and connection of that social, economic, or political or cultural history with referred global history (Aguirre-Rojas, 2000a, 2004a).

It is equally false to oppose quantitative, serial, mass, and anonymous history, supposedly more scientific inasmuch as it is more supported in the use of mathematics, to concrete history, lived by individuals, families, or small social groups that are supposedly more real. History is, at the same time, a history of the masses and individuals; therefore the same history of the general population bends, as does that of the individual drama of each peasant family that collapses because their land does not increase in size while the descendants of their children who should inherit such land grow in numbers.

If it is true that the quantification and construction of series of all types are very useful tools for the development of history, they are in the same way a microhistoric approximation and biographic reconstruction that we have already mentioned. It would be very difficult to learn the multiple diverse faces of history and the thousands of dimensions and realities imbedded in such history if we were limited only to one type of technique or method or to one sole paradigm, model, or one particular field of historiographic research. By no means does this signify that the recovery of an "eclecticism" or a false "ecumenism" is not attached to any "orthodoxy," neither in the methodological plane nor in the epistemological plane, as was done by French historiographer, Jacques LeGoff, in defending and justifying the project of the so-called *nouvelle histoire,* or new history but instead to recognize and acknowledge that, given history's enormous variety and extraordinary complexity, it shall become necessary to progressively recover and integrate all lessons, paradigms, models, concepts, and proposals that have been developed by truly *critical* historiography of the past fifteen decades, all are studied in terms of specific historic themes and problems that each historian chooses to address and develop and in terms of available sources, goals, or objectives of the historic survey—the approach that the studied object itself may allow and makes possible and specific dimensions or realities that the historian intends to obtain or capture.

The reason is that, far from being mutually excluding and alternative, the lessons of different authors who, throughout the 150 years that current contemporary history has covered, have been setting the foundations of a possible truly critical history where they supplement one another and come together in a general sense, inasmuch that all represent tools that are still being used and the yet-indispensable and essential referents of the construction of the same critical history.

We are aware that if one of the demands of this critical history—that of "multiplying the possible views" regarding any one historical fact, process, or phenomenon, in order to thus understand it and ulterior explanation more complex—such multiplication and increasing of complexity shall only be positive if we dissolve all these false dilemmas or alternatives and other similar ones that we have not addressed here. Dissolving and overcoming false dilemmas or alternatives will give us the capacity of going beyond these sterile antinomies and choices on our path of trying to recount, adequately, subtly, and complicatededly, the entire set of elements forming different historic realities that we attempt to explain scientifically in all their difficult, varied, and complex diversity.

This is a truly critical and scientific explanation of history, which in the same way that it cannot dispense with the study, the approach and later the teaching of the essential contents of the popular culture, lies within the lines that we have outlined, it also cannot ignore this perspective that is necessarily dialectic and tends to lessen rigidity at the same time that it is profoundly critical and complex as exemplified in the works of Carlo Ginzburg.

This in line of what social critic and philosopher, Walter Benjamin, reminded us of when he stated that "only that historian that has been imbued with the idea that not even the dead shall be safe from the enemy if the enemy happens to be the victor, shall have the right to light up the spark of hope in the past. …" It is indeed an urgent and essential task for critical, honest, and serious historians all over the world to be again "saving our dead," as well as helping the living to fight, keeping the "spark of hope" lit for some time, which from the grievances of the past and from conflicts of the present, is always looking ahead and beyond in search of a better future.

REFERENCES

(Translated from Spanish to English by María Elena Garza Quest.)

Aguirre-Rojas, C.A. (1993). 1968: La gran ruptura. *La Jornada Semanal, 225*, 18–22.

Aguirre-Rojas, C.A. (2000a). *Ensayos braudelianos.* Rosario: Editorial Prohistoria. Aguirre-Rojas, C.A. (2000b). Rethinking current social sciences: The case of historical discourses in the history of modernity. *Journal of World-System Research, 6*(3), 11–27.

Aguirre-Rojas, C.A. (2001). Chiapas, Lateinamerika und das kapitalistische Weltsystem. *Comparativ, 11*(2), 90–108.

Aguirre-Rojas, C.A. (2003a). *Antimanual del mal historiador* (8th ed.). Ciudad de Mexico: Editorial Contrahistorias.

Aguirre-Rojas, C.A. (2003b). *Contribución a la historia de la microhistoria italiana.* Rosario: Prohistoria.

Aguirre-Rojas, C.A. (2004a). *Fernand Braudel et les sciences humaines.* Paris: L'Harmattan.

Aguirre-Rojas, C.A. (2004b). *La historiografía en el siglo xx. Historia e historiadores entre 1848 y ¿2025?* Barcelona: Montesinos.

Bloch, M. (1983). L'ile de france, in M. Bloch (ed.), *Mélanges historiques.* Paris: EHESS—Serge Fleury, tome 2, 692–787.

Braudel, F. (1980). *On history.* Chicago, IL: University of Chicago Press.

Braudel, F. (1993). Renacimiento, reforma, 1968: Revoluciones culturales de larga duración. *La Jornada Semanal, 226*, 27–32.

De Certau, M. (1978). *L'écriture de l'histoire.* Paris: Gallimard.

Ginzburg, C. (1979). Premessa giustificativa. *Quaderni storici, 41*, 393–397.

Ginzburg, C. (1980). Introduzione, in P. Burke (ed.), *Cultura popolare dell'Europa moderna.* Milán: Giangiacomo Feltrinelli Editore.

Ginzburg, C. (1989). Folklore, magia, religione, in *Storia d'italia* (vol. 1, pp. 134–153). Turin: Giulio Einaudi Editore.

Ginzburg, C. (1991). *Ecstasies. Deciphering the witches' sabbath.* New York: Pantheon Books.

Ginzburg, C. (2003). Intervención sobre el paradigma indiciario, in C. Ginzburg (ed.), *Tentativas* (pp. 145–157). Morelia, México: Universidad Michoacana de San Nicolás de Hidalgo.

Levi, G. (1989). Les usages de la biographie. *Annales. E.S.C., 44*(6), 83–99.

Pirenne, H. (1937). What are historians trying to do? in H. Pirenne (ed.), *Methods in social science.* Chicago, IL: University of Chicago Press.

Veyne, P. (1979). *Comment on écrit l'histoire.* Paris: Editions du Seuil.

Wallerstein, I. (1991). 1968: Revolution in the world-system, in I. Wallerstein (ed.), *Geopolitics and geoculture.* Cambridge: Cambridge University Press/Editions Maison des Sciences de l'Homme.

White, H. (1973). *Metahistory.* Baltimore: John Hopkins University Press.

Contributors

Carlos Antonio Aguirre Rojas (1955) is currently a Researcher at the Instituto de Investigaciones Sociales of the Universidad Nacional Autonoma de Mexico. He has a PhD in Economics, from the UNAM, and a Posdoctoral degree in History from the École des Hautes Études en Sciences Sociales of Paris. He is a specialist in the field of Historical Methodology and also in the History of Historiography of the XIXth and XXth Centuries. More recently, he is studying the new antisystemic movements in Latin America 1968 - 2008, and the main lessons provided by those movements in order to radically reformulate the contemporary political theory.

Gordon Alley-Young is an assistant professor of Communication at Kingsborough Community College, a campus of the City University of New York. His research interests include experiential and multicultural approaches to education, critical perspectives on race and gender, and popular representations of education.

His research and essays are included in *ERIC, Education Review,* and *Programming* [forthcoming]. His book reviews appear in the *Canadian Journal of Communication, Feminist Teacher, Journal of Men's Studies, Scope: An Online Journal of Film Studies, The Journal of Religion and Popular Culture,* and *Canadian Ethnic Studies/Etudes Ethniques au Canada.*

Zvi Bekerman teaches anthropology of education at the School of Education and at The Melton Center for Jewish Education at Hebrew University of Jerusalem. He is also a research fellow at the Truman Institute for Peace at the Hebrew University. His main interests are in the study of cultural, ethnic and national identity, including identity processes and negotiation during intercultural encounters and in formal/informal learning contexts. Since 1999 he has been conducting, with the support of the Ford, Spencer and Bernard Van Leer Foundations, a long term ethnographic research project in the integrated/bilingual Palestinian-Jewish schools in Israel. Dr. Bekerman is also involved in the study of identity construction and development in educational computer-mediated environments

Nicholas C. Burbules is Grayce Wicall Gauthier Professor in the Department of Educational Policy Studies at the University of Illinois, Urbana/Champaign. He has published widely in the areas of philosophy of education, technology and education, and critical social and political theory. He is also the current editor of Educational Theory.

His most recent books include: Nicholas C. Burbules and Thomas A. Callister, Jr., Watch IT: The Promises and Risks of New Information Technologies for Education (Boulder, Colorado: Westview Press, 2000); Nicholas C. Burbules and Carlos Torres, eds., Globalization and Education: Critical Perspectives (New York: Routledge, 2000); and D.C. Phillips and Nicholas C. Burbules, Postpositivism and Educational Research (Lanham, Mass.: Rowman and Littlefield Publishers, 2000). His forthcoming books include Gert Biesta and Nicholas C. Burbules, Pragmatism and Educational Research, and Michael Peters and Nicholas C. Burbules, Poststructuralism and Educational Research, both with Rowman and Littlefield Publishers, 2004.

Mary M. Dalton is Assistant Professor of Communication at Wake Forest University (USA), and her research area is critical media studies. She is the author of *The Hollywood Curriculum: Teachers in the Movies* (Lang, 2004) and the co-editor of a forthcoming anthology called *The Sitcom Reader: America Viewed and Skewed* (SUNY Press, 2005). She is also a media critic for WFDD-FM, an affiliate of National Public Radio and an award winning documentary filmmaker.

Gonzalo Frasca is a game researcher, designer and entrepreneur. In 2002 he co-founded Powerful Robot, a game development studio based in Uruguay. The studio recently created Cartoon Network's most successful online game to date, Big Fat Awesome House Party, which reached over 13 million player accounts on its first year. As a researcher, Frasca focuses on games and communication, with a focus on politics and education. He holds a PhD in Game Studies from the IT University of Copenhagen and he blogs at Ludology.org

Virginia S. Funes is Tenured Professor of Image and Visual Communication Teaching and Methodology at the University of Lanús. Tenured Professor of Audiovisual Analysis in the Social Communication major at CAECE at Buenos Aires, Argentina.
Author of several publications specialized in communication and education Researcher in *"Glocal Youth, Testi e contesti mediatici per Giovanni del Nord e del Sud del mondo"*, a research project financed by the European Union.

Henry A. Giroux received his doctorate from Carnegie-Mellon University in 1977. He taught at Boston University from 1977 to 1983. From 1983-1992, he taught at Miami University. In 1992, he accepted the Waterbury Chair Professorship at Pennsylvania State University and served as the Director of the Waterbury Forum in Education and Cultural Studies. In 2004, he accepted a position at McMaster University in Canada where he is the Global Television Network Chair in English and Communication. He is on the editorial and advisory boards of numerous national and international scholarly journals. He also serves as the editor or co-editor of three scholarly book series. Professor Giroux was selected as a Kappa Delta Pi Laureate in 1998 and was the recipient of a Getty Research Institute Visiting Scholar Award in 1999. He was the recipient of the Hooker Distinguished Professor Award for 20001. He lectures frequently both in the United States and abroad and his research focuses on a variety of issues including cultural studies, youth, critical pedagogy, democratic theory, public education, social theory, and the politics of higher education. Professor Giroux has published extensively in a wide ranging number of scholarly jour-nals and books. His books include: Theory and Resistance in Education (Bergin and Garvey 1983); Schooling and the Struggle for Public Life, University of Minnesota Press [1988];Teachers as Intellectuals, Bergin and Garvey Publishers [1988];Postmodern Education: Politics, Culture, and Social Criticism (co-authored with Stanley Aronowitz), University of Minnesota Press [1991];Border Crossings: Cultural Workers and the Politics of Education, Routledge Publishing [1992]; 1992]; Disturbing Pleasures: Learning Popular Culture (Routledge, 1994 and Fugitive Cultures: Race, Violence, and Youth (Routledge, 1996),). His most recent books include: Channel Surfing: Racism, the Media and the Destruction of Today's Youth(St. Martins Press, 1997), Pedagogy and the Politics of Hope (Westview/Harper Collins 1997),The Mouse That Roared: Disney and the End of Innocence (Rowman and Littlefield, 1999); Impure Acts: the Practical Politics of Cultural Studies (Routledge, 2000); Stealing Innocence: Corporate Culture's War on Children (St. Martin's Press, 2001); Public Spaces/ Private Lives: Beyond the Culture of Cynicism (Rowman and Littlefield, 2001); Beyond the Corporate University (Rowman and Littlefield, 2001); and Breaking

Into the Movies: Film and the Culture of Politics (Basil Blackwell, 2002); The Abandoned Generation: Democracy and the Culture of Fear (Palgrave 2004); Take Back Higher Education: Race, Youth, and the Crisis of Democracy in the Post Civil Rights Era [co-authored with Susan Searls Giroux] Palgrave (2004); The Terror of Neoliberalism: The New Authoritarianism and the Eclipse of Democracy (Paradigm Press (2004). His forthcoming book, Henry Giroux on Politics, Culture, and Education, will be published by Palgrave in 2005.

Danah Henriksen is a doctoral student in the Learning, Technology, and Culture program in the College of Education at Michigan State University. Her areas of expertise include graphic design and educational technology.

Diana Silberman Keller received a first Ph.D. in education from the Hebrew University of Jerusalem, Israel. She has developed the Non-Formal Education Department at Beit Berl College and has created in the same institution the School for Multidisciplinary Studies. At this school she has developed the Interactive Communication Center Studies.

Her research interests are on ideologies and education, post-structural critique, informal education and cultural studies. She has published numerous articles on informal pedagogy, ideology and education and textual and semiotic analysis of educational texts. Diana Silberman Keller has engaged in a second Ph.D. degree program on Communication, Film and Internet at the European Graduates School at Saas-Fee, Swiss. She has participated in seminars by Giorgio Agamben, Avital Ronell, Slavoj Zizek, Alain Badiou, Siegfried Zielinski, Barbara Hammer and Wolfgang Schirmacher, Werner Hamacher and Hubertus Von Ameluxen.

She has submitted her dissertation named Mirrors triptych technology: Remediation and Translation Figures to the Division of Media and communications of The European Graduate School in Candidacy for the Degree of Doctor of Philosophy.

Kurt Squire is a professor at the University of Wisconsin-Madison in the Educational Communications and Technology division of Curriculum and Instruction . He is a former Montessori and primary school teacher and, before coming to Wisconsin, was Research Manager of the Games-to-Teach Project at MIT and Co-Director of the Education Arcade . Squire earned his doctorate in Instructional Systems Technology from Indiana University; his dissertation research examined students' learning through a game-based learning program he designed around/ Civilization III/. Squire co-founded Joystick101.org with

Jon Goodwin and currently writes a monthly column with Henry Jenkins for Computer Games magazine. In addition to writing over 30 scholarly articles and book chapters, and he has given dozens of talks and invited addresses in North America, Europe, and Asia. Squire's current research interests center on the impact of contemporary gaming practices on learning, schooling and society. Along with several other University Wisconsin-Madison faculty, he runs the Games and Professional Practice Simulations (GAPPS) initiative located at the Academic Advanced Distributed Learning Co-Lab .

Dr. Mary Stone Hanley, an assistant professor at George Mason Universitys College of Education and Human Development, has been an educator in public and higher education for more than 35 years. She earned a PhD in Curriculum and Instruction, with an emphasis in Multicultural Education, from the University of Washington in 1998. Her research interests include the Arts and Equity in Education. Her inquiries are about how the arts stimulate imagination and creativity and facilitate learning as a vehicle of culture and social justice, particularly with African American youth. Her studies of Hip Hop are an effort to understand the culture of youth from their perspectives. She is also a playwright, screenwriter, and poet. She has written several plays and two films produced for adolescent audiences.

Rebecca W. Black received her Ph.D. in Curriculum and Instruction from the University of Wisconsin, Madison in 2006. Her research centers on the literacy and socialization practices of adolescents from diverse cultural and linguistic backgrounds who are writing and participating in online, popular culture-inspired environments. Dr. Blacks work has been published in Reading Research Quarterly, the Journal of Adolescent and Adult Literacy, New Horizons for Learning, and E-learning. She is currently completing a book exploring how adolescent English language learners represent their cultural and linguistic identities through online fan fiction texts.

David Wong, Ph.D. is an associate professor in the Learning, Technology, and Culture program in the College of Education at Michigan State University. His areas of expertise include aesthetics, educational psychology, and educational technology.

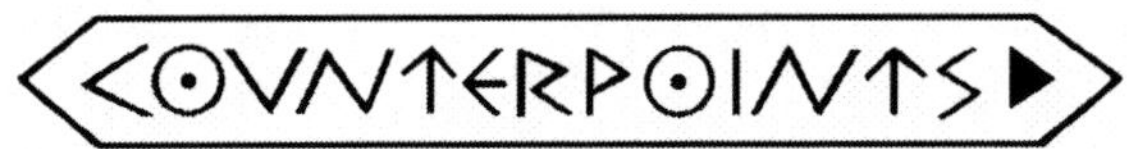

Studies in the Postmodern Theory of Education

General Editors
Joe L. Kincheloe & Shirley R. Steinberg

Counterpoints publishes the most compelling and imaginative books being written in education today. Grounded on the theoretical advances in criticalism, feminism, and postmodernism in the last two decades of the twentieth century, Counterpoints engages the meaning of these innovations in various forms of educational expression. Committed to the proposition that theoretical literature should be accessible to a variety of audiences, the series insists that its authors avoid esoteric and jargonistic languages that transform educational scholarship into an elite discourse for the initiated. Scholarly work matters only to the degree it affects consciousness and practice at multiple sites. Counterpoints' editorial policy is based on these principles and the ability of scholars to break new ground, to open new conversations, to go where educators have never gone before.

For additional information about this series or for the submission of manuscripts, please contact:

> Joe L. Kincheloe & Shirley R. Steinberg
> c/o Peter Lang Publishing, Inc.
> 29 Broadway, 18th floor
> New York, New York 10006

To order other books in this series, please contact our Customer Service Department:

> (800) 770-LANG (within the U.S.)
> (212) 647-7706 (outside the U.S.)
> (212) 647-7707 FAX

Or browse online by series:
> www.peterlang.com